Praise for *The Rise of Rage*

"For over twenty-five years, Julie has been studying, learning, and analyzing what causes anger and rage, and ways to harness and overcome these emotions. Julie's narratives in this manuscript allow the reader to become involved. Her sharing of experiences and perspectives helps one to identify the causes of anger issues, including outside influences. In doing so, she encourages the reader to leverage her knowledge in dealing with personal anger and helping others understand and adopt anger resolution techniques suitable to them. Julie writes, 'Wherever you go, you take you with you.' I might add, 'Whatever you do caused by anger, that also goes with you, often in the form of regret.'"

—**Alan Filer**, registered financial planner

"Julie has taken decades of experience as a therapist and distilled them down into bite-sized stories, helpful suggestions, and sage advice. Her words are a soothing balm. Read them, learn from them, and let the lessons she shares improve your relationships and create more love in your life."

—**Dr. Jeremy Goldberg**, author of *It'll Be Okay,*
and You Will Be Too

"I could hear Julie's voice throughout the entire book! Her writing style truly captures who she is as an educator, mentor, and storyteller. Her humor shone through, and I had many chuckles as I read. Perhaps more importantly, I found myself considering how 'Think, Say, and Ask,' acceptance, and forgiveness might change my relationship with myself and others for the better. The metaphor of resentment and anger being the weed that chokes out life and love packed a punch. I took many golden nuggets from this book that I know will help me become a better therapist, first responder, peer supporter, and response-able person."

—**Stephanie Gorrill**, first responder
and psychotherapist

"This book does an exceptional job of reframing our beliefs about unexpressed emotion and how to handle it. *The Rise of Rage* is the equivalent of many therapy sessions at a fraction of the cost. It comes with exercises you can work through at your own pace, and I was blown away by how much growth I experienced through the revelations I found even after a few pages. This work will not only break your own cycles but transform generational patterns that have impacted your family for decades."

—**Erin Skye Kelly**, author of *Get the Hell Out of Debt* and *Naked Money Meetings*

"*The Rise of Rage* is a wonderfully insightful book. My perspective regarding anger has been irrevocably shifted, following the realization that it is neither synonymous with aggression nor a shameful state that ought to be suppressed or avoided. This was a very enlightening read, and Julie commands the subject matter with absolute confidence and authority."

—**Jared Morrison**, author of *Of Dreams and Angels*

"Thank you to Julie Christiansen for sharing this brilliant book! There is so much in the content that I believe can and will apply to a very large audience. Many sections of the book are truly relatable. Her section on 'Simple Effective Tools,' including the 'Think, Say, and Ask' guidelines, is so important—even more important now with all the hostility and anger in our ever-shrinking world."

—**Barbara Mowat**, president, Impact Communications and GroYourBiz

THE RISE OF RAGE

Julie A. Christiansen

THE
RISE
OF
RAGE

Harnessing the Most
Misunderstood Emotion

Broadleaf Books
Minneapolis

THE RISE OF RAGE
Harnessing the Most Misunderstood Emotion

Copyright © 2024 by Julie Christiansen. Published by Broadleaf Books,
an imprint of 1517 Media. All rights reserved. Except for brief quotations in
critical articles or reviews, no part of this book may be reproduced in any manner
without prior written permission from the publisher. Email copyright@
1517.media or write to Permissions, Broadleaf Books, PO Box 1209, Minneapolis,
MN 55440-1209.

Library of Congress Cataloging-in-Publication Data

Names: Christiansen, Julie A., author.
Title: The rise of rage : harnessing the most misunderstood emotion /
   by Julie A. Christiansen.
Description: Minneapolis : Broadleaf Books, [2024] | Includes
   bibliographical references.
Identifiers: LCCN 2023011815 (print) | LCCN 2023011816 (ebook) | ISBN
   9781506492353 (hardback) | ISBN 9781506492360 (ebook)
Subjects: LCSH: Anger. | Temper. | Emotions.
Classification: LCC BF575.A5 C475 2024 (print) | LCC BF575.A5 (ebook) |
   DDC 152.4/7—dc23/eng/20230624
LC record available at https://lccn.loc.gov/2023011815
LC ebook record available at https://lccn.loc.gov/2023011816

Cover design: 1517 Media

Print ISBN: 978-1-5064-9235-3
eBook ISBN: 978-1-5064-9236-0

Printed in China.

CONTENTS

INTRODUCTION

Why Do We Need Another Book about Anger?

WHEN I FIRST wrote and published *Anger Solutions: Proven Strategies for Effectively Resolving Anger and Taking Control of Your Emotions*, my intention was to provide a step-by-step self-directed guide for readers who wanted to understand, express, and resolve the problems that caused their anger. It was meant to be a resource, something people could turn to if they felt uncomfortable with attending group or individual therapy. That book fulfilled its purpose in ways that I could not have foreseen back then. Not only is it a valuable self-help resource but it is also the guidepost for a vast network of *Anger Solutions* therapists, facilitators, and trainers. It's not a long book, but it packs a mighty punch.

The Rise of Rage was written with a different intent. At first, I thought this would be a great opportunity to do a complete brain dump of everything I have learned in my close to thirty years of studying anger and helping those who struggle with it. The question soon became: How do I fit all that experience into a book that people will want to read? Does anyone want to read a thousand-page tome? The truth is I could have written so much more than what you'll find between these covers. Sometimes too much talking, or writing, starts to feel like a parent lecture—you just can't wait for the speaker to stop talking so your punishment can begin. I did not want this book to feel like that.

The Rise of Rage is designed to get you thinking. I want readers to consider this content and process it within the context of their own values and experiences. Ask the questions: Is this me? Does this fit my reality? Is it possible that what I thought was the real world is only the world as I see it? Could it be there are other perspectives that make more sense than the one I have embraced?

Once you've processed what you've read, my desire is that you will take decisive action and proceed to implement what you've learned in ways that will produce radical transformation for you and those with whom you share relationships.

It's Been a Trip

From the launch of my career in mental health, I have spent countless hours deepening my understanding of anger, its process, and its many forms of expression. Much of what I have learned is distilled in the pages that follow, supported by research, and bolstered by stories informed by my professional and personal experience.

For better than ten years as an educator in the postsecondary space, I encountered many adult students who struggled with emotional regulation and coping with their big feelings. When you primarily teach subjects in psychology, students innately get that you understand their situation, and that results in them sharing loads of personal information. Students disclosed their struggles with depression and the pressure placed on them by an entire community to be successful in school because that community had invested to make their postsecondary studies possible. Students had psychotic breaks, uttered death threats, and openly shared their worst trauma experiences while in my classes. Many of my secondary school-aged students were homeless, abused, traumatized, forced to be adults and caretakers when they were still in their teens, trying desperately to adapt to a world they did not understand and trapped in cycles of addiction before their brains had fully matured.

In my role as a registered psychotherapist and mental health worker, I have encountered all manner of clients. Parents. Grandparents. Kids. Siblings. Whole families. Criminal offenders. Victims of crime. Law enforcement. Emergency responders. Military veterans. Couples. Addicts. Displaced persons. You name the mental health challenge, I have probably encountered it. Depression, anxiety, posttraumatic stress, chronic pain, childhood sexual abuse, addiction to drugs, addiction to gaming, addiction to pornography and compulsive sexual behavior, alcoholism, brain injury, stroke recovery, grief, bullying in schools, bullying at work, worker's compensation claims, motor vehicle accident recovery, coping with and recovering from narcissistic abuse, complex trauma, suicidal ideation, fetal alcohol syndrome in adults, suicidality, and the list goes on.

As a corporate trainer and public speaker, I have encountered bullying and harassment cases that have resulted in people acquiring severe physical disabilities. I have talked with people wracked by grief and visible, palpable anger because someone they loved "left them" by passing away. I have watched as employers bulldozed their way through team meetings hurling insults, uttering threats, and calling it "motivation." I have seen how office politics and abuse of power can decimate a team and pulverize productivity. I have seen what happens when policies are written but not enforced, and I have witnessed the fallout after one bad seed is empowered to poison the corporate culture.

All of this informs why I do what I do and why I am committed to leveraging individuals, families, and organizations into radical, positive, lasting change. It isn't enough for me to just listen and be supportive of my clients. They come to me because I am committed to working myself out of a job. What that looks like for me is that I equip clients with the knowledge, skills, and abilities they need to handle the stressors and challenges in their lives so effectively that they no longer need me. The greatest gift my calling and vocation give me is seeing my clients emerge from their cocoons beautiful, transformed, and ready to fly.

My journey to partnering with Broadleaf Books to bring you *The Rise of Rage* has been full of twists, turns, detours, and reroutes. It took many years of pushing through discomfort, pressing forward when I felt like quitting and relying heavily on my faith in God and His purpose for my life. While I always embraced my passion for serving others in the mental health space, circumstances directed me to the fields of journalism, business, public speaking, not-for-profit leadership, and back into mental health. Along the way, people came alongside to offer support, advice, and connection. One of those connections led me to Broadleaf Books. This amazing opportunity to give the *Anger Solutions* program a louder voice and a broader platform is one I do not take lightly.

Taming Your Inner Dragon

Sometimes when we personify anger, we conjure images of fire-breathing dragons, ancient dinosaurs with the power to destroy with their breath. Dragons are often depicted as raging, violent beings intent on destruction with no thought for the consequences of their actions. For us humans, *dino brooding* is what happens when we allow our downstairs reptilian brain to lead the thought process and guide the conversation. If we want to effectively resolve anger rather than just express it, we must step out of autopilot, stop dino brooding, and begin applying the principles shared in this book. I want people to consider the subjects discussed with a critical-thinking mind, a wise mind rather than their reptilian dragon brain.

Before they were depicted as harbingers of death and destruction, in ancient times, dragons were symbols of transformation and radical change. That's what I am all about. Back in the '90s, when I first saw a need for resources and support for people struggling with anger, there was not much out there. I pored over peer-reviewed articles that focused on aggression or criminality rather than exploring the root causes for antisocial behavior. Back then, anger *was* aggression—it was the dragon's fire; it was violence and destruction. The more I observed human behavior and studied the science of emotion, the more I came to realize there was something fundamentally wrong with the ways in which anger was conceptualized. The few clinical interventions that existed adhered to the medical model of assessment and treatment, focusing on symptoms rather than the root causes for behavior.

It occurred to me then that it made more sense to resolve the root issues rather than simply treating symptoms, which allowed the underlying problems to perpetuate and fester. I immediately set about trying to build a framework that would support this radical notion of resolving the problems that inform our emotions in place of pursuing the prevailing model of behavior management or modification. When I developed the *Anger Solutions* program, my instincts regarding its potential to create change were confirmed by preliminary results. It most certainly rewrote the narrative for my clients, and it was a game changer for *me*.

Throughout the process of developing the *Anger Solutions* model, I continually reflected on my own life and experience. Choice theory says we filter everything through our senses, values, and experiences. My experiences had informed my opinions about anger, conflict, and confrontation. I had swung to both sides of the pendulum—first as a submissive, compliant child, then as a passive-aggressive disrupter, and then as an overtly aggressive and sometimes dragon-like teenager.

Honestly, I despised all those versions of myself, but I most vehemently hated my dragon self. It occurred to me that I had been desperately seeking a vehicle through which I could express myself safely and appropriately, but for the most part, my attempts to communicate effectively had failed. I didn't know how to get my parents to trust me. I couldn't get through to my siblings. My friends recognized that I was different from them and had no problem telling me I didn't fit in. Boyfriends were attracted to the residual passive, compliant sides of me; they were shocked and repelled when the fire-breathing dragon showed herself. It almost made me sick—the revulsion I had toward the verbally aggressive things I said comingled with the feeling of power I obtained from finally getting my way.

I didn't know how to say no assertively; I had never been taught how. That submissive, passive, obedient child inside me still believed it was yes or nothing. The passive-aggressive preteen within protected my vulnerability: if people didn't trust me when I was telling the truth, I might as well do what I wanted and lie about it. Aggression was my only way of holding my boundaries; I didn't know any other way to do it. Assertive language and behavior were not encouraged, acknowledged, or rewarded—not just by my parents but by everyone I considered to be in authority.

I firmly believe I cannot lead people to a place that I have never been. Over the four years that I studied and refined the *Anger Solutions* model, I kitchen tested everything on myself. It was a four-year period of intense self-work. I prayed and cried often, had many a-ha moments, and made some commitments to myself that I would do better—not only for myself but also for my marriage, for our children, and for the communities I serve. You see, *Anger Solutions* is not an anger-management program. It is a journey of introspection, a systematic process of shifting out of limiting beliefs into empowering ones, and it is a powerful decision-making model that has the capacity to transform every interaction, every relationship, every conflict into something that produces radical, positive, and lasting change. Since its inception in 1994, tens of thousands of people have been shown how to change their lives by shifting their thoughts while learning to process their emotions and the problems that incited them.

The Theories Informing the Work

One thing I learned over the course of my professional journey is that there is no such thing as a one-size-fits-all approach to therapy. Thus, the work I do in psychotherapy is *multimodal.* What that means is I do not try to squish all my clients into a single treatment model. Most people think of talk therapy when they visualize counseling. There are many forms of talk therapy: Cognitive behavioral therapy (CBT)[1] is popular because it explores how shifting thoughts can impact feelings and subsequent behaviors, but it isn't for everyone. I apply elements of dialectical behavior therapy (DBT),[2] rational emotive behavior therapy,[3] solution-focused therapy,[4] mindfulness-based stress reduction (MBSR),[5] and psychiatric rehabilitation.[6] Most of all, my work is deeply rooted in William Glasser's choice theory, which informs reality therapy.

You will hear me refer to Glasser often. One of my greatest takeaways from his work is that there is no such thing as common sense; people do what makes sense to them. Using a multimodal approach rooted in choice theory makes sense to me. Choice theory is empowering for clients. It offers them a framework with which to combat the fallacy of control and to focus on what matters. Choice theory offers a framework for how anger develops that makes sense to me. And the best thing about choice theory is that when applied properly through reality therapy, I can use it to leverage people into choosing radical change for themselves rather than forcing it down their closed, change-resistant, unwilling throats.

You will also see a lot of Albert Ellis's rational emotive behavior therapy referenced in my work. Ellis was a bit of a psychological radical. He didn't mince his words, and his approach was much more in your face than the quieter, less aggressive CBT. Ellis's ideas around thoughts informing our feelings and behaviors are integral to all forms of talk therapy, and his simple strategies for effecting change still make sense for me and my clients. In the pages that follow, I have attempted to distill the key psychological theories that inform the work of *Anger Solutions* in a way that is interesting, engaging, and feels as far away from the parent lecture as possible.

Your Journey to Transformation Begins Here

Anger Solutions is about transforming your behavior—that is true. But it is so much more than that. *Anger Solutions* is a decision-making model that harnesses the power of your beliefs and thoughts, allowing you to wrest back control of the things you can while releasing all the things you can't. It is about using the right skills and knowledge to ask the right questions so you get the best answers. It is about forging healthy relationships through open and safe communication and the establishment of strong connections. It is about leveraging yourself into more positive outcomes by winning the fight that rages on the battlefield of the mind.

The Rise of Rage is about transformation—yours. You don't have anger problems; you never did. You have problems that cause you to feel angry. You have choices. You can choose to be a grumpy fire-breathing dragon that torches everyone and everything that crosses you, or you can learn to harness and leverage the energy of anger, using it to help you effectively express yourself and solve your problems.

This book will inspire you to unlearn everything you thought you knew about anger and its etiology. It will provide context for the factors that may contribute to anger, and it will share how one who is wise and concerned about creating positive outcomes might apply that knowledge. My hope for you is that you will not only release faulty beliefs about anger that have hampered your growth and ability to effectively solve those anger-inducing problems but that you will also experience the freedom that comes with knowing and loving yourself, setting clear boundaries, and using simple but effective tools to express your needs and solve your problems.

At the conclusion of each chapter, you will find a summary of the key takeaways as well as a suggestion for how you can actively integrate what you have learned so you can begin effecting the transformation you desire. Some of my suggestions may push you out of your comfort zone; if you want to grow, shift, or change, you must learn to get comfortable with the discomfort. I encourage you to push through and do the work. You won't regret it. Hang tight and read on. As one who has walked this road before, I assure you I'll be with you every step of the way.

—Julie

I

THE RISE OF RAGE

Talking 'bout My Generation

THE SLOGAN FOR the Republican candidate in the 2017 US presidential election was "Make America Great Again." Many folks who were not sold on the catchy phrase dared to ask the question: *When was America great?* Was it when criminals and debtors were being shipped to the New World as punishment by the crown, being forced to settle in a land they didn't know or understand? Was it when the First Nations of those lands were forced from their homes to make way for the colonizers? Was it great during the Boston Tea Party or when the gangs of New York were wreaking death and havoc on the burgeoning city? Was it great when immigrants escaping the potato famine were stigmatized and maligned for no fault of their own? Was it great during the several hundred years of slave trade, building the nation's wealth on the backs of people stolen from their homelands and sold like chattel? Was it great when lynchings were a reason to take kids out of school so they could watch or when burning Black people to death was documented in photos and then sold as postcard keepsakes?

Maybe America was great during the Salem witch trials or when Japanese Americans were forced into internment camps. Perhaps it was during the '60s when the civil rights movement began to gather steam or during the '70s when the antiwar protests and free love movements became a thing. Was America great when Black Wall Street was bombed, businesses burned to the ground, and business owners shot without legal or moral consequence? Was America great during the Great Depression or when the banks were buying and selling people's mortgages in some complicated scheme that eventually culminated in the housing market crash of 2007? Was it great when police were video recorded as they choked the life out of a man pleading for his mother?

Now, listen. Before you return this book and cancel me, please understand something. I am simply repeating the questions I heard from detractors of the MAGA slogan. I realize that like every other powerhouse nation in history, the United States of America has experienced incredible moments of greatness. That said, it is also true there is much in US history (as it is for every nation on the planet) that reflects the depravity, greed, and callousness of its government and its people. That's harsh—also true.

My point in highlighting the darker moments of US history is not to malign a nation or its citizens but to demonstrate that human behavior in the best of times *and* the worst of times is driven by emotional states. Fear, anxiety, sadness, disgust, contempt, disrespect, greed, selfishness, superiority, entitlement, and, of course, anger have informed many poor choices—if not every poor choice—made by every leader in history. Allow me to take you on an annotated journey through history as it relates to anger.

The Angry Gods

Anger and wrath have historically been paired with visual imagery or mythology of powerful, malevolent beings who felt justified in meting out punishment for perceived injustices. The underlying message was threefold: (1) anger is unbridled power; (2) anger is violent, dangerous, and/or harmful; and (3) anger is the privilege of the powerful.

Anger always seemed to be the response when the gods' rules were broken, their boundaries violated, their commands disobeyed, or their expectations not met. Regardless of the culture in which they originated, stories were told of angry gods who poured out their wrath on disobedient or disloyal subjects. The God of Israel sent plagues, serpents, and earthquakes and even allowed his chosen people to be taken into captivity because they violated the boundaries and broke the rules he had set in place for them. The Buddha noted that anger is a "moral blemish"[1] and a form of suffering, while Christianity lists anger as the fourth of the seven deadly sins.

Within the context of mythology and ancient religious texts, one might assume the following three things:

(1) Anger is the prerogative of supernatural beings who are justified in how they express it, even if the form of expression is painful, punitive, and violent or results in widespread misery and death.

(2) Anger in individuals has disruptive and divisive effects that contribute to social disorganization and aggression between groups.

(3) Anger control is essential because it helps maintain political and social stability and manage the behavior of the masses.

The earliest written texts from across the world describe anger as something to be feared, avoided, and appeased. Ancient documents referred most often to the anger of the gods, with similarities in mythological lore despite diverse origins (Sri Lanka, China, Norway, Greece, Italy, Africa, South America, and the Middle East). Common themes in those early texts describe anger as paired with malevolence, evil spirits filled with ill intent, and angry gods who punished disloyal or disobedient subjects with natural disasters and social disruption.

Several myths about anger pervaded the thinking of the ancient day. Anger was believed to lead to the abandonment of morality—that those expressing anger would become animalistic and no longer human. It was believed that anger led to sorcery and that anger was vain or self-serving and without purpose. Anger in humans disturbed the gods. Anger often resulted in aggression that could culminate in deadly violence. In Greek tradition, anger was triggered by insult, rejection, and perceived injustice. It was manifested by nonverbal cues such as facial expressions or self-harm and acted on with physical aggression, assault, or murder.

Aristotle described anger (the Greek *orge*) as the desire to be avenged for a perceived injustice. Throughout early history, anger was conceived of as the strongest of emotions and was often perceived as the mechanism by which humans could achieve pleasure while avoiding pain.

In warrior cultures, anger was cultivated as an altered state that made soldiers such as the Norse berserkers, the Celts, or the Thracians fierce in battle. In Southeast Asia, the Malay word *amok* is meant to describe a murderous frenzy coupled with temporary insanity, intense fury, or rage. Interestingly, this word, with its roots in seventeenth-century Southern Indian warrior classes, is attributed almost exclusively to men.

If we were to examine how anger has been conceptualized through the ages, we might say it was first framed as bestial passion—irrational, maladaptive, impairing judgment, and breeding disorganized thought and action.

Even Sun Tzu taught that anger was a weakness that when found in his enemies, could be capitalized on. Marcus Aurelius also believed that giving in to anger was a weakness. He preferred serving up revenge after the heat of anger had dissipated.

Seneca is supposed to be one of the first anger scholars. He believed anger should be eliminated or eradicated in favor of cultivating a peaceful mind. Pythagoras believed conscious restraint of anger (that is, anger expressed in word or deed) would encourage patience and self-control.

Fast forward to the twentieth century, when many of these ancient ideas prevailed in more modern conceptualizations of anger. Psychologists coined terms like *anger attacks, road rage,* and *intermittent explosive disorder,* implying that anger is pathological and results in irrational or aggressive behavior that can only be moderated with medication. The notion that anger is part and parcel of psychopathology and can be diagnosed and treated, or that it is some form of mental defect, is still common today.

What I find amusing are the many breaks in the lines of logic for these early conceptualizations of anger. Anger was touted as a sign of weakness, yet it was called on as a form of strength for those going to war. In Greek culture, *orge* was perceived as hot, immediate, and manly, while *cholos* anger was weak, cold, delayed, and attributed to women; after all, revenge is a dish best served cold. But wait a minute . . . wasn't it Marcus Aurelius who said that? The overarching themes related to anger support the implication that it is something that must be controlled.

So Mad Right Now

Consider what we have learned so far. Anger has historically been linked to words like *malevolence, punishment, fear, unbridled power, dangerous, violent, harmful, insanity, aggression, bestial passion, sorcery, vanity, inappropriate, amoral, childish, shameful, murderous, weakness,* and the list goes on. Do any of these words come close to describing anger?

Here's the thing. These words are descriptive in nature, creating word pictures in our minds of what anger is *like.* They are metaphors that encourage us to feel a certain kind of way about anger, but they do nothing to help extract anger from the mythical restraints that have enshrouded it for millennia.

We can look at examples throughout ancient and current history (revolutions, world wars, conscription, the antiwar movement of the late '60s and '70s, civil rights movements, the struggle for independence from colonial rule, political unrest, protests against austerity measures, Black Lives Matter, the storming of the US Capitol, and Canadian trucker convoys) that we might say prove the rule that anger leads to intragroup aggression and social disorganization. Is that the whole story?

There are many common misconceptions about anger: what it is, what it isn't, how it works, why it works, what it's for, and how to express it. Anger is one of those great emotional paradoxes. We as human beings experience anger on a regular basis, but unlike happiness, sadness, and fear, we struggle with its expression. When we're happy, we laugh. When we're sad, we cry. When we're afraid, we tremble, run, fight, or hide. But when we're angry, we somehow get stuck. Somehow, throughout the course of time, we have come to believe that anger is too volatile, too dangerous, too violent an emotion.

I suppose if you look at the history of mankind, from Cain to Judas to Jack the Ripper to Hitler to the political and social dysfunction of the twenty-first century, the examples we have for coping with anger haven't left us much we can, in good conscience, use. However, there are two sides to every story and two ways to learn from history. When I think of Joseph, Jesus, Churchill, Gandhi, Mother Theresa, Mandela, Malcolm X, or Martin Luther King, I see another side of anger—that is the limitless potential for human beings to make the right choices even in the throes of intense negative emotions.

Anger may be a tool employed alongside fear by the powerful to control society, but it can also be a catalyst for positive change. The truth is that every human being under the sun experiences varying intensities of anger from time to time. With the burden of historical texts and more recent anger research weighing heavily on our consciousness, we have come to believe that since anger is best identified through behavior, anger *is* behavior.

The past several years of chaos and unrest have proven that anger is a stable, enduring part of the human construct, and no number of anger-management tactics will make it go away. What we have also seen in light of worldwide Black Lives Matter protests; political supporters rioting, storming, and vandalizing public buildings; unprovoked assaults; school shootings;

hate crimes; and an outpouring of vitriolic abuse on social media platforms is an apparent inability of modern society to manage big emotions like anger. Emotions need to be felt and acknowledged. Once acknowledged, they need to be expressed, not managed or controlled. Once expressed, the problems that ignited those emotions must be addressed and, if possible, resolved.

I realize there are many problems in this world that cannot be solved easily, if at all. There are too many opposing views; there is too much greed; there are too many conflicting political agendas, too many narcissists, and too many powerful corporations that have no concern for the greater good. I can't change those things. It is unlikely that you can either. What you and I can do is learn to recognize and acknowledge our big feelings and express them in ways that are safe and appropriate, ways that help us get our needs met without causing harm to others.

Why Bother?

Of all the human emotions, anger is probably the most misunderstood. Why is it important to understand anger at all? The answer to that question lies in your decision to read this book.

You need to understand yourself. I'll venture the reason you decided to pick up this book and read it has something to do with your desire to finally do something about the way you currently deal with your anger. You have experienced the rise of rage within you. Perhaps you are fed up with feeling angry and not having any way to express it. Maybe you no longer want to hold it all inside. You're sick and tired of feeling sick and tired, and you are fed up with being everybody's doormat.

Maybe the anger inside you is starting to build, and you're afraid that if it explodes, you may do something you'll regret later. It could be that your relationships are suffering because you tend to act out your anger more aggressively. You don't know why you blow up so quickly or why certain things make you mad. You just know you're ready to change, and you need some help. You need to understand what anger really is, how it develops, and why you feel the way you feel. This book will help you accomplish all of that and more.

You need help understanding others. Perhaps you live with an angry person, or you know someone who does. Maybe your biggest need right now is to better understand your loved one who has difficulty expressing anger. Maybe your challenging person is someone with whom you work—a boss, a colleague, or an employee. You like your job, but you don't like the tension and toxicity that pervade the office. After two-plus years of working from home, you have no idea how you'll readjust to such a negative work environment. You're looking for a new perspective—some tools to help you break the ice and at least work comfortably with your coworkers.

You're not sure what you believe about anger. Many of our beliefs about anger are based on our personal experiences or what we learned from television and the movies. The way we were punished as children often affects our ideas about anger as well. In the early pages of this book, your traditional beliefs about anger will be challenged, and you will find yourself gaining new insight about what anger truly is. You'll come to understand that your beliefs determine how you behave. If you better understand anger, your beliefs about this emotion and how you express it will undoubtedly change.

Perhaps your self-esteem is in the toilet. When anger is expressed inappropriately, people react—and their reactions are bound to affect those expressing their anger. What if you have been expressing your anger in a way that makes people withdraw from relationships with you, thereby causing you to feel guilty, ashamed, or embarrassed? What if people are avoiding you or treating you in a way that makes you feel small or unloved? What if you are using anger to feel powerful, unique, or heard?

Perhaps you are struggling with guilt because of the things you have said or done in the heat of anger. Garnering a better understanding of anger and how it develops has helped my clients in this boat to change their behavior. When they began expressing themselves in less destructive ways, they found themselves able to recover some of those lost relationships and rebuild some of what was broken down. A bonus of this result is a decrease in guilt and an increase in self-esteem. Perhaps by exploring new ways to express your anger, you will experience the same results as those who have walked this road before.

It is imperative we understand that much of what occurs in our lives on an emotional level happens without our conscious awareness. Our first goal, then, is to increase our awareness about what is happening, how we feel about it, and what we should do about those feelings. How do we do that?

Let's begin by delving deeper into the myths that have been perpetuated about anger and debunking them.

Summary

1. Anger has historically been equated with aggression and punitive or retaliatory behavior.
2. Emotions must be felt, acknowledged, and expressed.
3. The problems that ignite big feelings must be resolved.

Reflection

What are your motivations for reading *The Rise of Rage?* Of the possibilities I presented, which of them resonates most deeply with you? Journal your thoughts in preparation for the next chapter.

2

WHAT WE DON'T SEE

We do not see things as they are; we see things as we are.

—*Anaïs Nin*

AVERY, THE GENERAL manager of the local luxury vehicle dealership, storms out of his office, screaming at the sales team for their low sales numbers last month. After shredding them to bits, he huffs a deep breath and stalks back into his office, slamming the door behind him.

After making a valiant attempt at damage control with his team, the exhausted sales manager, Jim, steps silently out of his office at the end of the day. He closes the door gently but firmly, nods farewell to his colleagues, and steps out to his car. Stopping at his favorite watering hole, he hands the bartender his keys and asks for his usual drink with the order to "keep 'em coming." As he nurses his drink, he plots ways he can ruin Avery's career without anyone knowing he is behind it.

While Avery stands hollering at his team, the office manager, Sue, surreptitiously but desperately fishes through her purse for her ulcer medication as a spasm of pain rips through her midsection. Later that evening, after an argument with her partner, she retreats into the bathroom, locking the door behind her. She runs a hot, foamy bath and muffles her sobs as water fills the tub.

Bob, a member of the sales team, heads to the gym on his lunch break. By his own admission, he has a short fuse. It doesn't take much to set him off. He screeches his way through traffic, cursing every red light, every bad driver, every delay that stands between him and a smooth ride to the gym. On arrival, he straps on his boxing gloves and heads straight to the heavy bag. After thirty minutes of picturing Avery's face and beating the sand right out of the bag, he is physically and emotionally spent—for now.

Debbie, Avery's wife, has had a rough day of her own. Avery comes home venting drive plasma,[1] as he seems to do every other day. She is fed up with his constantly angry, critical, and emotionally abusive behavior. In her typical fashion, she quietly serves him dinner, delivering only monosyllabic responses to any conversation directed her way. He has no idea, but in another month, she will have enough money set aside, and when she does, she's taking herself and the kids and getting far, far away from Avery and his lousy attitude.

Avery, Jim, Susan, Bob, and Debbie are all angry. How do we know it? What is anger anyway? What isn't it? How is it possible that all these people, with their unique responses, are filled with rage?

If we look at Bob, the fellow with the short fuse, right away we say, "Of course he is angry. Look at what he is *doing*: he is cursing, driving recklessly, yelling at the traffic." What we just described is Bob's behavior, not how he is feeling. It is easy to label Avery's behavior as anger—yelling, hurling abusive insults, slamming doors. It's no secret that he is angry, right?

If we examine Sue's behavior, we might assume she is depressed, maybe grieving. Perhaps she is just in pain, hence her need to soak in the tub. Then there is Jim. Simple observation reveals nothing at all. He is just a regular guy, stopping for a drink before going home at the end of the day. How, then, do we reach the conclusion that he is angry? Even Debbie, going quietly about her plans, is seething inside, but you would never know it to look at her.

The Anger Iceberg versus the Iceberg of Behavior

Traditional anger management says anger is a secondary emotion. It declares that we see anger while underneath the surface is a host of other emotions. Anger, it is said, is what emerges to "protect" us from our other emotions such as fear, sadness, or anxiety. When one feels attacked, they might respond with aggression to protect themselves. That aggression is perceived as anger. If an illiterate parent is embarrassed by their inability to read a story to their child, they may respond with criticism or by shouting, "I'm busy! I don't have time to read to you" to deflect from the truth that they cannot read. That outburst is labeled as anger.

The Anger Iceberg

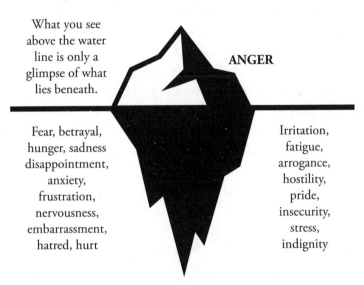

What you see above the water line is only a glimpse of what lies beneath.

ANGER

Fear, betrayal, hunger, sadness disappointment, anxiety, frustration, nervousness, embarrassment, hatred, hurt

Irritation, fatigue, arrogance, hostility, pride, insecurity, stress, indignity

There is a grain of truth in this model. Certainly, behaviors typically associated with anger may be used to protect us from a perceived emotional or physical threat; however, the anger is not what we see. What you *see* is behavior. You then interpret the behavior and make meaning of it—deciding

The Iceberg of Behavior

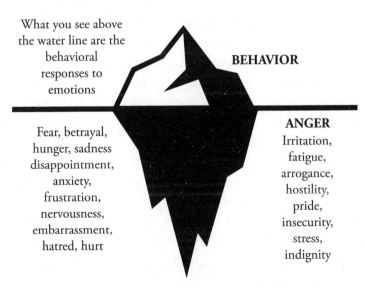

What you see above the water line are the behavioral responses to emotions

BEHAVIOR

Fear, betrayal, hunger, sadness disappointment, anxiety, frustration, nervousness, embarrassment, hatred, hurt

ANGER
Irritation, fatigue, arrogance, hostility, pride, insecurity, stress, indignity

that what you see is reflective of this emotion or that. You see someone smiling and interpret the smile to reflect happiness. You see someone crying and decide the person is sad. You see someone scowling, and you assume they are feeling frustrated or angry. What you are seeing is *behavior.*

Anger is not behavior. It is an emotion. It is not something we do or can necessarily see; it is something we *feel.* Avery, Jim, Sue, Bob, and Debbie all experience varied intensities of anger; however, their behaviors—their anger styles—represent their own unique choice for expressing their anger.

Emotions are not readily measurable or even visible. Dr. Paul Ekman's work in deception detection supports this. He notes that it is possible for human beings to mask their true emotions by schooling facial features, mincing words, and using both practiced and unconscious nonverbal behaviors to conceal true emotional states.

You don't even have to go to the science to see proof of this. Just think of that time you asked your friend, spouse, sibling, parent, or coworker if everything was okay, and their response muttered through gritted teeth was "I'm *fine.*" You knew they were not fine, but you went with it anyway. Why? You didn't want to call them out on the suspicion that they were concealing their real feelings.

If emotions are felt experiences that inform behaviors but may also be concealed or internalized, this is where the philosophers of old and psychologists of the nineteenth and twentieth centuries got it wrong. They focused on the behaviors that are assumed to always accompany the emotion—so much so that in conceptualizing the feeling, they excluded it from the equation. Instead, they bought into the lie that anger is dangerous, and they sought to do as Seneca suggested—to "eradicate anger in favour of a tranquil mind."[2]

Dr. Paul Ekman, a leading researcher and scholar in the areas of emotions and emotional expression, adheres to the theory of anger as a primary or basic emotion, one that is universally experienced and recognized simply by facial expression. Basic emotions theory advocates note that anger may be expressed as early as the end of the first year, when infants are able to make meaning of the means and ends of their behavior, and they perceive that their attempts to attain an objective may be blocked or thwarted. In simpler terms, when babies develop to the point where they can recognize that something they want is not immediately attainable due to obstacles or their limited motor control, they experience and express anger.

I recall my granddaughter at that age learning how to attach and detach building blocks. Attaching them was easy, and the pleasure of the accomplishment was plain to see in her facial expressions and physical reactions. Pulling the blocks apart was a different story. She lacked the muscle coordination and upper body strength to detach the blocks with ease. Her frustration built quickly, and soon she was scowling, crying, and tossing the blocks away. My little grandbaby had made the connection between her attempts to achieve a goal and a seemingly insurmountable obstacle, and this caused her to feel angry. She expressed her feelings by acting out.

Nova's tantrum was not her anger. The tantrum was her *vehicle* for expressing an emotion she was too immature to name. Anger is a part of the human construct, a basic emotion, just as much as happiness, sadness, or fear. Anger is an emotional response to an undesirable stimulus.

The Greek language has many words for anger. *Chalepaino* means "annoyed." *Kotos* is the word used for "resentment." *Cholos* is "bitterness." *Thumos* represents "zeal" or "energy." *Orge* is used to describe "rage" or "madness." In English, we, too, have many words to describe anger. The thing is we do not often associate those words with the visual images of danger, violence, or aggression that we have come to equate with anger. Frustration akin to what my grandbaby felt, irritation, deep disappointment, and upset, as well as being mad, rageful, livid, and incensed, are all words we could use to describe angry feelings.

I Don't Have the Words

I had a friend who defined every emotion she ever experienced with the words *happy, sad, afraid*, and *upset*. She would watch an episode of her favorite television series, and when something happened to a character she liked, she would say, "I'm so *happy* this happened to them." Her response was the same when she bought a pair of shoes at the sale price; she felt *happy*. When she gave birth to her first child, she expressed feeling *so happy*. Conversely, if she went to the store to purchase a sale item and there were none left, she would feel *upset*. She verbalized experiencing the same emotional response of *upset* when her marriage broke up.

It was incredibly difficult for us to converse about anything on a deeper emotional level because she did not have a base in her vocabulary to support anything but talk of shallow topics. I found it both fascinating and sad that she had such a limited vocabulary with which to express herself. She was completely unaware that her inability to accurately define her feelings was a hindrance to her ability to communicate with others.

Knowing how you feel and having the ability to accurately express that feeling are essential. Try this little experiment right now as you are reading. Think back to the happiest moment you have ever experienced in your life. Focus on that moment and place yourself in that gladdened state. Now sit back and smile as broadly as you can. With that wide, broad, ecstatic grin on your face, say as loudly as you can, "I'm so depressed!" Monitor what happens to your body as you say the words. You will likely feel your facial muscles struggle to convert your smile into a frown. You might find your posture changing as you say the word *depressed*.

Interesting phenomenon, isn't it? Have you ever noticed that the more you talk about feeling a certain way, the more you feel that way? It is vital that you carefully define the emotion you are experiencing before you express verbally how you feel. Think of it like this: there are varying degrees and intensities for every emotion we experience. If you regarded happiness as a continuum or a *valence* from, say, content to blissful, there would be a plethora of emotional degrees in between.

content   pleased   happy   joyful   ecstatic   blissful

Now, if I bought a pair of shoes and got them at 50 percent off the lowest ticketed price, I might be fairly pleased about that. I most certainly wouldn't be feeling blissful about it. Conversely, if my wedding day was indeed the happiest day of my life, had I expressed my emotional experience as being "just okay" or "content," that would not have nearly begun to accurately depict how I was feeling.

Consider this valence in terms of anger.

frustrated   angry   upset   furious   livid   red-hot rage

Suppose you are in a busy parking lot during the height of the holiday shopping season and you are having difficulty finding a parking spot.

Would *furious* accurately describe your emotion, or would *frustrated* be a better word?

Now try that other exercise again. Put yourself in a totally relaxed position and breathe out the words "I am so furious!" What happens to your body? Does it tense up? Do your fists tighten? How do those words come out of your mouth? Is your face still relaxed, or are your teeth clenched tight as you say the word *furious*? Is heat radiating from your body as though you could breathe fire?

I trust that you see the power our choice of words has over our behavioral responses. It is imperative that we choose our feeling words wisely so that we do not inadvertently escalate mild feelings into intense emotions.

Let us then clarify anger for once and for all. Anger is defined in the great book of Webster as "a strong feeling of displeasure and usually of antagonism." Oxford dictionaries describe anger like this: "a strong feeling of annoyance, displeasure, or hostility." The *Cambridge Dictionary*'s definition is closer to that of Aristotle's *orge*: "a strong feeling that makes you want to hurt someone or be unpleasant because of something unfair or unkind that has happened." The common denominator in each definition is the phrase "a strong feeling." There you have it. Anger is an emotion. Where we tend to get stuck is when anger manifests as *orge*, and people act on their desire to "hurt someone or be unpleasant."

What's Your Style?

Where it gets dicey is that traditional anger-management models focus on behavior and call it *anger*. The challenge is there are many people who internalize their behavioral responses to anger rather than externalizing them. Take Susan, for example. Sue communicates in a passive style. She rarely asks directly for what she wants, preferring to beat around the bush. She has difficulty making eye contact and saying no to unreasonable requests, and she defers to the decisions of others so as not to rock the boat. When something angers Sue, she holds that negative energy inside, choosing not to point out the injustice, the broken rule, or the unmet expectation; instead, she says everything is "fine." After many years of everything being "fine," Sue develops a peptic ulcer, high blood pressure, and chronic migraines. She is not fine. In *Anger Solutions*, we call this the Bottler style of anger expression.

Sue uses behavior to mask her true emotions; however, those emotions are still being expressed, albeit badly. The energy is indeed active, and it is creating a result—one that is primarily harmful to Sue. She accepts this harm as reasonable in favor of maintaining the status quo, avoiding conflict, and maintaining her easygoing reputation.

Over my many years of working with people to resolve anger, I have identified nine additional anger styles. A close cousin of the Bottler is the Controlled Blaster. Controlled Blasters tend to contain their angry feelings and energy for as long as they are capable until that final straw falls, and they explode. The explosion is typically not directed at the person(s) or situation(s) that caused their anger; rather, it impacts the person or situation that represents that final straw. The fallout is messy. Trust is eroded. Apologies must be made. And in the end, while the Controlled Blaster feels better for a moment, the lasting result is guilt, the need for reparations, shaky relationships, and unresolved problems.

The Chronic Venter is one who talks around issues instead of about the issue that has generated angry feelings. Chronic Venters are the Wendy and Willie Whiners of the family or the office. They complain much and often to people who cannot help, or they do so to avoid addressing the real problem when talking with people who can help. Chronic Venters talk *a lot*, and it is the same old story. Because of this, people stop listening because, frankly, same old song, different tune—and it's boring. For the Chronic Venter, this means the problems that sparked the anger in the first place remain unresolved.

Avery and Bob share characteristics of the Scrapper and the ACME Poster Child. Scrappers take their anger out on people or things that can't or won't fight back. They often resort to aggression because it makes them feel powerful and in control. The challenge is it is difficult to trust people who say they love you, but they often hurt you—and let's be clear: when aggression is used in place of communication, relationships fall apart. The ACME Poster Child is short-fused, exploding and de-escalating quickly. ACME Poster Children are often unaware of how their outbursts impact others and lack insight into how damaging their behavior can be to relationships. This lack of insight prevents ACME Poster Children from focusing on the problems that ignited the explosions; it also impairs their ability to see what reparations must be done after the fallout because they honestly do not believe the outburst was that bad to begin with. The inevitable outcome for both styles is that the underlying problems remain unresolved.

Silent Debbie is what I call the Iceberg. Make no mistake, she is seething inside; the fire of her anger burns so hot, it's blue. She knows her quiet anger is no match for Avery's boisterous, aggressive style. If ever he might emerge from his narcissism and self-absorption to notice her icy silence, she would reassure him that she is *fine*. She uses her silence as a buffer against his verbal abuse because she believes there is no point in telling him how she feels and what she needs to make the relationship work. He will likely respond by hurling accusations at her as to why the relationship challenges are her fault. So she forges ahead in silence, biding her time until she can walk away. Of course, the problems informing this life-altering decision will remain unsolved.

Bob's anger style is also reflective of the Conductor. Ideally, Conductors take the negative energy of anger and channel that energy into something positive. In Bob's case, he takes it to the gym and beats the heavy bag until he is ready to pass out. Others might clean obsessively, organize a closet or a desk, or do something creative like composing music or generating a piece of art on canvas or paper. There are also negative conductors, people like Jim, who take that negative energy and channel it into choices with poor outcomes such as drowning one's woes in alcohol.

Jim's path to alcoholism is a choice to numb his feelings rather than acknowledge them. His choice to seek revenge is representative of the Snake anger style. This passive-aggressive style of anger response is typical for those who feel powerless to confront aggression or abuse head-on, but knowing they can cause the aggressor pain in an indirect or covert way is immensely satisfying. Passive-aggressive behavior ranges from more overt nonverbals such as eye-rolling, loud impatient sighs, sarcasm, veiled threats, and backhanded compliments to more underhanded tactics like leaving people off important email threads, "forgetting" to tell others about the impromptu sales meeting, stalling on tasks that will help others get their jobs done on time, or playing nice in public while assassinating character behind closed doors.

Another style we see Avery using in his relationship with Debbie is that of Captain Criticize. An extension of the Scrapper and the Chronic Venter, Captain Criticize is all about what others *should* do and how they *could have* done things differently or better, mostly for his pleasure. Hurling constant criticism at others erodes intimacy, and without the trust, safety, and camaraderie that are inherent in intimacy, relationships quickly wither and die on the vine. Because the focus of Captain Criticize is on the *people* rather than the problems, the problems that caused the anger will never be resolved.

Lastly, the style we endorse combined with the Conductor—more on this later—for effective anger resolution is called Give and Take. This approach puts emotional expression and problem-solving first. It is about focusing on the *problem* instead of the person. It is about valuing relationships enough to seek to understand before being understood. It is about using effective, assertive, and compassionate communication to solve the problem, preserve the relationship, and release the energy that is attached to the emotion. The Give and Take style seeks to engage in collaborative conflict or problem resolution, aiming for a win-win or a fair-fair result that produces both short- and long-term gains for both parties. Only once this process is accomplished should the Conductor style be applied to release any residual angry energy.

In as many ways as anger can be experienced, it can also be expressed. The worst mistake we could make is to assume that one size fits all for anger expression and to embrace the fallacy that anger is always aggression or that anger is easily recognizable by one's behavior. Helen Keller once said, "The only thing worse than being blind is having sight but no vision."[3] Let's not get it twisted. Just because you see things a certain way doesn't make them that way. Effective anger resolution is all about paying attention to the things we don't see.

Summary

1) Anger is an emotion—a basic emotion that is universally experienced and recognized.
2) There are ten common styles of expressing anger:
   a. Bottler
   b. Controlled Blaster
   c. ACME Poster Child
   d. Chronic Venter

e. Scrapper

f. Iceberg

g. Conductor

h. Captain Criticize

i. Snake

j. Give and Take

Reflection

Which anger styles do you tend to use the most? Where did you learn these styles? What are the benefits of using them? What are the negative consequences of using each of your preferred styles?

Action Step

As you journal your responses, consider how things might improve if you found a way to express anger that garnered all the benefits you want without any of the negative consequences.

3

I'M A BELIEVER

SOME YEARS AGO, I was engaged to provide *Anger Solutions* coaching to a client of another therapist who was employed with an Employee Assistance Program provider. The client had been targeted by a workplace bully, and the harassment had escalated, eroding my client's ability to cope. He had said some threatening things about the bully, and his workplace immediately sent him off to get counseling and told him he could not return to work until *he* was safe to work with. Y'all know I could write for *days* about what was wrong with that picture. My client had progressed well and had regained the confidence to return to work and to resume therapy with his primary counselor. One day, his counselor called, and she was very upset.

"He has *relapsed!*" she cried. "He just called about an incident at work, and he *yelled* at me. The treatment obviously didn't work; he is still angry!"

Let me break that down. Her expectation was that by participating in fifteen weeks of *Anger Solutions* coaching, our client's "anger problem" would be *fixed*. She identified his yelling as the problem rather than trying to figure out the reason he was yelling. Not only had she mistaken my client's yelling for the problem but she also sounded afraid of the client because of his anger. That fear was palpable; I could feel it oozing through our telephone connection.

I asked her a question, knowing that she dealt primarily in addiction therapy. "What do you tell a client who has fallen off the wagon?"

She replied that she would encourage that client to return to Alcoholics Anonymous. She would tell them that it is okay and that people make mistakes. She would explore what triggered the return to substance use, and then she would work on helping them build resiliency and resistance so they could be more successful in the future.

I explained to her that her words of support and encouragement were warranted for our client as well. You see, we fear what we don't understand,

and my colleague did not understand anger. She believed the lie that anger and aggression are the same thing. She interpreted our client's yelling as "a relapse" into aggression rather than a frantic cry for help. I reminded her that anger is not a disease, nor is it something we need to fear. Once I challenged her beliefs, and we explored the reasons for his outburst, she came to understand that the client's feelings were justified despite his poor attempt at expressing them.

Actor and comedian John Belushi was one of the first performers on *Saturday Night Live*. He was known for his legendary characters, including one-half of the Blues Brothers, and his hilarious sketches on the show. A brilliant entertainer, Belushi performed with a manic, boisterous energy that has yet to be replicated. Belushi perished due to an overdose of heroin and cocaine in 1982. I recall watching his biography on television, and I was fascinated by the rise and fall of someone whom everyone agreed was remarkably and uniquely talented. Of course, one of the aspects of his life that I found most interesting was his beliefs and how they informed his behavior.

One of John Belushi's core beliefs was that drugs enhanced his performance on stage and on the screen. Perhaps that belief was informed by his fans' lackluster response to the roles in which he played the straight man. They wanted the wild, manic character they loved, and they wanted that guy to show up in every role. Because Belushi believed that drugs enhanced his ability to perform, it didn't matter how many barriers his friends and family placed between him and drugs; he was driven to find a way to obtain and use them. It didn't matter that his drug use led to his dismissal from *Saturday Night Live* on more than one occasion. When push came to shove for Belushi, it is no wonder that he turned to drugs to achieve enhancement of his mood rather than seek out the comfort of his friends and family.

In his article "The Human Side of Addiction: What Caused John Belushi's Death?" Stanton Peele considers the effect that a negative self-image had on Belushi's death: "*A negative self-image is so deep and pervasive that no amount of praise or achievement can allay it. Always living down a negative sense of themselves, they frantically seek experiences which [**they believe**] will relieve their pain.*"[1]

Note that I included the italicized words above. The *belief* that drugs will relieve the pain is what drives one to seek out the experience of taking drugs. Not everyone turns to drugs when they are suffering because not everyone **believes** that drugs are the answer. Peele further explores the possible effect of negative belief systems on Belushi's life and death: "*People only learn to hate themselves when those on whom they count for their earliest support and respect instead teach them that they are worthless or despicable. When a child has learned this message, he may spend the rest of his life trying to prove it is true and reacting with discomfort to any information or person which says it is not true.*"[2]

How does this relate to belief systems and anger? If Peele's theory is correct and Belushi had learned to believe either early in childhood or from his unforgiving fans that he was "worthless," that fundamental core belief would have served as the foundation for many others that would build his system of beliefs. *I am worthless, therefore:*

- I cannot succeed (worthless people cannot succeed, at least not on their own).
- I may be a success now, but it won't last—I'm not worthy of it.
- I cannot love myself (How can I love what is worthless?).
- I am not worthy of love (because I am worthless).
- I will never be thin, drug-free, or abstinent from alcohol and nicotine (my lack of self-worth prevents me from doing what is necessary to quit my bad habits).
- It doesn't matter if I die from an overdose (if I have no worth, I have no reason to live).

The insidious nature of negative beliefs is the extent to which they can shape our lives. As it was for Belushi, so it is for many members of our society. Low self-worth coupled with faulty core beliefs can send people into a downward spiral of poor coping mechanisms, anger, depression, and unfulfillment.

Let us now examine the power of belief to shape our experience and expression of anger. We will start by examining the most common myths that we accept about anger.

Myth 1: Anger Is Behavior

I know you are likely getting tired of reading this over and over again, but a wise man said, "Repetition is the mother of skill."[3] Hear this again: Anger is *not* behavior! Anger is experienced as a negative emotion, one of the basic emotions that we as humans experience, along with happiness or enjoyment, sadness, anger, fear, disgust, and surprise. We do not *do* happy, or sad, or afraid. Why, then, should we expect to *do* anger? We do not use the term "I'm getting happy!" on a regular basis, but it is not unusual for one to say, "I'm getting mad at you!"

I have found this myth to be the most widely believed in society. It is what I call a *foundational* belief because almost every other myth that exists about anger rests on this first one. Just as my colleague perceived the client's behavior—yelling—to be his anger and responded with fear and panic, many other people who ascribe to this belief may respond in kind. It is imperative that we go right to the heart of the matter and change this foundational belief. Once this myth is dispelled, the other myths will melt away like the Wicked Witch of the West.

Myth 2: Anger Is Bad

You get this, right? If anger is a behavior, then of course it is bad—that goes without saying. If anger equals hitting, yelling, screaming, slamming doors, and all the other behaviors we see as negative, then no wonder we see anger as bad. The truth is that experiencing the emotion of anger in and of itself is not "bad," although it never feels good to be cross, mad, furious, or livid. The *ways* we choose to express anger can sometimes be labeled as *bad* or *unacceptable.*

Myth 3: Anger Should Not Be Expressed

If anger is an emotion, then it follows that we should be free to express our anger as freely as we express our other basic emotions. No one thinks it odd that humans express their happiness, sadness, or fear. In my seminars, I have heard it explained this way: "Anger is dangerous," "Anger is sinful," "Showing your anger doesn't help you in the end." Think about this: Unexpressed anger has its repercussions as well. Unresolved, unexpressed anger can lead to a wide range of physical problems such as ulcers, high blood pressure, migraines, heart disease, and stroke, to name only a few. Not expressing anger can hold far more consequences for the angry person in the way of ongoing emotional problems as a result of the unresolved feelings.

Myth 4: Anger and Aggression Are the Same Things

This is a myth propagated and reinforced daily by the media and Hollywood. In the movies or on TV, when people get angry, they almost always resort to violence as a means of resolving their anger. It is most important to remember that anger is an *emotion*. Aggression is only one of many possible behavioral responses to anger.

Unlike animals, the choice for humans to attack or flee is not such a simple one. We have higher reasoning abilities, which enables us to determine the best course of action or reaction toward the perceived threat. The physiological response to anger ends at the point of making a choice. Any action taken in response to the heightened physiological effects of fight or flight is solely the responsibility of the person taking the action.

Myth 5: Women and Children Should Not Express Anger

Historically, women and children who expressed anger outwardly were depicted as "lacking moral instruction, cognitively immature, or having an underdeveloped rational mind."[4] The Greeks believed that we were born angry but that anger was a precursor for disease in infants. The Darwinians popularized the use of the word *tantrum*, assigning it to children rather than the adults it had originally been attributed to. Parents were encouraged to punish tantrums so as to break the will of the child.

This philosophy perpetuated the belief that anger and the behaviors associated with it are the domain of those in authority—in this case, the parents—and it was fine for them to mete out punishment even if it meant using the same angry behaviors for which the child was being disciplined. Even as recently as the 1990s, studies exploring sex differences in anger expression concluded that while men express their stress, anger and frustration by acting out, women "tend and befriend."[5] Studies like these perpetuated preexisting stereotypes, reinforcing that outwardly expressed anger in women was against the norm; therefore, it was inappropriate and somehow representative of emotional dysfunction.

Children are often scolded for expressing their anger—even if many times they are only doing what they learned from their parents or other role models. How many times do we tell our children that hitting or yelling or stomping away is "bad" without offering alternatives to their behavior? Little children are concrete thinkers, and they associate their behavior with the way they feel. If we reprimand them for their behavior without separating it from their emotion, we ingrain in them the foundational belief that anger is behavior *and* that anger is bad.

From an early age, children learn that it is better to repress anger than to express it since expressing anger is typically cause for punishment or admonition from a parent or an authority figure. Think of how this foundational belief is supported through the school years. Steve and Billy are fighting in the schoolyard. The principal calls them into his office and suspends them both. They are punished for attempting to resolve their anger in an inappropriate way; however, no alternatives are given outside of the customary "shake hands and say you're sorry."

What the principal doesn't know is that Steve has been encouraged to bully Billy because Billy doesn't look or sound like Steve. He hears all about the "foreigners coming here to steal our jobs" from his parents. He listens closely when the adults around him justify racial violence using arguments around "Black-on-Black violence" or "guns don't kill people."

The principal thinks he is teaching the boys to resolve their differences like men; in fact, the differences remain—there has been no dialogue, no resolution, and no agreement to disagree. Let's not even bother with the fact that Steve and Billy are only ten years old. They have no idea what "shake hands like men" even means. The principal hasn't asked about nor addressed the reasons the boys have been fighting. Steve and Billy are still angry at one another; they just know that fighting is out of the question.

Steve will most likely take the bullying underground and make sure that if they fight, it will be somewhere not on school property. Billy may develop the belief that defending himself is useless since he received the same punishment as the instigator of the aggression. Worse yet, the beliefs that lie beneath the motivation for the fight are still intact. What should the boys do to deal with their anger? They're still not sure. To top things off, they will inevitably face punishment from their parents for getting suspended. The underlying reason for the suspension may not be addressed in a way the boys can understand.

For women, it has long been an unspoken rule that they keep their anger to themselves. Women who were assertive or made bold moves in business or expressed confidence in their bodies and their sexuality were frowned on; similarly, it was not "proper" for women to openly express their anger. While men stereotypically act out their anger with aggression, violence, or risk-taking behaviors, women are expected to keep it in, explaining why so many use the Chronic Venting method of anger expression, or they use more passive styles like the "Iceberg." Although, over the years, women have become more empowered within society, effective and assertive ways of anger expression must still be taught and encouraged among the female populous.

Myth 6: If I Express My Anger, Bad Things Will Happen

We have established that anger is an emotion; as such, it should not be judged as "bad" or "dangerous." Yet the popular belief remains that anger, if expressed, can only lead to "bad things." What people choose to forget is that our choices and actions determine our outcomes, not the feelings that preclude them. I can be hopping mad and stay silent. I could also be slightly irritated and snap at someone with sharp words. The methods we use to express our emotions are what inform our outcomes, not the emotions themselves.

Think of the good that has been done in the world because someone got angry enough to push for change: The abolition of the trans-Atlantic slave trade. The civil rights movement. Voting rights for women. The #MeToo movement. Think of how many lives have been saved because of the Mothers Against Drunk Driving (MADD) program. Think of the early storm-warning systems now in use. All because someone or a group of *someones* decided enough was enough and there needed to be a change. Feeling angry doesn't invariably lead to bad outcomes. Choosing poorly how that anger will be expressed may well lead to negative consequences. Here's the thing: The choice is yours. Every time.

Which of these myths have you always believed is reality? With which of these are you already arguing? Think about it for a while. Think of your own anger style and the behaviors you typically choose to express or conceal your anger. Why do you choose those particular behaviors? Could it be because you believe either one or more of these myths to be true, and that belief governs the behaviors you choose? You see, belief truly *is* the basis of action.

The Neurobiological Explanation for Anger

Why do we fear anger so much? Could it be that for all the talk of anger management, road rage, and the like, we still lack an understanding of the emotion? A secondary belief that emerges from the notion that anger is bad, and that anger equals aggression, is that anger is dangerous. Dangerous things are to be feared, are they not?

Neuropsychiatrist Daniel Siegel, MD, and parenting expert Tina Payne Bryson, PhD, conceptualized the model of the upstairs and downstairs brain to help parents explain brain behavior to their children. This model has been adapted by eye movement desensitization and reprocessing experts to help people understand the neurobiological basis of anger.

As you are reading this, take your left thumb and tuck it into the palm of your left hand. Close the remaining fingers around it, making a fist. Imagine that this fist is your brain.

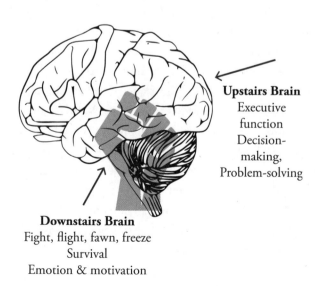

Upstairs Brain
Executive
function
Decision-
making,
Problem-solving

Downstairs Brain
Fight, flight, fawn, freeze
Survival
Emotion & motivation

The thumb represents the downstairs brain. This area—the limbic system and the amygdala—is responsible for your fight-or-flight response, your emotions and motivation, bodily functions, and survival. This part of the brain is professional at *acting before thinking*.

Those fingers surrounding the downstairs brain represent your upstairs brain, the cerebral cortex. This mass of gray matter, particularly the frontal lobes, is responsible for decision-making, higher-order and critical thinking, executive function, emotional regulation, self-awareness, and more. This part of the brain helps you *think before acting*.

When the brain reacts to a perceived threat, the downstairs brain activates and overrides the upstairs brain functions. The body's metabolism rate increases, as do heart rate, blood pressure, and breathing. Saliva and mucus dry up, increasing the size of the air passages to the lungs. Surface blood vessels also constrict to reduce bleeding in case of injury. These changes are the downstairs brain preparing the body to engage in its survival functions— fight, flee, fawn, or freeze. They do not tell the individual which path to choose. That is the purview of the upstairs brain—but remember, the upstairs brain is put on standby whenever the limbic system is activated.

Note that I mentioned the brain reacting to a perceived threat. Sometimes what we perceive to be threatening is as benign as downy-soft ducklings. Other times the threat is real. Your perception is based on your experience, values, and senses, and if you believe what you see, you will react or respond in kind. So if your prior experience tells you that the circumstances you are facing right now are like another experience that proved threatening, you will immediately respond first on an emotional, then physiological, then intellectual level.

First, the brain makes meaning of the circumstance and registers the perceived threat. Then the downstairs brain will put the body in a state fight or flight so that whatever happens next, the body will be prepared for it. Lastly, the limbic system lands on a course of action, which will hopefully bring us the immediate desired result—that is, the removal of the threat.

In this scenario, the upstairs brain will not reengage until after the action has been taken. The downstairs brain excels at shooting first and asking questions later. Sadly, this technique does not often produce satisfactory long-term outcomes. As we move forward, we will examine strategies to reengage the upstairs brain so that the choices we make when feeling angry do not create negative consequences or blowback. Any effective strategy will necessarily include the challenging and shifting of faulty beliefs.

Motivation and Emotion—Pleasure and Pain

History tells us that John Belushi believed that drugs made him a better actor/comedian. He acted in accordance with those beliefs despite the best efforts to keep him clean by all who loved him. He didn't realize that his pursuit of pleasure on the one hand was causing him pain and that it would lead to the ultimate pain for himself, his family, and his friends.

The hedonic theory proposes that human behavior is motivated by the pursuit of pleasure and the avoidance of pain. This notion was conceptualized as early as 435 BCE by Aristippus and Epicurus, who believed pleasure was the ideal to which all should aspire. Plato and Aristotle also shared their thoughts on pleasure through a holistic lens, whereas Aristippus was all about the pleasures of the flesh.

In Britain, hedonism was explored through the lens of what would most benefit the societal and political systems of the day. British philosophers agreed that humans are motivated to pursue pleasure and avoid pain. Some went as far as to suggest that reason—historically touted by philosophers as the answer to keeping our baser passions in check—was powerless against the human's need and quest for pleasure. French philosophers also argued that the primary motives of humans should be the pursuit of pleasure and avoidance of pain. The thoughts of nineteenth- and early twentieth-century psychologists were influenced by a line of thinking that insisted hedonism makes evolutionary sense as it is the only type of behavior that ensures humans will experience more pleasure than pain.

Freud expanded on hedonic theory, developing the unpleasure/pleasure principle and the reality principle. In effect, he noted that people suffering from what he labeled *neurosis* used fantasy to escape the painful realities of their lives; in other words, it was their way of avoiding pain and seeking pleasure. He noted that "every neurosis has an effect . . . of forcing the patient out of real life, of alienating him from reality. The neurotic turns away from reality because he finds either the whole or parts of it unbearable."[6] Kind of sounds like Belushi, doesn't it?

In effect, Freud believed that neurotics would always do more to avoid pain; the ensuing pleasure—that is, the escape from reality—is a natural consequence of that avoidance. The question is: does avoidance of pain inevitably lead to pleasure, or does it only act as a temporary reprieve from the reality at hand?

Let's take this further and make a broad, sweeping, universal proposal. Let us first assume that neuroticism is universal. After all, every personality and temperament profile out there includes a scale to measure neuroticism. This means that every human has a measure of neuroticism; some are more neurotic than others, and most certainly, traumatic experiences or other significant events may lead to an increase in neurotic experience and behavior. Let us next propose that human beings will almost always do *more* to avoid pain than they will to gain pleasure. When a hand touches a hot surface like a stovetop, the immediate reaction is to snatch the hand away because it hurts. Sinking the burned hand into a vat of cold water may immediately provide some relief, but it may prove worse for the burn and for the process of healing. This is not to say that humans will not also work hard to seek pleasure, but why else would we do so if not to avoid pain?

Some years ago, my husband and I took our then toddler daughter to Jamaica to visit my parents. We drove from Kingston to a Jack Tar village on the north coast to spend a few idyllic days on the beach. On the second day, the gas stove exploded as my mom attempted to light it. The gas had been leaking for days, and the blast was so powerful that it shook the windows. We found my mom outside the cottage sitting on the stoop, completely dazed and confused. Her eyebrows and the hairs on her arms and legs had been singed off, and the evidence of flash burns was beginning to show on her legs. We had no idea what to do.

Some men came over from an adjacent cottage to find out what happened. One of them said, "I know what to do. I served in Vietnam, and if you put damp salt on the burn, it will soothe the wounds and leave no scars." I didn't believe him, but he seemed to know what he was doing. He packed wet salt on my mom's burns, and within a few hours, she was able to move about without discomfort. This man had a process for removing pain and increasing comfort, and it worked, even though it didn't seem to make sense to us. The long-term effect of this intervention was nothing short of miraculous. My mother suffered no scarring and no other physical evidence of her close call. The short-term intervention intended to avoid pain provided both immediate and long-term positive outcomes. By the way, I now fully believe in the use of wet salt to treat burns.

When I was a child, new to Canada, I almost froze to death walking home from school on a particularly frigid Ottawa winter day. My brother found me passed out on the path to our home, picked me up, and got me back to the house. We didn't know anything about frostbite or its effects—it was our first experience with winter, and the temperatures that year dipped as low as –35 degrees Celsius. All we knew was I was freezing, and I needed to be warmed up as quickly as possible. My grandmother ran hot water and placed my hands under the tap while vigorously rubbing my hands. The objective was to avoid the pain associated with my frozen hands and feet. The result was a seven-year-old girl screaming at the top of her lungs because the pain of hot water on freezing hands was beyond excruciating. I would have happily returned to the cold pain; that would have been more pleasurable or acceptable than the hot pain. The attempts to avoid one pain inadvertently led to an even greater measure of pain.

What happens when there's a lack of pain? Are we even alive if there is no pain? Suffering, the push-pull between pain and pleasure, the quest for homeostasis—the tendency of the body to maintain a steady state—and the concept of a comfort zone stem from the idea that pain or discomfort is an intrinsic motivator of human behavior. Where there is no pain, there may be comfort for a time; however, over time, the comfort itself becomes uncomfortable.

The psychology of motivation—whether it be theories regarding behaviorism, instincts, drives, needs, or arousal—all has this in common: negative stimuli (pain) drive us to act ostensibly to either move away from or avoid those stimuli or to move toward or approach other stimuli that we *believe* will create a different, more positive emotional state. When we are hungry, we eat. When thirsty, we drink. When cold, we seek warmth. When overly hot, we seek refreshment. When lonely, we seek companionship. When bored, we seek activity. Pain could very well be our primary source of motivation.

What happens when there's a lack of pleasure? This is a little trickier. You see, if it is true that humans will do more to avoid pain than to achieve pleasure, one might assume there would have to be a palpable, measurable absence of pleasure before one would become dissatisfied. Think of the story of the great Exodus. The Hebrews subsisted on a diet of manna for years. At first, they had nothing to eat. They were starving, and they complained they would die in the wilderness if they weren't provided food. Then God miraculously sent manna from heaven every morning. In those early days, folks were excited. They couldn't wait to get out there and harvest this miracle food. Hunger = pain. Food = pleasure or comfort. Then over the passage of time, they became bored with manna. It stopped being pleasurable. Boredom = pain.

There have been many models of human needs, from Maslow's hierarchy of needs to William Glasser's choice theory model of needs. Tony Robbins conceptualizes human needs as six universally experienced drives that we experience in different intensities. While all six are necessary, they often are in conflict with each other.

Consider the first set of conflicting needs—certainty and variety—through the lens of the Exodus. The Hebrews had a basic need: hunger. Once manna started falling from the sky every day, they had a sense of *certainty* that they would have food to eat for the day: pleasure. Then they ran out of recipes and ways to make manna interesting. What was once pleasurable and *predictable* had become boring: pain. Soon they returned to complaining: "We're tired of manna cakes, manna waffles, ba-manna bread, and manna burgers. We want real food." They had real food! What they wanted was *variety*. The thing is, too much variety creates anxiety. They needed balance between the certainty that they would eat while maintaining a little spice in their menu.

The second set of conflicting needs is the need for *love and belonging* (inclusion or connection) and the need for *uniqueness* (identity). Think back to your high school days. That need to find a place to fit. To belong. Isn't that why you signed up for clubs and teams, played chess, or hung out with the artsy kids? Or were you one of those who dyed your hair black and wore Docs and skinny jeans with black nails and black lipstick, lurking on the fringe of things? Were you a loner who marched to the beat of your own drum? The thing is that too much inclusion in a group means you risk losing your identity. Too much exclusion breeds loneliness and isolation.

The third set of needs is identified as the needs of the spirit: the need for *growth* and for *contribution*. What is the point of learning, growing, or becoming an expert in your field if you never have an opportunity to share that knowledge with others? What is the point of becoming obscenely rich if you never give to charity? I know the skeptics would argue that rich people only give to charity so they can get the tax benefits. But seriously, what good is wealth if it is not shared?

For each of these dialectics, there must be balance. I can set my life up so that I have a measure of certainty, but I can also pursue new things, act spontaneously, and take a few calculated risks so that I can still experience the joy and spice that is variety. I can find my tribe and align myself with people like me—family, friends, faith communities—and find joy in the connection I have with those groups, but I can also engage in activities that nurture my passions, that are uniquely me. I can be part of a writing community, but I don't have to copy the writing styles of my peers. I can study, learn, exercise, eat healthy, meditate, pray, and do all the things I believe are essential for my personal growth. I can also choose the ways in which I will contribute to my community—whether through volunteerism, pro bono counseling services, or donations to charity. It can be both/and rather than having to choose one over the other.

Back to the question of what happens when there is no pleasure: people will do more to avoid pain than to gain pleasure, right? Let's say you live in the 'burbs, and new neighbors move in. They wear leathers, have haircuts with a biker club logo, and ride motorcycles instead of driving in "cages." They are also polite. They shovel your driveway in winter. They bring in your garbage cans for you on garbage day. Always respectful, never loud or boisterous, lights out by eleven even on weekends. They prove themselves to be predictable in how they behave, and you feel *comfortable* and *safe* with them.

What if, over time, things began to change? A party here, a motorcycle backfires there. Some rowdy friends come over and hang out for too long. One of their guests ogles and catcalls your teenage daughter. Lights stay on longer. No one clears your driveway after that blizzard dumped thirty centimeters of snow. No more pleasantries, politeness, or overt respect. The pleasure is gone, but it might not be enough to push you over into the realm of pain. Their behavior would have to escalate until the point that your frustration over noisy, disrespectful neighbors drives you to make a change.

You see, the pleasure/pain principle is more than just doing more to avoid one and gain the other. You must exceed your threshold for discomfort before you will be motivated to effect change. Consider the frog, who when placed into a pot of cold water heated up gradually doesn't know it is cooking until it is too late. You and I are that frog, my friend. We often do not realize that our circumstances have been cooking us until we have reached our threshold for physical or psychological pain tolerance. We can be very content living in an environment where there is no pleasure as long as the pain is tolerable.

At the end of the day, what you believe to be pleasurable or painful will determine your choices and actions. You might believe smoking is dangerous, but because that danger or harm is deferred, there is no need for you to quit smoking today. You might believe you are still safe to drive after two or three drinks, even if the law says otherwise. You might believe your avoidance of family dinners is best for everyone involved. You might believe your obsessive behaviors give you a sense of control over your environment. It is a good idea to check your beliefs and evaluate them objectively to see if they compel you to engage in approach or avoidance behaviors that could inadvertently cause more pain in the long run.

Summary

1) Belief is the basis of action.
2) We busted certain myths about anger and found the following:
   a. Anger is an emotion.
   b. Anger should not be judged as bad or wrong.
   c. Anger is to be expressed, not controlled.
   d. Anger is not aggression.
   e. Women and children are entitled to feel and express emotions.
   f. Expressing anger does not necessarily result in negative outcomes.
3) When anger is ignited, the upstairs brain steps back, while the downstairs brain runs the show.

4) We are motivated by pleasure and pain; however, humans are more motivated to avoid pain than they are to seek pleasure.

Reflection and Action Step

Make a list of the things you believe. You may use the Beliefs Cheat Sheet found in the Rise of Rage workbook, downloadable from the website. What do you believe about religion, money, family, politics, education, the world of work, travel, the environment, or life in general? Consider which of your beliefs are limiting or empowering. Do any of your beliefs need to be reviewed, challenged, or upgraded?

4

WHAT DID YOU EXPECT?

The Slap Heard around the World

ON THE EVENING of March 27, 2022, spirits were high. The who's who of Hollywood's elite gathered at the Dolby Theatre at Ovation Hollywood to celebrate the best of the best in the moviemaking industry. Will Smith was pegged as a strong contender for best actor for his role as Richard Williams, father and long-time coach of Serena and Venus Williams. The Williams family had turned out in support of the film, and everyone was wired with anticipation of how the events of the night would unfold. Would the film receive an Oscar? Would Will win the coveted award? What transpired that evening was proof positive that the right trigger matched with an anxious, unregulated mind and a captive audience could create a perfect storm resulting in the shipwreck of a promising career and a pristine reputation.

I did not even watch the Oscars that night, but I certainly heard about the slap the next morning. People were quick to pile onto Will, and a host of people in the media superciliously armchair-quarterbacked the events, saying, "There is this little thing called impulse control." Here's the facts, folks. When your limbic system—aka *downstairs brain*—has hijacked your faculties, your frontal lobes, which are responsible for impulse control, have already left the building. They're not functioning right now. They're on hiatus while your limbic system is running the show. And if your limbic system says a slap is what's needed, then a slap is what will happen.

I want to break this down for you using my thought matrix. Whenever your brain attends to something—a stimulus of any kind—it begins to make meaning of it. This is a complex series of mechanisms and functions working in concert for conscious thought or cognition to take place. There are three functions of human memory: attending—paying attention to a stimulus; encoding, or storage—making sense of the stimulus, deciding if it is worth remembering, and moving the stimulus and its meaning from your short-term memory into your long-term memory banks. The final function of memory is retrieval—or recovering the memory for future reference. Also working to inform your memory functions are sensation and perception. Your five senses input data into your brain, and your perception works to make meaning of the sensory data. In effect, cognition is the process of all the above and more. Let's not forget the various parts of the brain—occipital lobes for vision; parietal lobes for sensation; frontal lobes for focus, attention, and giving language to the sensory data; temporal lobes for auditory sensation and memory—that work in concert, seamlessly cataloging, labeling, and interpreting every bit of sensory input 24/7. Everything that follows is contingent on the direction your thoughts lead you.

Thoughts inform our feelings. Once meaning has been assigned to a stimulus, your brain then "chooses" a feeling state that is appropriate for the meaning. The late Princess of Wales once said that she had such little privacy in the royal palace that she could not even relieve herself without someone standing close enough to hear. I don't know about you, but for me, the meaning I would attach to having to use the privy while someone stood close enough to hear my most personal bodily functions is "This is embarrassing." Someone else might choose the word *humiliating*. Now apply those feeling words to yourself, and see how your physiology shifts in response. If someone else had a bit of a twisted sense of humor, they might apply a different meaning: "This is funny. Let's see how loud I can be." Now apply that meaning to yourself, and see how your physiology shifts. So, you see, your thoughts inform your feelings.

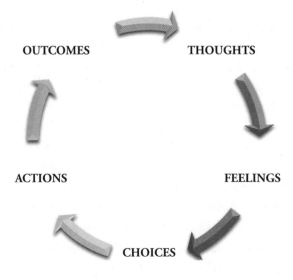

OUTCOMES   THOUGHTS

ACTIONS   FEELINGS

CHOICES

Here's where it gets dicey. When you have a thought like "This is humiliating or embarrassing," the immediate desire that arises is that of eliminating that feeling. No one wants to feel humiliated, embarrassed, hurt, disappointed, furious, or shamed. It is natural to follow the instinct to remove that feeling as quickly as possible. It's painful. It doesn't feel good. We want away from that, and the sooner the better. Remember, humans will always do more to avoid pain than they will to gain pleasure. So what humans tend to do when they are overcome by a negative emotion that feels uncomfortable is run to a quick fix. The quick fix is a choice of action driven by the limbic system and often unregulated by the frontal lobes because, remember, they are currently on hiatus.

The problem with quick fixes is that they are exactly that: quick. Because they are usually decisions driven by the downstairs brain, there is little if any thought given to *consequences*. In Will Smith's case, his brain demanded satisfaction and protection of those he loved. It gave little thought to what the slap itself might mean for his reputation, for his career, for the award he was about to receive, or for his future. Had he been exposed to *Anger Solutions*, he would have had the tools to express his displeasure with Chris Rock without causing damage to his reputation or brand. He would have found a way to get satisfaction for the insult while keeping his image intact.

There is no need for things to go sideways if you have a good understanding of how your brain works and you have tools to help keep it on task. Rather than allowing the downstairs brain to take over, determining which choices (finding a quick fix to alleviate embarrassment and anger) and corresponding actions (slapping Chris) are most appropriate, you can apply a workaround to reengage the frontal lobes so that you can process your thoughts and feelings and then choose a course of action that is directed at an outcome you desire rather than the inevitable backlash that comes from using quick fixes.

Much of what happens when our limbic system hijacks the upstairs brain is due to lazy brain work accompanied by a defeatist mindset. What I mean by *lazy brain work* is the human tendency to float through life on autopilot. You get up, shower, eat breakfast, rush the kids out the door, and then sit in traffic while mainlining coffee. You arrive at work, but you cannot remember how you got there—the route is so embedded in your memory that you can get to and from work without thinking about it. Your evening schedule is the same: have dinner, check the kids' homework, walk the dog, watch some television, read, or watch the nightly news. Some perfunctory small talk with the significant other. Plan for the next day. Go to sleep. Rinse and repeat.

Maybe this isn't your story at all, but that doesn't mean you don't spend a fair amount of your day on autopilot. Just think of that time you needed to make a stop on the way home from work, but once you got in the car, on the bus, or on the subway, the autopilot kicked in, and you found yourself walking up the driveway before you remembered the necessary errand. There is no shame in this. My autopilot switches on at least once a week, if not more frequently. It is just a fact of life. We can, however, develop strategies to help us be more present.

Return to the thought matrix for a moment. Thoughts inform feelings. When those feelings are uncomfortable or painful, instinct directs us to remove the painful stimulus or to remedy the situation so we no longer feel uncomfortable. Once the choice is made, a behavior is activated, one that the user hopes will fix the feeling. What typically happens, as it did in the case of Will Smith, is that the behavior leads to even more uncomfortable outcome—feelings of deep embarrassment, shame, and remorse.

Now pair this *lazy brain work* with a defeatist mindset, one that says, "This is just how I am. I can't change." A defeatist mindset when it comes to emotional expression is one that chooses the path of least resistance without considering the long-term consequences for the behavior. A defeatist mindset typically results in someone making a poor choice when they're angry and then defending that choice with a statement akin to "I couldn't help it. I didn't mean to." The goal, then, is to redirect our thoughts so that we may achieve more favorable outcomes. This is not impossible, but to achieve those favorable outcomes, we must switch out of autopilot and start thinking and acting with intention.

Here's the deal. Anger management says to take a deep breath, count to ten, and walk away. You might stay angry, but that doesn't matter—just don't hurt the other person. Anger *resolution* is about solving those problems that caused the anger in the first place. The problem that caused Will's anger was an ill-timed, inconsiderate joke about someone he loved. The problem was that he did not feel like it's okay for anybody to talk about his wife that way. Add to that the feeling of helplessness to stop it, coupled with an overwhelming need to protect his family and the people he loves.

E + R = O

Before we make deeper sense of this, consider another concept that dovetails nicely with the thought matrix, one I learned many years ago from Jack Canfield: E + R = O. *Event* plus *response* equals *outcome*. In effect, it is not the event (the joke) that determined Will Smith's outcome; rather, it was his *response* (the slap). Imagine the different responses Will could have chosen.

1) He could have waited to confront Chris backstage or later in a private conversation.
2) He could have gathered up his wife and his entourage and quietly exited the building.
3) He could have leaned over, kissed his wife's bald head, and flipped Chris Rock the bird (off camera, of course) in a joking manner.
4) He could have waited until he had an opportunity to speak (ahem, "The winner is . . .") and addressed the distastefulness of the joke while educating the audience and the world about alopecia.

Any one of these responses would have netted him a different outcome than being banned from the Oscars for ten years and the major hit to his reputation. To be sure, his response was the determining factor for his outcomes then and even now.

Should've, Could've, Would've—The Language of Unmet Expectations

This brings me to the language we use when we are reflecting on those events that lead to angry responses. Did you notice anything about the options I provided for Will? They all contained the words *could have* or *would have*. This, my friends, is the language of unmet expectations. I'll wager that late that night in the privacy of his own home, Will and Jada discussed what he could have, would have, or should have done. Will's downstairs brain demanded immediate satisfaction, and for a millisecond, it achieved that outcome. What the downstairs brain didn't account for—what it never accounts for—is how the quick fix will negatively impact the actor in the moments following the fleeting sense of satisfaction. The downstairs brain is unconcerned with long-term outcomes. Therefore, we must reengage the upstairs brain to ensure the achievement of favorable long-term outcomes. Just remember, every time you hear someone say, "I should've said" or "If things were different, I would've" or "I could've been a contender," you are hearing the language of an unmet expectation.

William Glasser suggests that there is no such thing as common sense; people do what makes sense to them. Following this line of logic, in the heat of the moment, when Will's downstairs brain hijacked his executive function, it made perfect sense for him to get up on that stage and plant a full-bodied open-handed slap on Chris's left cheek. It made sense to him because Chris's joke triggered one of the four core reasons people get angry.

1. Broken rules. Perhaps Will had an unwritten, unspoken rule that nobody disrespects his wife.
2. Unmet needs or expectations. Will may have had an expectation that on such a big night for him, Jada, and the Williams family, the jokes would be directed elsewhere.
3. Violated boundaries. Making fun of such a sensitive topic as Jada's alopecia could be perceived as a boundary violation.
4. Thwarted goals. Will may have perceived that Chris's insensitive comments were in direct conflict with one of his personal or professional goals.

Consider yourself doing something as simple as navigating traffic. The entire premise of driving is that everyone will obey the rules of the road so that motorists, cyclists, and pedestrians can arrive at their destinations safely. The destination is your outcome. Your preferred way of getting to your destination is driving. You get in your car with the expectation that people will obey the rules of the road and you will arrive safely. Then some fool in a luxury car zips by you, cutting you off in your lane, and the driver has the audacity to flip you an obscene hand gesture as you slam on your brakes to avoid a deadly collision. How would you react in that situation? Would you speed up, try to overtake the offensive driver, and shout at him through your tinted windows? Would you return the favor by cutting him off? Would you try to run him off the road and then slash his tires to teach him a lesson? And wouldn't he deserve it? After all, he violated the rules of the road, making it unsafe for himself and all the drivers within his proximity. Any of the above options is a quick fix. None of them guarantees safe arrival at your destination, which is your desired outcome.

How, then, should you break out of this pattern of reacting with a quick fix?

Step 1: Begin with the end in mind. Yes, I borrowed that from Stephen Covey, but it applies here. Before you ever get in the car, set your intention for what kind of a commute you want and be clear about your desired outcome, which is to arrive at your destination safely.

Step 2: Evaluate the situation objectively, with your end in mind. How, you might ask, should you do that?

Choice Theory

William Glasser's choice theory provides us with a simple yet effective framework for evaluating our circumstances. Choice theory proposes that we experience and make sense of three worlds. The *real world* is what truly exists inside and outside of our environments. Once we receive the sensory data of the real world, we pass it through our internal perceptions—our senses, our values, and our experiences—to make meaning; this is the *perceived world*, or the world as we see it. Everyone also has a mental picture of how things would be, could be, or should be for them to be happy. This is what Glasser calls the *ideal world. Frustration* results from a believed mismatch between the *perceived* world and the *ideal* world.

In the *real world*, my employer tells me I should take more initiative in my job. My past experiences with negative criticism, compounded by my belief that even constructive criticism means I am not doing everything right, cause me to *perceive* my boss as challenging my ability to do my job.

In my *ideal world,* no one would ever criticize my actions. The lack of congruence between my perceived world and my ideal world sends a *frustration signal* to my brain. In this case, the frustration signal manifests itself in the form of anger (defensiveness): "I take plenty initiative around here. If he thinks he can find somebody better to do the job, I dare him to try!"

According to Glasser, frustration is what motivates an individual to act. Frustration is defined in choice theory as any stimulus that causes you pain (physical, psychological, or emotional). We have already established that there cannot simply be an absence of pleasure for one to be motivated to change. One must arrive at the threshold between the absence of pleasure and the presence of pain. You must be dissatisfied enough with a situation before you make the move toward change. Therefore, if behavior is manifestation of frustration, and the problem that informed the anger is not resolved, individuals can respond in one of two ways. They can turn the anger inward or outward.

Anger Turned Inward

Think of the Bottler style of anger expression. The effects of this style are generally physical in nature as the angry person is usually the only one who knows they're angry. Some examples of somatic responses to this style are ulcers, headaches, colon problems, eating disorders, insomnia, or generalized anxiety—ailments I call the *diseases of holding on.* We could say that the act of turning unresolved anger inward is the result of *thinking without acting.*

Anger Turned Outward

Imagine the Controlled Blaster or the ACME Poster Child. Unresolved anger turned outward can present itself as verbal aggression, verbal abuse, physical aggression and/or physical abuse, passive-aggressive behaviors, or a combination of these. We might say that the act of turning unresolved anger outward is the result of *acting without thinking.*

In both cases, there is an obvious lack of balance in these responses and actions. How, then, does one achieve balance? Glasser says that the individual performing a *self-evaluation* at the point of experiencing the frustration signal will achieve balance.

Let us return to the scenario of your commute to work. Your desired outcome is to arrive at work safely. You are confronted with a fellow motorist who has not only violated the rules of the road, making them unsafe for you, but he also implied you were to blame for his poor driving. Rules have been broken, and expectations have been unmet. The goal of self-evaluation is to strike a balance of thinking and *then* acting. First, you have to reengage your upstairs brain, which went on vacation right about the time you slammed on the brakes and shouted an epithet or two. The same is true for a Will Smith / Chris Rock type of scenario. First, one must reengage the area responsible for executive function so that one can make wiser decisions and choose more careful, intentional actions.

Breath work is the best and fastest way to reengage the frontal lobes. This is where taking a deep breath and counting to ten is warranted; however, don't count to ten with the expectation your anger will *go away*. Count to ten so that your deep, diaphragmatic breaths enable you to reoxygenate the frontal lobes and get them operating again. While you are breathing deeply, hold that breath so the oxygen has an opportunity to navigate the bloodstream and then slowly exhale. That precious time allows your higher-order thinking to reengage.

Think, Say, and Ask

The process I devised to work through Glasser's model for self-evaluation is called TSA: think, say, and ask. This process is heavy at the point of thinking because, remember, everything on the thought matrix is guided by your cognitions. What you think about a stimulus will determine the meaning you make of it, which will inform the emotions that emerge. If the emotion feels bad, the pain/pleasure principle will kick in, driving you to try for a quick fix, which will inevitably lead to unhappy long-term outcomes.

Think

Before you do anything else, think about what is happening, what it means, and how you feel. Remember, acting before thinking is basically not thinking. Will Smith chose a course of action and then committed to it as he was walking up on stage. Even a split second taken to evaluate the situation and how he was feeling in it may have changed his anger response. *Thinking* is the process of evaluating the situation and your perceptions about the events. Thinking with intention enables you to consider the possible outcomes and options for attaining the best possible short- and long-term outcomes. Some questions you might consider include the following:

- What is happening? Step out of your feelings for a moment and evaluate the facts of the situation.
- What does it mean to me? The meaning you assign to any situation will determine how you feel about it and what you will want to do next. Think carefully of what this situation means for you.
- How do I feel about it? Carefully evaluate your feeling state and assign a word that best describes your emotions.
- What is my desired outcome? How would you like this to turn out? What would be the best outcome in both short and long terms? Don't just think about fixing your feelings in the now; what are the "big" things you would like to see happen because of or despite this event?
- What can I do to achieve that outcome? Run through all the options available, even the ones that sound implausible.
- What is the best thing that can happen if I act on option A, B, or C? What is the worst thing that could happen? You need to ensure you are fully informed of the pros and cons of each action. Too often, we only focus on the worst that could happen, and we avoid the action because of fear. Sometimes, choosing to only focus on the best thing that could happen results in making choices with horrible consequences. Consider all points of the spectrum.
- What is the lifetime value of this event? If this event has no lifetime value, maybe the best thing to do is to walk away and forget about it. Perhaps you need to say something to stop the situation from getting worse, but you may not need to do a full dialogue because there is no lifetime value. When the situation involves people you love, family, close friends, teachers, coaches, police, or other authority figures, you will need to be more intentional about how you proceed with your communication.

Will Smith's inner dialogue might have sounded like this, had the *T* part been applied to the showdown at the Oscars. *What's happening?* "Chris Rock just made a joke about my wife's baldness. She doesn't seem happy about it. Everyone is laughing uncomfortably." *What does it mean?* "It means he insulted Jada. It means she has been attacked, and it is my job to protect her. It means my rules have been broken, and my expectations for tonight are unmet." *How do I feel?* "I feel angry. Embarrassed. Inadequate." *What do I want?* "I want to enjoy the evening with my wife. I want to celebrate the success that is *King Richard*. I want to win an Oscar and make a great acceptance speech. I want to party after the awards ceremony with the people who made this amazing evening a reality." *How can I achieve that outcome? What's the best thing that can happen if I slap Chris? What's the worst thing that can happen?*

All that time, Will would be engaging his breath so his upstairs brain gets reengaged and helps him to make better decisions. His upstairs brain would help him to realize the slap that would be heard around the world may not be all that good for his career. It most certainly would not be good for his brand image or his self-esteem.

Say

Explain your perception and interpretation of what has happened. Express your feelings. Separate the people from their behaviors. Stick to the issue. State your expectations. Assertiveness is the key to anger resolution. Passivity leads to anger turned inward. Aggressiveness is anger turned outward. Saying how you feel gets it off your chest so you don't stew. It also opens an opportunity for you to resolve your anger with the other party.

Ask

Open up a dialogue. The other person may not even know they are making you angry. Dialogue empowers both parties to make a change and to contribute to the process of change. Ask for a response. Focus on questions that presuppose a positive outcome and, if possible, the outcome that is best for both parties. The outcome that follows will be a direct result of the dialogue that ensues between you and the other party. Remember that your outcomes will be tied directly to the response you choose, so choose carefully.

How many of these skills do you feel you have? Which are you comfortable using now? Which ones make you feel uncomfortable or vulnerable? If you already use some of these skills, do you feel you are using them effectively? As you ask yourself these questions, you are continuing the process of self-evaluation. Life is a series of questions looking for answers. We tend to go through the process at a subconscious level *on autopilot*, which is why we end up getting such crummy answers a lot of the time. By performing conscious self-evaluation, we increase our awareness not only of our surroundings and how they affect us but also of how our behavior affects others.

TSA in Action

There was that time I was alone on an airport shuttle on my way to New York City. There was a torrential downpour, and I commented to the shuttle driver, "It's so wet outside." The driver replied in his best attempt at a sultry deep voice, "I thought women liked to get wet." *Yup. He said that.* My brain exploded. I was so angry, I could barely breathe. Then somewhere in the back of my mind, a little voice said, "Don't kill him, Julie. He isn't worth your reputation." After that first thought, all that played on repeat through my mind was *TSA. TSA. TSA.* So I took a deep breath disguised as a gasp of shock and ran TSA.

Think: what is happening? I am on a shuttle with a man that I need, but he just said something gross and horrible. *What does it mean?* It means I need to be careful in how I respond because I don't have time to get off this bus and try to wait for another shuttle. It means I might be unsafe, so that's another reason to choose my response carefully. *What is my desired outcome?* I want to go to New York City. I want to get to the airport as quickly and safely as possible. I want him to drive and not to speak. *How do I accomplish that?* I ran down a bunch of possible solutions in my mind and ran them by the A/B split test: What's the best thing that can happen if I do that? What's the worst thing that can happen if I do that?

Say: After a speed-thinking rundown of possible responses, I settled on channeling my mother, who did righteous indignation like no one else. In a low, menacing voice, I bit out four words: *"I. Beg. Your. Pardon."* No lie, the driver sat up straight, eyes front, hands at ten and two, and rumbled off toward the airport. Not another word was spoken, and I was ecstatic that it worked!

Now to my favorite question about the lifetime value of this event, had this been a relationship that I valued, I would have included the final component in TSA—ask—but I did not want to further a dialogue with a perfect stranger who thought it was appropriate to be so rude and disgusting to a customer. Some people might say I was wrong to not have filed a complaint, but, remember, my desired outcome was to get to New York City, not to get some random dirty-minded stranger fired. I thought it through, chose an appropriate response in line with my desired outcome, and said what needed to be said to get me that outcome. The lifetime value of this event for me is that I now have a perfect object lesson to demonstrate the effectiveness of TSA. That's the power of TSA: think, say, ask.

Next time you find yourself feeling triggered toward anger, think it through. Ask the questions I asked above. Get clear on what is happening: which rules have been broken, which expectations or needs have been unaddressed, which boundaries have been violated, and which goals appear to be thwarted. Determine how you feel and what you want. Not just the momentary satisfaction, but what is your optimal, desired outcome? Choose your words wisely and say something to the person who can help you solve the problem. Finally, ask them to work with you to solve the issue that made you angry in the first place. That's what *Anger Solutions* is all about.

Summary

Anger develops when our experiences do not meet our expectations; we feel a frustration signal every time our perceived world is in negative balance with the ideal world.

E + R = O: event plus response equals outcome. It is not your experiences that create your outcomes; it is your responses to those experiences.

The decision-making engine that leads to immediate and lasting transformation is TSA.

Think: What is happening? What does it mean? How do I feel? What is my desired outcome? What can I do to achieve that outcome? What is the best/worst thing that can happen if I choose option A, B, or C? What is the lifetime value of this event?

Say: This is how I feel about this presenting problem. I need, want, believe. . . . These are my expectations, boundaries, or rules.

Ask: Are you willing to help me solve this problem? What can we both do differently so that we do not have this problem in the future?

Reflection

List one personal example for each of the ways in which anger can be triggered. How did you respond in those situations? Can you identify the anger style of expression you used? What was the outcome in each case? If you could revisit each experience using TSA, how might the result have been different?

Action Steps

1) If you have not already done so, go to the website and download the workbook. Find the TSA Cheat Sheet.
2) Use the TSA Cheat Sheet whenever you are faced with a conflict, confrontation, or problem that evokes a frustration signal.

5

YOUR CIRCUS, YOUR MONKEYS

UNBELIEVABLE. I WAS naught but a speck in an endless line of vehicles crawling at a snail's pace along the Highway 401 corridor. How could this have happened? I'd left home early, and traffic had seemed reasonable—that is, until I hit the 427 North headed to the 401, and everything became gridlocked. I was stuck in traffic en route to facilitate conflict resolution training for the Department of National Defense Land Force Area headquarters. It was official. This was a nightmare. I couldn't believe it—I was going to be late for an event with the military!

Fortunately, this was the age of cell phones. I called ahead to the commander and let him know I was trapped in traffic with no foreseeable way out of the gridlock. After giving him my best estimate of when I would arrive, I clicked off. Now what? I could sit in traffic, thinking thoughts that would agitate and escalate my anxiety, which would in turn result in me arriving to DND late and flustered. If I showed up like that, I certainly would not be in the right headspace to deliver conflict resolution training. At the very least, I would not be prepared to bring my A game to the presentation.

Considering that doing the best job possible for our military was my desired outcome, I settled on another strategy to get me through the drive from Hades. Back when I had been a certified seminar leader for Pryor Resources International, I had learned that the average commute for an American totals more than three hundred hours a year. At PRI, we used to talk about "universities on wheels" and that if we used our commutes with intention, we could acquire a new language, develop a new area of expertise, or learn a new skill. To that end, I had hours upon hours of workshops, seminars, and training material on CD stored in my car. I picked out something that would be informative yet calming, plugged it in, and focused my attention on deepening my expertise and building my confidence. By the time I arrived at DND, I was calmer and in a better headspace so that I could, as I had hoped, deliver my A game.

Can you imagine how my client and my audience would have responded had I walked into the meeting room late and flustered and venting loudly about the terrible traffic and what a nightmare it had been to commute to their location? How often does this scenario play out with frustration and irritation being vented to the wrong person for a situation completely outside of their control? How much more often do families and friends become the whipping posts for situations that had nothing to do with them?

Rage Misdirected

The ACME Poster Child and Controlled Blaster anger styles have in common the tendency to direct their blasts at things or people that have little to do with the problem informing their anger. Sometimes anger is directed at the symptom because it is perceived as safer or easier than to speak directly to the source of the problem.

Case in point: Dad has a secret, one that is tied to a deep sense of shame. Three-year-old Jimmy idolizes his dad, and while he loves getting bedtime stories from his Mom, he really wants this bonding time with his father. Most nights, though, Dad always has an excuse for not being available, but as most little ones can be, Jimmy is persistent in his efforts to get his dad to read his favorite story. Finally, one evening, Dad explodes in anger: "I don't have time to read you a stupid story! Just get yourself up to bed and stop pestering me!"

Jimmy is devastated. Everyone else is shocked into silence. Dad retires to his room, but he can't sleep. He is shrouded in shame. He loves his wife and kids more than life. He just doesn't know how to tell them he doesn't know how to read.

Why is it so difficult to be direct, open, and honest in communication, especially with the people we hold most dear? Could it be that our limiting beliefs get in the way? After all, if belief is the basis of action, it should be possible to infer one's beliefs based on one's actions.

Freud—both Sigmund and Anna—would propose that any challenges humans have in communication are due to thwarted goals that occurred during a crucial stage of development. Anna Freud would suggest that our defense mechanisms activate to protect our fragile egos from further damage. Those of the school of cognitive behavioral therapy would argue that distorted or irrational thinking is at the heart of poor communication.

Crooked Thinking

A bias is defined as "an inclination or prejudice for or against a person or group, situations, or things, especially in a way considered to be unfair."[1] Biases are informed by *heuristics*, or shortcuts in thinking. Heuristics enable us to make decisions unconsciously and quickly without having to process all the available information. The use of heuristics, rooted in the Greek meaning "to discover," is a problem-solving approach that relies heavily on prior knowledge and personal experience. One may apply self-education, evaluation, and feedback to reduce decision-making time, producing better or faster results. The simplest form of heuristic is an educated guess. While it is advisable to have as much information as possible before coming to a decision, heuristics are most effective in situations where precision is not as important as speed. In your favorite TV word game show, the players apply heuristics to guess the correct answer. Hangman is a game of heuristics, as are crossword puzzles.

Here's the thing: applying heuristics to arrive at quick conclusions doesn't guarantee you will arrive at the *correct* conclusion. What if I asked you to tell me a six-letter word for *relative*? What would your first response be? My first guess was *family*, but there are other words that also fit: *member, people, allied* (because the word *relative* has different meanings), *auntie, mother, father, nephew, sister, cousin*—you get the idea. Using heuristics when you have little information or the wrong information will often bring you to the wrong conclusion.

Albert Ellis proposed that one's way of thinking about events rather than the events themselves leads to unhealthy emotions and behaviors. Ellis asserted that all humans are born with a gift for illogical or "crooked" thinking, which impedes their efforts to achieve satisfaction in life. However, he believed firmly that individuals have the capacity to change, and this belief led to the development of rational emotive behavior therapy, which was the foundation for cognitive behavioral therapy, brought to popularity by Aaron Beck.

Rational emotive *behavior* therapy highlights the relationship among cognition, emotion, and behavior. The goal of REBT is to help people modify their irrational thought patterns to overcome the psychological issues they face.

ABCs

To explain how thoughts and meaning-making contribute to mental and emotional distress, Ellis developed the ABC model:

A—Activating event: something happens in the environment.
B—Beliefs: a belief is formed about that event.
C—Consequence: an emotional and/or behavioral response to the belief is developed.

In the world of behavior therapy, ABCs represent *antecedent, behavior,* and *consequence.*

A—Antecedent: the activating event, trigger, or stimulus
B—Behavior: the response or reaction to the activating event
C—Consequence: the equal and opposite reaction to the behavior

I often used the ABC chart in therapy to help people develop greater awareness of how their actions inform their consequences. That said, there is something missing from the equation despite its similarity to E + R = O (event plus response equals outcome). What is missing is the process of thought, which Ellis had included in his model. Revised, we might conceptualize the process like this:

A = Antecedent or Activating event
B = Belief or thought about the activating event—the assignation of meaning
B = Behavior (reaction or response)
C = Consequence or outcome

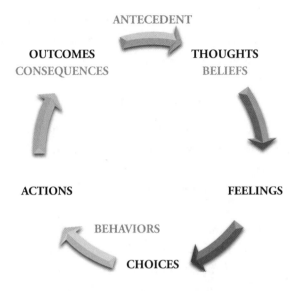

When we conceptualize the ABC model in the context of the thought matrix, we can see how the ABCs align with the cycle. The activating event or stimulus triggers a cascade of thoughts. Illogical or crooked thinking informs beliefs that may be distorted or irrational, which contribute to feelings of distress. These undesirable feelings inform the need to *feel better now*, the choice to fix the feeling rather than address the problem, with behavior following on the heels of that choice. We know that for every action, there is an equal and opposite reaction; the natural consequences of the behavior will inevitably inform how we think about future activating events.

Now, Ellis believed that understanding an individual's emotional response to an event requires that we first understand the beliefs to which they ascribe. He identified four types of irrational or crooked thought processes in which people tend to engage:

1. Demandingness—developing and holding on to rigid, unrealistic expectations of oneself, other people, or events
2. Awfulizing—more commonly known as *catastrophizing*—believing the worst possible consequences of an event
3. I can't stand it-itis—or low frustration tolerance—believing oneself incapable of emotionally managing or coping with certain experiences

4. Generalized negative ratings of self or others—forming an overall negative self-evaluation or low opinion of others based on very little information about the person or event

Irrational Beliefs

It is important to note that just because one has an undesirable experience does not mean it should automatically lead to psychological distress. It is only when the activating event is interpreted with dysfunctional thoughts and beliefs that problems arise. Remember, very little in life has meaning except the meaning that you assign to it.

REBT ascribes to the notion that belief is the basis of action. If one wishes to change one's behavior, the place to start is at the point of belief or thought. Ellis suggested that irrational beliefs are often distinguishable by rigid, absolute, and grandiose demands, typically expressed in the form of *musts*, *shoulds*, and *oughts*—very much like the language of unmet expectations, *should've*, *could've*, and *would've*. It isn't just expectations of others that get caught in the web of irrational thinking. Ellis classified three key categories of irrational demands that he believed lie at the core of psychological dysfunction. The common denominator is unrealistic ideals or expectations of self or others.

1. I *must* be successful and earn others' approval.
2. I *should* or *must* be treated well; others *should* do the right thing.
3. Life *must* be easy; it *should* be free of discomfort and *should* never be inconvenient.

I think of the many scenarios I have processed with clients over my many years as a therapist and the ways in which these irrational beliefs and demands have interfered with their ability to enjoy experiences or to progress in employment or personal relationships.

Scenario: Ice-skating on a pond. The ice is eighteen inches thick; the water beneath is only knee deep. "*If the ice breaks and I fall through, I would just die.*" Interpretation through an REBT lens: *Life must be easy and convenient. If I fell through the ice, it would be awful because I would be embarrassed, and I couldn't stand that.*

Scenario: Client quits his job on the first day. *"I knew they were laughing at me, and I figured anytime now, I would get fired, so I left before they had a chance to fire me."* Interpretation through an REBT lens: *I am stupid and unable to be successful. All the people in my new workplace obviously can see how much of a failure I am. This is awful. I cannot stand it. I must exit this situation because it is too painful; I am unable to cope.*

The endgame for REBT is to identify the irrational beliefs that inform an individual's emotional distress and then to challenge these beliefs, replacing them with more realistic ones. For example, the person mentioned in the second scenario might learn to adjust his thoughts along these lines: "The employer wouldn't have hired me if he thought I was stupid. Perhaps these people are laughing because they enjoy their job. Not everything has to be about me. And even if it is, I am happy to have a job, so I won't leave until they ask me to. Although it would be unpleasant to be fired, I can cope with it. After all, I was unemployed before I had this job. I already know that I can stand being unemployed again. I can go back to the employment agency, and they can help me find a new job."

How Distorted Beliefs Are Formed

Now that we have an idea of what distorted beliefs are and the demands that inform them, how do these beliefs come to be rooted in our minds in the first place? Julian Rotter conceived of the locus of control (LOC) in the 1960s, and this personality construct remains one of the most studied in the social sciences. LOC reveals the degree to which an individual will perceive outcomes as related to personal behaviors and characteristics versus external factors. Existing along a continuum, individuals considered to have a more internal LOC tend to see outcomes as being contingent on their own actions, whereas those considered to be more external tend to believe that outcomes are a result of external forces such as luck, fate, chance, or powerful others.

People with a more internal locus of control perceive and make meaning of negative stimuli differently than those with a more external locus of control. Two people are carpooling to work, and they are stuck in traffic. The driver has an external locus of control and, as such, believes that this is a continuation of his bad luck or karma or that the universe is out to get him—that is why he is going to be late for work. The passenger, who has an internal locus of control, considers ways in which they might change their actions to affect different outcomes. They could leave earlier so as not to get caught in the rush, or they could choose a different route to avoid heavy traffic on the way to work. The driver will invariably experience more distress during the commute because he feels he has *no control* over his current circumstances.

An external locus of control shifts attention away from monitoring and regulating our own emotional states and toward laying the blame or praise for our emotional states on external factors beyond our control. The truth of it is that too many of us do not attempt to control our thoughts because *we are too busy trying to control our emotions instead.*

The fallacy of control suggests that by saying or doing a certain thing; or by being a certain way; or by wishing, hoping, or dreaming for a certain outcome, then we can control that outcome. This is not true. I cannot tell you how many of my psychotherapy clients struggle with anxiety, depression, and posttraumatic stress because they experienced an event that shattered their illusion of control.

REBT, LOC, and the Fallacy of Control

My manager was on my case again. It seemed like every week she had me in her office, demanding to know what I was doing, how I was doing it, and accusing me of being the reason we would not meet our government-mandated quotas. I was beyond stressed. You see, I had bought into the narrative of the administration, which was that I should be happy I had a job. I should be amenable to whatever abuse was directed at me by my peers or my supervisors, and regardless of the challenges I was presented with in doing my job, I should always perform to their standards. I was drowning in *shoulds!* Despite my every attempt to control my work environment, I was feeling more unwell, losing sleep, and suffering headaches and other serious health issues due to the magnitude of stress I was under.

One day, I reached my breaking point. I turned back to TSA because I had run out of strategies for controlling my circumstances. A funny thing happened when I walked myself through the decision-making model. I recognized I was trying desperately to control a situation that had nothing to do with me! When I finally took stock of the elements of my job situation that I could control compared to what was outside of my wheelhouse, I realized there was very little I could or can control. Furthermore, I remembered something I had learned years previous from Brian Tracy: that I am the CEO of my own career.

I had an epiphany. If I am the CEO of my own career, then my future in that job was not up to my employer; it was up to me. When I walked through the questions outlined in TSA, it sounded a lot like this.

1. *What is happening?* My boss keeps accusing me of failing the team, but she keeps sending me all the hardest-to-serve clients because I get the best results. The challenge is that those results don't materialize within the government's expectations, so while I'm doing excellent work, it still looks bad for me on paper. What's happening is that she keeps threatening to fire me, thinking it will motivate me, but all that's happening is that the stress is interfering with my performance, and it is making me sick.

2. *What does it mean?* It means I need to decide whether the paycheck and benefits are worth the toll this job is taking on my emotional and physical health. It means I need to consider my options should she fire me before I'm ready to move on. It means I need to ask that she spread the hard-to-serve clients more evenly across all the caseloads instead of them all being assigned to me.

3. *What do I want? What is my desired outcome?* What I want is to do my job without interference. I want to help people achieve their goals, and I want to help create radical, positive, lasting change.

4. *How can I obtain that outcome?* I could stay in this job for the steady paycheck and intrinsic satisfaction. I could move on and work elsewhere. I could pursue my own professional goals and create a system for creating radical change that is uniquely mine.

5. Here's the best part: *What's the worst thing that can happen if she fires me?* I won't have a job at this place. *What's the best thing that can happen if she fires me?* I won't have a job at this place. Listen, friend, when I realized that getting fired meant I wouldn't have to

work in such a toxic environment any longer, I was released from the need for control. It was like my downstairs brain finally shut up, and my frontal lobes started filling in the blanks. I had an impressive résumé, loads of work experience, a concurrent under-grad degree, and a stack of certificates from all kinds of additional training. My upstairs brain reminded me that I could find work elsewhere if I wanted it, and I also knew I could make a go of my business if I so chose.

6. *What is the lifetime value of this event/situation?* The realization came to me that this was a pivotal moment in my career. I could knuckle under the pressure of my employer and continue to strive toward meeting her impossible demands, or I could wrest back control of those things within my power to direct—my thoughts, my beliefs, my choices, my actions, my responses.

When next she summoned me, I walked boldly into her office and asked her point-blank, "Are you going to fire me?" She stared at me, stunned. I asked the question again. "Because if you are going to fire me, I'd like to know in advance so I can get my résumé ready."

Woohah! The backpedaling began immediately. "There's nothing in it for me if I fire you," she replied. Huh. All that bark, and there was no bite.

"Well, then," I smiled, "if I'm not fired, can I get back to work?" That was the end of that. Within a few months, *she* was gone, and I learned that she never had the authority to hire or fire. A few months after that, I gave my notice, and I have never, ever looked back.

While the external locus reinforces the fallacy of control, the simple truth is that we can control nothing in our external environment. Not the weather. Not the length of the checkout line at the big box store. Not the flow of traffic on the interprovincial or interstate highway. Not the attitude of the server in your favorite restaurant. You cannot control the moment your water breaks, the gender of your unborn child, or whether the doctor will do an expert or a butcher job on your C-section. You cannot control if the driver behind you will stop or crash into the back of your car. You cannot control the decisions your company's management will make, the behavior of bul-lies, or the use of microaggressions, overt racism, and discrimination in the workplace. You most surely cannot control what comes out of your partner's mouth, nor can you control the emotions you feel when you hear what comes out of your partner's mouth!

In my seminars on stress management and anger resolution, I often have the audience participate in an exercise in which they partner up with someone and share a situation in their lives they want to change. Each partner takes a turn sharing the story and describing what they cannot control in their situation. They then describe what is left that they can control. Most people will have the same answers, which are reflective of a more internal locus of control: I can control my attitude. My reactions and responses. The words I use when I communicate. The way in which I will communicate.

I control my choices. I can choose when to confront someone on their behavior and when to step back and say nothing. I can choose who I will allow in my life, and I can choose to set boundaries. I can choose whom to trust. I can choose to forgive. I can choose to take care of myself. I can choose to seek help for my problems, and I can choose if I want to do the work required to create a better life for myself. I can control my choices, and the thoughts I think are there by my choice. Therefore, I can train my brain to think differently so that I can influence my outcomes in a more positive way.

Invisible Interpretations

We have established that the emotion of anger is not something one can always readily identify through visual stimuli. The ways we make meaning are a lot like this. First, our *external* or sensory perception does its job of receiving sensory data in our immediate environment. Our eyes, noses, ears, mouths, and skin receive information. Our *internal* perceptions—our thoughts, constructs, and beliefs—interpret and make meaning of the data we receive. Imagine if you had the inability to receive sensory data through touch due to nerve damage or spinal cord injury. Imagine if you could touch things but you had no way of making meaning of the things you felt. How would you know that a surface is too hot to touch? Would you recognize *heat*, or would you only recognize the *pain* caused by the heat? The key lesson here is that just because you see it a certain way doesn't make it so.

Case in point—make sense of this sentence: **IAMNOWHERE**.

Some of you will immediately see "I am nowhere." Others will see "I am now here."

Every reader sees the same letters in the same order of presentation, but the meaning that is derived from the letters is dependent entirely on *how you look at it.*

You are the ringmaster of your own circus. Every thought you entertain that contributes to anxiety, angst, frustration, or depression is a lead actor in your circus act. For me, the circus ring usually presents itself when I am driving—hence, the copious references to road incidents. I happen to have very clear expectations of myself and other drivers, and I hold a reasonable expectation matched with a level of trust extended to other commuters that we will all obey the rules of the road to keep each other safe so we can all arrive alive. When people violate those rules and expectations, I tend to entertain the monkeys that start chattering in my downstairs brain.

Many years ago, I was driving along the 427 North toward my destination of Yorkdale Mall to meet a potential client. I was on a hands-free call when a blue BMW flew past me, cut me off, and the driver flipped me the bird as though I had violated his driving rules. I hit the brakes to avoid a collision and carried on, a bit flustered but none the worse for wear. The monkeys in my circus started their standard chatter: "What a jerk! What did I do to him? I'm just over here driving, minding my own business. Somebody hasn't had their coffee yet. I should gesture back or something. He needs to know he is wrong!" On and on the chatter resounded, but since I had an audience via my Bluetooth, I kept my outside voice in check, preferring to keep calm and carry on.

A 2006 survey by the Traffic Injury Research Foundation (TIRF) found that some 670,000 Canadians admit they like to take risks while driving, "just for the fun of it."[2] The study also found that over twice as many males engage in aggressive driving compared with women.

The TIRF noted that aggressive driving includes behaviors like excessive speeding, running red lights, honking horns, risk-taking, and, in extreme cases, physical violence. Aggressive, careless, or risk-taking drivers may not intend to harm, but their behavior increases the risk of collision for everyone in their path. Speed kills, and taking risks like driving impaired or running red lights is dangerous for the driver, any unfortunate passengers they might have, and all the drivers around them. This type of driving often results in road rage—other drivers retaliating with even more aggressive driving or with violence.

In my case, I chose to ignore the monkey chatter; instead, I applied my traditional approach of thinking it through and determining my desired outcome. Sure, I was angry at the BMW driver. He was rude. There was no need to cut me off. Certainly, the flip-off was not warranted since the driving violation came from him, not me. But my desired outcome was to arrive at my destination on time and unharmed. So I took a deep breath, managed my anxiety, and kept on driving responsibly. I chose to take no risks, to forgo any attempts at retaliation, and to just stay chill.

Here's the fun part. That was back in the day when I had door magnets on my car with my photo, my name, and my phone number along with a tagline, "Solutions for Anger and Stress." Unbeknown to me, while I was happily rolling along, having forgotten all about the blue guy, he had slowed down long enough to record my phone number. A few minutes after I had settled down in a food court at Yorkdale Mall with Starbucks latte in hand, I received a text. It said, "Sorry for cutting you off this morning. Blue BMW, tinted windows."

I was, and always am, the ringleader of my own circus. My choice to keep the monkeys in check by refusing to retaliate was cause enough to make the Beemer driver reconsider his actions—likely through some act of self-evaluation—and apologize. I achieved my desired outcome of arriving alive, and he shifted his long-term outcomes by thinking through his actions and choosing to take responsibility. Road rage crisis was averted, and we both ended up having a better day because of it. That, my friends, is leverage.

The bottom line is this: Sometimes the way you see things is not how they truly are. If the monkeys take over the circus, you may find yourself escalating arguments that never needed to take place. Just because you see it one way doesn't mean that is how everyone else sees it. Remember that your perceived world is informed by your senses—external perception—your values, and your experiences, which inform your internal perceptions. No two people share the same values or experiences. We can certainly have things in common, but no two experiences are identical. There will always be minute, if not massive, differences in how you and others interpret your surroundings and your experiences.

No matter how you interpret what is happening in your life, you still have power in that you get to decide who the key players in your circus are or if you even want to keep running a circus at all. Just know that if you decide to let the monkeys loose, you better be ready for chaos to ensue.

Summary

Heuristics, or thinking shortcuts, inform biases or the assumptions we make about people, groups, situations, or things.

Faulty, irrational, or distorted thoughts lead to poor choices and even poorer outcomes.

We can control nothing in our external environment.

The key to shifting away from crooked thinking is to first challenge irrational beliefs and then replace them with more realistic ones.

Action Steps

1. Find the worksheets for this chapter in your workbook: Putting Crooked Thoughts on Trial and Destroying the Fallacy of Control.
2. As you work through the exercises, consider if you have an internal or external locus of control. How can you continue to practice processing your experiences from a more internal locus of control?

6

MUDDLED MINDSET

The Cinderella Syndrome

ONCE UPON A time, there was a young woman whose mother died when she was very young. Cinderella, better known as Ella, was the beloved only child, and her father doted on her, but as she matured, he felt she should have a female role model, so he married a woman with two young daughters around Ella's age. This "wicked stepmother" reviled Ella for her place in her new husband's life, and when Ella's father suddenly passed away, leaving her in the care of her stepmother, she was treated worse than a servant—bullied, abused, and isolated—while the stepmother and the stepdaughters squandered Ella's father's fortune trying to elevate themselves in society.

When the ruler of the land desired for his son to take a wife, it was decreed that all the women in the land should attend a ball so that the prince could choose a wife from the crowd of fair, eligible young maidens. It was devastating for Ella when, after she was promised to go to the ball, that promise was broken, her expectations shattered. With no dress, no transportation, and no hope, Ella was left feeling so very inadequate and helpless.

Enter the fairy godmother, who solved all of Ella's problems with the stroke of a wand. Suddenly, Ella was beautiful, dressed to impress, and had a cadre of "servants" to accompany her to the ball in a fancy carriage. Even though she only had until midnight, Ella met the prince, they fell in love at first sight, and after she disappeared, he moved heaven and earth to find the woman he loved. Of course, once he found her and all the wrongs were made right, they lived happily ever after.

Why Do We Love Ella?

If I am to be completely honest, as a child, I liked the story, but it always bothered me a bit. It wasn't until I was much older, with children of my own, that it occurred to me why this fairy tale troubled me so. Here's the thing: I realized that Ella had *all* the resources she needed to shape her own destiny, but the barrier to her success was that she lacked a problem-resolution mindset.

Now, to be fair, Ella's life experience had not fully supported the development of a success or problem-solving mindset. Let's review the facts of Ella's case:

1. Her mother died when she was very young (trauma and loss).
2. She was doted on by her father, who indulged her every whim (lack of self-efficacy).
3. Her father remarried, but he chose poorly. This decision had a negative impact on Ella's life (bullying/emotional abuse/negative transfer—a side effect of bad heuristics).
4. Her father died suddenly (more trauma and loss).
5. The emotional abuse escalated, and her status was reduced significantly (erosion of her self-esteem).
6. By all appearances, every choice Ella wanted to make was dependent on the whims of her stepmother (lack of self-efficacy, lack of autonomy).

It is clear no one was out there consistently showing Ella how she could think for herself, act for herself, or make informed choices to determine the course of her own future.

In and of itself, the fact that Ella is written this way really bothers me. I like stories that feature strong female leads, so Ella, as a beautiful but weak protagonist, picks away at my sensibilities. That aside, the appearance of a fairy godmother who solves everything for Ella reinforces the narrative of a beautiful but witless and helpless creature who couldn't tie her own shoes without the help and support of a third party. Even the fact that the prince swoops in and saves the day sends a message to little girls everywhere that what men are looking for is someone lovely to look at who is kind, loving, and compassionate; who can take mountains of abuse and still emerge unscathed; but who can't make a single decision for herself—in other words, she is easily controlled. Blech.

Now don't get me wrong. I love romance, and my guilty pleasure is a well-written romance novel. But seriously, in real life, Ella would need some in-depth psychological treatment for her complex trauma experiences as well as some talk therapy to help reconcile her interpretation of her life experiences with the myriad of other choices she had available to her.

ACEs and Their Ability to Muddle Mindsets

Consider Ella's ACEs for a moment—her *adverse childhood experiences*. ACEs could be events of abuse, neglect, or household challenges that happened in childhood. They can be any highly stressful experience that happened or might happen before the age of eighteen. An ACE could be a single event, or it could be several circumstances in which your safety, security, trust, or sense of self is threatened or violated. These types of events fall into three categories:

- Abuse—physical, emotional, or sexual
- Neglect—physical or emotional
- Household challenges such as divorce, incarcerated parent, substance use or abuse, domestic violence, mental illness, poverty, homelessness, and so on. Other forms of ACEs include discrimination based on race, ethnicity, gender identity or sexual orientation, religion, learning disabilities or other disabilities. It can also include poverty; racism; other violence like bullying or witnessing violence at school, work, or in the community; intergenerational or cultural trauma; removal into foster care; migration or immigration; bereavement/survivorship; or having adult responsibilities as a child.

Consider Ella's experiences: the loss of both parents presumably before her eighteenth birthday. Emotional and physical abuse. Neglect. Poverty or the threat of it. Having to take on adult responsibilities as a child.

According to the tenets of rational emotive behavior therapy, traumatic experiences including ACEs have the potential to cause you to question who you are, shattering the self. Trauma also has a way of stealing your voice. Because the limbic system, the downstairs brain, is laser-focused on keeping you safe, you respond to every stimulus through the lens of trauma or your ACEs. Remember Glasser's assertion that we filter our real world through our senses, our values, and our *experiences*. Ella's experiences, being what they were, had taught her to do the same. Her mindset said, *If I want to be loved, I must comply with the wishes of others even if they are to my detriment.* Her mindset said, *I am helpless to design my own destiny. I am at the mercy of those more powerful than I.* Her mindset said, *If I work hard enough, if I please others enough, I may eventually get what I want.*

For Ella to create the radical, positive, lasting change she wanted for herself, she would have to learn how to think, speak, and choose for herself after a lifetime of having others do so for her. She would have to revisit those limiting beliefs, challenge them, and amend them. She would have to become fully cognizant of her thought processes and have the will and the wherewithal to shift her thoughts so that she could focus on her long-term desired outcomes. She would have to consider what she wanted for herself rather than focusing on only helping others to get what they wanted, all for the sake of a semblance of acceptance.

In truth, without some intense self-work, Ella would likely not live happily ever after; rather, she would *expect* to experience the same kind of mistreatment and emotional abuse from the queen mother as she received from her stepmother. She would likely be incredibly insecure in her new role as princess, having never had authority like that before. Even though being catered to might be a bit of throwback to her life pre-stepmom, she might feel uncomfortable with being pampered and waited on because at this point, she would feel more kinship with the servants than she would with the monarchy.

Now that I have ruined this fairy tale for you and your children, let's look at Ella's mindset as it is developed in her story. When we examine the story carefully, we will find that Ella had *everything* she needed to get herself to the ball. She didn't need a fairy godmother to fix it for her.

1. She had access to her stepsisters' dresses, shoes, hair supplies, and makeup.

2. There was a wagon in the courtyard that she used to run errands for her stepmother.
3. There was a horse in the barn that Ella used to cart the wagon.

When the fairy godmother showed up, she turned a pumpkin into a carriage. Didn't need that—there was already a wagon. She turned mice into horses but didn't need to since there was already a horse. Then she turned the horse into a footman, which Ella would not have needed; she was perfectly capable of climbing into the wagon herself—*she did it all the time*. The fairy godmother "magicked" a dress, glass slippers, and a wicked updo and then sent her off to "find her destiny." All I'm saying is Ella could have done it on her own, if only she had the right mindset.

What Contributes to a Muddled Mindset?

One of the biggest barriers to effective thought processing is what psychologists call *functional fixedness*, a cognitive bias that limits a person from using any object except in the way it is traditionally used. Functional fixedness is to some degree a function of temperament—our innate nature. It reflects a lack of sensitivity to probability and poor usage of our brain's plasticity in relation to problem-solving. Functional fixedness prevents us from opening our perceptions to see things from different perspectives.

This cognitive bias makes problem-solving more difficult because it limits innovation and out-of-the-box thinking. Functional fixedness is referred to as a *negative transfer* because it appears when our past experiences and the meaning we make of them interfere with acquiring or applying new information. Conversely, *positive transfer* happens when our past experiences and the values we attach to them make it easier to acquire and apply new knowledge.

Functional fixedness is contributed to by age, experience, and mental sets. The older people get, the more set in their ways they become, and they may have difficulty with innovative thinking. A *mental set* could be conceived of as a specific way of looking at a problem. We could say that a mental set is a framework or a *set of beliefs* one has developed to help identify, process, and solve problems. Note the interplay of perception, meaning-making, and beliefs in the development of a mental set. Imagine Ella spending her formative years first in grief, then to feel loved and treasured for a time, only to be mired in more grief brought on by traumatic loss, compounded by abuse and neglect. How might her ACEs inform her mental set?

Let's say you want to cut a piece of paper with scissors, but you have misplaced the only set of scissors you have in your house, office, or classroom. Functional fixedness says the only way one can cut paper is with some scissors. *If I don't have some scissors, I guess I can't perform this task.* Applying plasticity and sensitivity to probability allows us to look at all the other ways in which we might be able to complete the task.

Just think about it. There must be at least three ways to cut paper without some scissors.

- You could fold it carefully and tear along the folds.
- You could use a carpet knife or kitchen knife.
- You could use a letter opener.

I wouldn't be surprised if you came up with some other options than the ones I just provided here. The more flexible the mindset, the easier it is to solve the presenting problem.

There was that time I was moving my daughter out of her apartment; she had taken off somewhere, and we were to meet up in an hour or two. I left her building and locked the door behind me, leaving the key on the stove. Only when I got to my car did I realize I had left my cell phone inside the apartment. I will not divulge my secrets, but I will admit that without contacting the landlord, I was able to gain access to the apartment to retrieve my phone. Had I been mired in functional fixedness, a minor inconvenience would have evolved into a big, hairy deal. Instead, I applied my creative problem-solving skills using every possible innovative idea that popped into my head until I was able to successfully unlock the door to gain access.

I expect that learning to adjust to life in the palace would be near impossible for someone like Ella, whose ACEs had her trapped in negative transfer thinking. For Ella, a dress, hair products, or shoes not belonging to her were not available to her even in a pinch. A wagon was only to be used for chores. The horse was only to draw the wagon to the market and back.

A lock could only be opened with a key. A servant's purpose was to serve, and she identified more as a servant than she ever would as a princess.

If You're Fixated on Only One Solution, All Others Will Remain Invisible

What happens when you get fixated on the solution you think you *need* rather than the alternatives you *have*? You will feel:

- angry
- upset
- frustrated
- disappointed
- scared

Ella's first mistake was trying repeatedly to please others *and* in wishing for love from and acceptance by her stepfamily. They were never going to accept her. Hoping for them to change led to an increase in depression and hopelessness. Her futile attempts to influence a different outcome with the same behavior was "crazy-making." All these efforts were rooted in faulty thinking—her own form of functional fixedness. Her motivating thought was this: "If I do what they want, they will love and accept me."

Ella's second mistake was buying into the fallacy of control. Remember, the fallacy of control suggests that by saying or doing a certain thing, or by being a certain way, or by wishing, hoping, or dreaming for a certain outcome, then we can control that outcome. Ella had not learned to release her need for control, nor had she learned that the feelings, intentions, and behaviors of others were never within her control in the first place. Striving to control things one cannot leads to heightened anxiety and feelings of low self-worth.

Her third mistake was the thing that contributes to insanity in the extreme and poor mental health on a daily basis—that is, she fostered unrealistic expectations about her stepfamily's ability and willingness to love and accept her. She was focused on the dream rather than the reality of what was in front of her. Maya Angelou said when people show you who they are, you should believe them. Ella did not want to believe her stepfamily was so wicked. She was fixated on holding out hope that they would love her if only she pleased them enough.

If the language of unmet expectations is *should've*, *could've*, and *would've*, then expectations are at the root of every negative emotion. Think of the expectations you had that turned out to be unrealistic and, therefore, impossible to meet.

- You expected them to be loyal.
- You expected them to love you the way you loved them.
- You expected your pet to live longer.
- You expected there would be time to say goodbye.
- You expected to feel safe or to be safe.
- You expected your friends to look out for you.
- You expected to be rewarded for your hard work.

Who before Do

Albert Ellis and the proponents of REBT say that trauma shatters the self. How can one expect to "recover" when the very things that define them have been torn to shreds? Many people talk about overcoming trauma, but here's the thing: you cannot overcome the trauma itself—you can't overcome something that has already happened. What you can overcome is the memory of it, the stain of it, the shame of it, the pain of it. The traumatic experience will forever be a part of the fabric of your life's tapestry, but it does not have to own you, define you, or restrict you any longer.

Ella defined herself by her traumatic experiences and the meaning she had been forced to make of them. She believed herself unlovable, unworthy, undeserving because her family continued to ram that narrative down her throat. For Ella to become the princess she had the potential to be, she first had to discover and own who she was born to be and who she was *right now*. Only then could she change the choices she would make and the actions she would take. Who before do. How could Ella transform into her happily-ever-after self when all that was done for her by the fairy godmother was only skin deep?

Imagine you have a lovely mantle clock that is beautiful to look at, but it doesn't keep time. Its hands stay forever locked in the one o'clock position. If you only looked at the clock at 1:00 a.m. and 1:00 p.m., you might assume the clock is working fine. But when you check it randomly throughout the day, you notice it is not working as it was created to work.

You decide to move it to a new location. It still won't work. You shine it up pretty so it gleams and sparkles, but it still won't work. You yell at the clock. Tell it to get itself together, toughen up, and get back to work. It still won't work. You change the batteries. It still won't work. You try the soft touch, speaking gently to the clock. You encourage it to start working again, to be the best it can be. Yet it still won't work.

See, nothing you do externally will make the clock magically start working again. You've done all you can do; there's nothing left but to reach out to an expert—a clockmaker, a horologist, who knows and understands the inner workings of clocks. The horologist's only concern is to get the clock working again. They will go inside the clock to examine all the moving parts, find what is no longer functioning or what is stuck, and fix it.

Wherever You Go, You Take You with You

You and I—and Ella too—are like that clock. Often, when we feel things aren't right, we try to make surface changes. We move to a new place, new home, new job, new relationship. In Ella's case, she had a fairy godmother who dressed her up in fancy threads and lots of glitter, but the fairy godmother did none of the deep work of helping to shift Ella's mindset. She still felt unloved, unworthy, undeserving. Like Ella, you may still feel some pesky emotions despite the attempts to shine yourself up—because wherever you go, you take you with you.

You might try to work out. Make that body shiny and new. Hey, exercise is good for you, so this isn't a bad idea, but it will only do so much for your emotional state. You might color or cut your hair, start wearing makeup, grow a beard, or otherwise alter your appearance, but emotional messes are heart deep, not skin deep.

You might berate yourself, or others close to you might do it for you. If anything, this will make you feel worse and do nothing for your already messy emotional state. You could try positive affirmations and speak kindly to yourself. This is also good for you, and it may help somewhat, but if the root cause of the messy emotions remains, you will continue to feel less than okay.

What is needed, then, is a non-invested third party, an *expert* in the field of emotions—enter the therapist—who can examine your inner workings, look at all the moving and stuck parts, and walk alongside you to reach your goal of optimum mental health. A therapist can be like a teacher, a voice of support, validation and collaboration, a mentor, or a guide. Therapists are charged with holding your heart safe as they work through your messy emotions with you. With the meticulous care of a master weaver, they help you gather the threads of your seemingly shattered existence and help you stitch together the tapestry of your life. Sometimes it's just one small thing that needs to be replaced or removed to get everything running smoothly again. Sometimes more intensive repair work is needed. Either way, a therapist is your ally in your journey to wholeness.

Can I just add one thing here? I said that you are *like* the clock. You are *not* the clock. Clocks can break. In the physical sense, it is true that humans are also breakable. We are not immortal, nor are we invincible. Having messy emotions or a muddled mindset doesn't mean you're broken. It just means you're human.

Let's return to the notion of identity work as an innovative tool to counter the shattering effect of trauma. Please allow me a little creative license with the retelling of Ella's happy ever after. With a little help from her therapist, some personality assessment tools, and a definitive statement about who she was, Ella discovered the person she was born to be, the person she was before trauma shattered her sense of self and stole her voice. She embraced her true self and came to recognize how her trauma responses were betraying the person she was meant to be. Ella remembered how loved she was by her father and recognized that while he meant well, he had chosen poorly, and she was the beneficiary of his bad decisions. She learned how to take ownership of the things that were hers alone and to place the responsibility for everything else with the people to whom it belonged.

Then when the prince came looking for a bride, he found a beautiful, resilient, resourceful woman who had been dragged through the fires of hell and survived. He found someone who had empathy for servants and would treat them with care and respect rather than with arrogant disdain. He found someone who would be respectful to his parents but would not be a push-over. Someone who valued love, connection, and family but who would not sacrifice her self-worth or her values in exchange for that connection. He found someone with whom he could partner in life, someone who would one day be his queen. Told you I love romance!

Remember that the key to radical, positive, lasting change lies in the thoughts, feelings, choices, and actions you engage in, which contributes to your outcomes. Remember, too, that often things that happen—those things outside of your control—are not your fault. It wasn't Ella's fault that her mom died or that her father married a shrew. It was not her fault that her dad died too. It wasn't her fault that her stepmother and stepsisters were evil. It wasn't even her fault that her attempts to please them failed. Ella owed these people nothing.

Do not take ownership of the things in your life that you can't control, whether they are biological, socioeconomical, relational, or psychological. Focus your energy on the things you can control: Your responses, your choices, your thoughts, your reactions. How you fuel your body, how you care for your health. Choose your thoughts wisely and check your mental sets often to ensure they are working for you and not against you. Talk to someone! There is no shame in talking to a non-invested third party like a therapist. Expand your mental sets by learning new coping skills and embracing innovative methods of problem-solving.

Remember, Ella had everything she needed at her fingertips to be successful, but because of her functional fixedness, she was blind to the answers sitting right in front of her. All the resources you need to solve your problems are right in front of you—all you need to do is embrace and apply them.

When Thoughts Attack

When the monkeys inside our heads take over the circus and thoughts attack, what to do? Crooked thinking informs yucky feelings, which lead to the choices we will make. Psychologist Richard Lazarus conceptualized stress as the perception that the resources we have at our disposal are insufficient for the perceived demands. He notes that the sources of stress include pressure—urgent demands or expectations emerging from an outside source; uncontrollability—the degree of control that one believes one has over a situation or an event; or frustration when people's efforts to achieve a goal or fulfill a need are thwarted. Does any of this sound like Ella's life?

Kurt Lewin tells us we have three types of choices when faced with conflict: avoidance/avoidance, approach/avoidance, and approach/approach. The avoidance/avoidance choice—meaning that no matter which option you choose, the expected outcome will be a bad one—is the most stress-inducing of all choices because no matter what, it is a lose-lose situation. With the approach/avoidance choice, both choices have good and bad sides to them. You might take job offer 1, which has great pay and benefits but will require you to work nights, and you will never see your partner, who works solid days. Or job offer 2, which is solid days but has lousy pay, no benefits, and no guarantee of permanent employment. These types of choices are stressful too, but at least in each choice, there is some benefit to offset the risks. Consider the married man who is attracted to someone at work. He loves his partner, but he wants to be with this other person. If he cheats, he will have betrayed his vows and may have additional fallout of the loss of his marriage. If he remains faithful, he will have the pain that comes with abstaining from something he really wants—to pursue the attraction. This is also a type of approach/avoidance choice.

Lastly, there is the approach/approach choice. This is the least stressful of the choice types because no matter what you decide, it is a win-win. Since either goal or potential outcome is favorable, it does not really matter which choice you make.

My theory is this: when you have entertained the biases that inform negative transfer, which in turn affects your emotions, and you are confronted with uncomfortable feelings, you will be faced with one of four choices: to approach, to avoid, to aggress, or to acquiesce. Sadly, when we are faced with feelings of fear, anxiety, depression, or loneliness, we tend to choose either fight or flight—in other words, we will choose to aggress or avoid. These types of choices translate to actions taken. Avoidance shows up this way: *avoid* conflict, avoid having difficult conversations, avoid problem-solving, choosing behaviors that will, in the short term at least, avoid emotional pain. Alternately, we might choose to *aggress*: start fights, use inflammatory language to deflect from our negative feelings, bully others to redirect attention from our own perceived shortcomings, or target people who appear to be threats to our self-esteem and success. To choose *approach* means using the *Anger Solutions* model of TSA, thinking things through objectively and rationally, determining your desired outcome, identifying the person who can best help you solve the problem as you perceive it, and then entering into a dialogue with them about how to solve the problem. Ella's conflict resolution style of choice was to *acquiesce*, in hopes that by fawning or people-pleasing, she would eventually win love and acceptance.

Anxiety and Anger—Avoiding Quick Fixes

Ella's transformation from scullery maid to princess at the hands of her fairy godmother was the penultimate quick fix. It felt good and looked good, but it lasted only until midnight, and then Ella was back to her ragged, dirty, seemingly unlovable self. The thought matrix demonstrates how choices are informed by feelings and emotional states. *Reacting* to an uncomfortable feeling with a quick fix like avoidance, aggression, or acquiescing will most usually result in a temporary reprieve from the uncomfortable emotion followed by even more discomfort.

Self-awareness is essential to helping us to shift from reacting to responding—hence, the TSA tool for processing and resolving the problems that triggered the emotional state. When my clients express feelings of distress at their tendency to gravitate toward quick fixes—self-soothing behaviors, anxious tics, stress spending, or angry outbursts—I encourage them to work through this process.

Aware: Direct your awareness to what you are doing in the moment—hand-wringing, biting nails, snapping at others, stress eating.
Acknowledge: "I see that I'm wringing my hands again." "I notice I am irritable and snappy."
Accept: Be okay with the way you are acting in the moment. Don't judge it. Do not blame, shame, or complain about your actions. If you can accept the behavior but acknowledge that you want to

change it, you can then plan how you will move toward change or what you will do instead. Try to do this all without judgment.

Assess: How am I feeling in this moment? Am I anxious? Nervous? Bored? Lonely? Angry? Sad? Tired? Am I just doing this out of habit? If I am trying to fix a feeling, what might I do instead that would be more effective? Is there something I am thinking that is contributing to this feeling? If I shift my thoughts, might the feeling change? If the feelings change, it is likely my anxious behaviors will stop.

Adapt and Adjust: This is where you actively embark on extinguishing the old behavior and introducing a healthier choice.

Problem resolution doesn't always come easy, especially when you are fixated on the wrong aspect of the problem. Muddled mindsets caused by functional fixedness, flawed mental sets, lack of self-awareness, and resistance to innovative thinking will hijack your ability to arrive at a reasonable, safe, or appropriate response to your problems. As much as I would love to say that anger resolution is as simple as TSA, it is not that elementary. To seize control of your own destiny, you must relinquish the fallacy of control and be open to different perspectives and new ways of seeing things. You may require the intervention of therapy to help unravel and reweave the threads of your tapestry, to help you challenge and adjust your mindset and shore up your resiliency. When you learn to do these things and school your thoughts to influence your feelings and subsequent choices, you'll create the radical, positive, lasting change you seek.

Summary

1. ACEs and the ensuing trauma can negatively impact or contribute to the way we respond to events as we grow and mature.

2. Functional fixedness and mental set can impede effective problem-solving and may contribute to feelings of being stuck.

3. When attempting to process and shift anxious thoughts or behaviors, follow this model: become *aware* of what you are doing or thinking; *acknowledge* the behavior without judgment; *accept* that it is happening in the moment; *assess* the reasons for the behavior

or thought; *adapt* and *adjust* your thoughts and choose alternative behaviors.

Reflection

Can you identify areas in your life that are affected by functional fixedness? Are there aspects of your mental set that need to be shifted or adapted? Have you ever found yourself in a situation wishing like Ella that someone would just come and "magic" a solution for you? Knowing what you know now, what would you do differently if you ever find yourself in a similar circumstance?

Action Steps

1. Go to the website and download the worksheet, Bring Your "A" Game.
2. Practice processing your anxious thoughts or those driven by a frustration signal.

7

KILL THE MONSTER
WHEN IT'S A BABY

Monsters in Training

WHY DO BULLIES get ahead? Because people don't have the will or courage to kill the monster when it's a baby. My boss used to holler all the time, "You teach people how to treat you!" He was right. Every time bullies engage in aggressive, abusive, intimidating, or passive-aggressive behavior; every time bullies lie or twist the truth to their advantage; every time they gaslight someone who calls them out on their tactics and they are free to continue to do these things with impunity, we are in effect teaching them how to treat us.

Young children are monsters in training. The off-duty police officer/dad notices a couple of young boys on their school property "ghost riding" or pushing their riderless bikes into traffic. That's mischief and reckless endangerment. He then watches as they roll their bikes toward teachers' electric vehicles parked in the charging station of the school parking lot. A collision causing even a minor scratch and dent could result in thousands of dollars in damage to a teacher's vehicle. That's vandalism. He chooses to be a responsible citizen, steps in, and tells them to stop, flashing his badge so they will take him seriously.

The next day when dropping his kids off at school, he is met by another officer, who says one of the boy's moms called to complain about his intervention. She defended her son's behavior by asking, "Why is the police officer's son allowed to play in the field, but my son is not allowed to play in traffic?"

True story.

True. Story.

That mom is teaching her son how to treat people by allowing and defending his defiant, deviant, and dangerous behavior. She is feeding the monster rather than starving his appetite for mischief. By empowering her son to defy the law rather than respect it, she is growing her very own monster.

Run!

Why is it that in almost every monster movie, everyone starts out saying how cute it is as a baby? Don't they realize that T-Rex or Velociraptor is going to grow up and act on its nature? A predator is a predator no matter how cute it is when it is little. Take bullying behavior, for example. The signs of lack of empathy, which contributes to bullying behavior, can be seen in children as early as age four. When I started eleventh grade in a new high school, my social studies / homeroom teacher encouraged us to tell a story about ourselves so the rest of the class could get to know us better. One of my classmates divulged that she was expelled from kindergarten. The story goes that on the first day of kindergarten, she saw another child sitting in the playground sandbox. She noticed the child was sitting directly under the teeter-totter, and her first thought was, *I wonder what would happen if I. . . .* Well, she did indeed flip the teeter-totter up, bonking her little classmate on the head, resulting in her subsequent suspension.

By the time I knew her, my classmate was a perfectly lovely human, but what if that behavior and the attitudes informing it had gone unchecked? What if she had been allowed to grow into a full-fledged bully? Bullying is defined as *"repeated aggression characterized by the intent to inflict harm, in which there is a power differential between the person who is bullying, and the one being victimized."*[1] While bullying behavior is not unique to the classroom, schoolyard, office, or boardroom, research shows that most of it discontinues as children mature; thus, most bullying behavior occurs among children of elementary-school age. While bullying certainly continues throughout high school and into adulthood, research demonstrates that it peaks during the preteen years—in seventh and eighth grades—and, for most, declines as they mature throughout their secondary school years. The majority will grow out of this behavior trend, but there is a percentage of the population that will not mature enough to discontinue their bullying tendencies. This outlier group will continue to engage in aggressive and hostile behaviors through adulthood.

Whether you are eight, eighteen, forty-eight, or eighty-eight, the experience of being abused can be shameful and humiliating. When bullying occurs, the targets will try everything they can think of to stop the abuse. If they are unable to stop the bullying, a third party is needed to disrupt the power imbalance, to remove the negative power from the one engaging in the abusive behavior, and to protect and empower the one who is being victimized. In the case of school-aged children, this third party is almost often an adult responsible for the children, such as a teacher, principal, or coach. When the targets are supported by adults, other children who witness bullying may also become part of the solution rather than part of the problem. Renowned Canadian bullying experts Debra Pepler and Wendy Craig found that when a child has the courage to respond and call out bullying, the behavior stops within ten seconds 57 percent of the time.

Glasser said that every problem is, at its heart, a relationship problem. Pepler and Craig's research affirmed this suggestion when they reached the conclusion that bullying is a relationship problem that requires relationship solutions to protect victims from bullying. Relationship solutions will help both bullies and victims integrate into positive peer relationships and strengthen their social skills and adaptive coping abilities.

No two victims or bullies are the same; in fact, some bullies may often find themselves the victim in other settings. If we are to stem the tide of bullying behavior, we must start where the behavior begins—in childhood. Placing bullies and their victims in a room together and telling them to "work it out" is not a viable solution. First, it revictimizes the target by putting them in the direct path of their tormentor. Second, in the case of children, if they could work it out, they would have already done so. Without the guidance of someone more mature who can demonstrate empathy and explore the attitudes that inform the bullying, any such so-called attempt to resolve the conflict will surely fail. Third, this kind of "intervention" is a perfect example of feeding the monster instead of killing it. It empowers the bully to control the narrative; when the bully says, "It's handled," and the adult believes them, they can now take the bullying behavior underground and continue to torment the hapless victim in subtler ways that adults won't recognize.

Supports for targeted children must be based on their individual strengths and weaknesses, as well as the quality of their relationships both inside and outside their school. First, targeted children must be protected from the abuse they experience at the hands of their peers. This responsibility falls primarily on the adults in their lives. Some victimized children may experience challenges with emotional or behavioral regulation, depression, anxiety, or social and assertiveness skills.

Coaching victimized children to address the destructive challenges they face when being bullied is called *scaffolding*, and this skill can be provided through steady in-the-moment support from parents, teachers, and peers and through structured programming. Learning healthy relationship skills while supported by adults and peers will enable targeted children to find refuge from the torment of bullying and develop with confidence the friendships they desperately want and need. Adults need to take responsibility for monitoring the victimized child's safety, well-being, and social experiences and to ensure that the bullying has stopped.

Focusing all the interventions on supporting the target of bullying is also a mistake. Keeping kids in from recess under the guise of "keeping them safe" while the bullies are allowed to go out and play reinforces the bully's behavior while punishing the victim. Early and immediate interventions must be applied to bullies not only because their behavior is damaging to others but also because of the harm they may cause themselves with this type of behavior.

Left unchecked, bullying may persist into adulthood and impact employability, socioeconomic status, future relationships, and even criminality. There is a strong positive correlation between bullying and conduct disorder. Bullying in childhood is a predictor for antisocial behavior as bullies age. Utterly Global[2] reports that from grades 6–9, children who bully are 6 percent more likely to be convicted of a crime by the age of twenty-four. Bullies who started in childhood are five times more likely to have a criminal record. Adult bullies are six times more likely to fight, ten times more likely to lie, and almost three times as prone to engage in workplace harassment as adults who did not engage in childhood bullying behavior.

Different Strokes for Different Folks

People choose to bully others for different reasons. This means their motivations must be addressed in different ways. Some people bully because they want something, but they lack the necessary social skills to ask for what they want. Social skills programs that teach empathy and encourage prosocial behavior and nonviolent problem-solving skills are recommended in this case.

Bullies may have little or no experience cooperating with others. They are used to getting what they want and are unaccustomed to having to negotiate or to compromise. The values, habits, and traditions of their family of origin may have informed the tendency to bully others, either because family members modeled such behavior or because home life was so frustrating that the bullying had a trickle-down effect. Opportunities to engage in cooperative learning experiences are important. Research in social psychology has found that placing bullies and their targets in a position with a problem that can only be solved by group cohesion and full participation decreases feelings of discrimination and hostility, encourages cooperative interaction, and builds feelings of kinship.

Bullies sometimes have a strong need to lead or control others. They might bully others because they can; there are no recriminations or sanctions that act as deterrents to their behavior. Remember, there is no such thing as common sense; people do what makes sense to them. People who choose bullying behavior do so because it makes sense for their immediate goals. The role of parents, teachers, and administrators, then, is to help children who bully to understand that bullying doesn't make sense. This means that bullies must experience the negative *consequences* of bullying—this may be through the loss of privileges, full suspensions, or restrictions from extracurricular activities. They must also be encouraged to engage in prosocial behavior with the introduction of positive reinforcements for treating people fairly and respectfully. When this is done effectively, students with a past reputation for bullying have so reformed that they end up taking a leading role in school antibullying committees and practices.

School Violence on the Rise

Where bullying is largely a result of inadequate impulse control, students can sometimes be helped through exercises promoting more thoughtful delayed responses. Any such interventions must be carefully planned and executed, and they must meet the child where they are. I encourage teachers to stay on top of current research about bullying and its impact on the classroom environment. Teachers and school administrators need to be aware of the various forms of bullying—including relational bullying, which is the most impactful—and be trained on how to address bullying, intervene on behalf of the victim, and how best to consequence bullying behaviors.

May I be frank? In this age of cancel culture and litigation for every little thing, school administrators have become too fearful of liability. In my experience of advocating for my clients who have been bullied, I tire of hearing "We're investigating" or "We can't divulge that information due to privacy." All I and my clients hear is "We don't want to take responsibility for this. We don't want to be sued. So we will act like we're doing something, and we'll hide behind the veil of *privacy* so you won't know that we're not really doing anything at all." What I hate to hear even more is "We have a zero-tolerance policy for bullying and aggression in our school." Tell me, school admins, how's that working for you?

The Facts about School Violence

While crime in US schools has consistently dropped, the trend regarding juvenile violence over the past several decades tells a dramatically different story. The arrest rate for *violent juvenile crime* between 1967 and 1997 increased by 143 percent. From 1960 through 1991, the US population saw an increase of a mere 40 percent; however, over the same period, violent juvenile crime increased by 500 percent, murders by 170 percent, and aggravated assaults by 600 percent. The prevalence of aggression, violence, and bullying in schools is an acknowledged challenge for students, teachers, staff, and administrators. The ensuing concern has caused many schools to seek out and implement anger management and impulse control-based programs for at-risk students in hopes of preventing further traumatic events; however, these interventions are applied in an ad hoc fashion, and the lack of standardization across school boards and inconsistency in administrative approaches mean that most of the students needing intervention fall through the cracks.

As it is in most other contexts, within the educational setting, anger is often equated with violence and aggression. The APA's recent task force on violence and aggression in schools noted that over 35 percent of school administrators, 25 percent of staff, 30 percent of teachers, and 15 percent of school counselors were victims of violence by students during COVID-19, from July 2020 to June 2021. The numbers were even higher for rates of parental aggression.

The mass student killings at Columbine High School in Littleton, Colorado, were once touted as the deadliest school massacre in America's history, with thirteen dead and more than twenty injured. A 2001 report from the National School Safety Center documented 321 school-associated violent deaths in the United States from 1992 through 2001. Since that report, countless other deaths have occurred due to violence in schools, including the more recent shooting in Ulvade, Texas, where nineteen elementary students and two teachers lost their lives, eclipsing Columbine as the deadliest school shooting in the United States.

Since Columbine, the *Washington Post* submits that more than 300,000 US students have experienced gun violence. In Canada, one-third of gun violence is committed by someone under the age of twenty. While the Ecole Polytechnique shooting in 1989 remains the most tragic school shooting in Canadian history, aggression and deadly violence are sadly becoming more the norm in Canadian schools. According to Global News, in 2006, at Dawson College, Laval, Quebec, an eighteen-year-old girl was killed and twenty others were hurt when a twenty-five-year-old gunman shot them with a semiautomatic weapon. At C.W. Jeffreys Collegiate Institute in Toronto in 2007, a fifteen-year-old boy died from a single gunshot wound to the chest. Two teens were charged with first-degree murder. In 1999 in Taber, Alberta, a fourteen-year-old grade-9 student shot three students; one was fatally wounded. In February 2022, an eighteen-year-old student died after a shooting at a Toronto high school. In December 2022, eight girls age thirteen to sixteen swarmed a fifty-nine-year-old homeless man, stabbing him to death. And the hits just keep on coming.

There have also been increasing reports of death by suicide of children and youths who experienced severe bullying from their peers, the most notable of these cases perhaps being that of Amanda Todd, who died by suicide in 2012; the man who coached her to die by suicide was only just convicted in 2022. For those children who survive bullying and peer-to-peer violence, mental health problems including posttraumatic stress disorder, anxiety, depression, and adjustment disorder may persist for years following exposure to the aggression. It would be reasonable to assume that early interventions within the education system with a view to killing the monster while it is still young might prove helpful in stemming the tide of apparently increasing violence and aggression in schools.

The prevailing conceptualization of anger as behavior has led to much of traditional anger management focusing its research on behavior management rather than emotional expression or problem resolution. Despite the trend toward behavior management, in recent years, there has been a shift toward helping people learn effective skills for expressing and resolving anger.

A meta-analysis of sixty articles comprised of both published and unpublished research grouped existing school programs into four types:

(1) coping-skills training
(2) emotional awareness and self-control
(3) relaxation strategies including breathing techniques
(4) role-plays or modeling activities

The first significant finding suggests that anger-management interventions reduced children's negative emotional and behavioral outcome measures of anger, aggression, and loss of self-control when compared with the control group. The second finding was that the anger-management interventions reviewed were equally effective, except for role-play or modeling. Thus, anger-management programs focused on coping-skills training, emotional awareness and self-control, problem-solving, and relaxation appeared to be statistically effective, whereas no significant behavior change was found when role-play was the *central* focus of the intervention.

Cultured versus Culture

A kindergarten teacher feels helpless to slay the baby dragons in her classroom. One little boy tells her to f*$# herself every day. When she complains to her principal, she is told there is nothing she can do because his father says, "It's cultural," and if she disciplines the boy, neither the union nor the school will stand behind her. What kind of foolishness is that? Since when is disrespecting a teacher "cultural"? Another boy in her class hits her because in his "culture," he doesn't have to respect women, nor does he have to respect or honor the religious or celebratory holidays of people from other cultures, religions, or ethnicities. She is again informed by the school that she must suck it up because they cannot speak out against the boy's culture. Since when is blatant disrespect protected by culture?

When I worked in brain-injury rehabilitation, one of the agencies I worked for allowed all sorts of violent and aggressive acts by the residents to occur, excusing it all because "it was the client's brain injury" that contributed to the behavior. Listen, folks—culture, upbringing, religious beliefs, bad attitudes, or brain injuries are all *reasons* one might behave in a particular way, but they are not *excuses* for the behavior. And let me assure you, in my culture of origin, if you disrespected an adult, your sister, your sister's friend, your mom, your mom's friends and neighbors, and your granny and all her friends would be lining up to give your hide a good tanning.

Imagine taking these young boys and teaching them only how to mimic appropriate behaviors without explaining to them why those behaviors should change or challenging the mindset that informs those behaviors. How long would they maintain the new habits before reverting to their old ones? Something more than modeling or role-playing preferred behaviors is required.

Mental Health Crisis in Education

The adverse childhood experiences scale predicts the health risk associated with traumatic events from childhood. High ACEs are positively correlated with an increased risk for heart disease, cancer, depression, and both physical and emotional health problems during pregnancy and the postpartum period. Conversely, other factors, such as strong interpersonal relationships, may decrease risk. It is important to note that a health risk factor is not the same as a health problem.

As ACEs are based on experiences from birth to age eighteen, does it not make sense to provide tools to help children and teens resolve their ACEs before they graduate? How much money would be saved in the first year of college? How many students get to university or college and drop out in the first year due to mental health issues?

The mental health of postsecondary students is on the decline. Lethbridge College participated in the National College Health Assessment (NCHA), a measure of student health and wellness across all Alberta postsecondary populations. The data confirmed increased stress and mental health issues for college students with contributing factors including finances, dysregulated sleep, and poor mental health. Also interesting was a 44 percent increase in students dealing with depression and a 25 percent increase in those experiencing anxiety as compared to the 2013 study. Other research documents that 46 percent of postsecondary students believe their depression impairs their ability to fully function. The number of students with recognized mental health issues has more than doubled over a five-year period.

The Center for Addiction and Mental Health (CAMH) Ontario Student Drug Use and Health Survey collected and aggregated data on all aspects of student mental health from 1991 to 2015. It reported the following results of interest:

- One in five students reported visiting a health professional for a mental health issue at least once in the previous year of study.
- More than 5 percent of secondary school students were prescribed medications for anxiety, depression, or both.
- Three percent of students sought counseling over the telephone, taking advantage of such services as Kids Help Phone.
- From seventh to twelfth grades, 28.4 percent of students reported needing mental health supports but not knowing how to access them.
- A total of 16.5 percent of students rated their mental health as fair or poor, but 34 percent of student respondents met the criteria for moderate to serious psychological distress as measured by the Kessler Six-Item Psychological Distress Scale.
- Of respondents, 12.4 percent experienced suicidal ideation, while 3 percent of respondents admitted to having made at least one suicide attempt.
- A total of 23.6 percent of students report being bullied at school.
- Approximately 8 percent of secondary school students reported having problems in the areas of psychological distress, antisocial behavior, hazardous/harmful drinking, and drug use/abuse.

It's Time for an Education Revolution

Could we make *Anger Solutions* a part of early education school curriculum, particularly before kids get to sixth grade, when antisocial behavior like bullying begins to escalate? Most school programs focus on behavior. They also target children who display problem behaviors or impulse control issues. Why not level the playing field and normalize prosocial behavior and therapy for *everyone*?

Given the rising rate of violence in adolescents—which in turn negatively impacts the school experience for students, faculty, administration, and the broader community—offering programs within the school setting that focus on emotional expression (assertiveness) and problem-solving could result in a reduction of aggression or violence as a tool to meet one's needs.

We have established that *Anger Solutions* approaches anger as a primary emotion that emerges when needs are unmet, boundaries have been violated, goals thwarted, or rules have been broken. Over the years of applying this program in various settings such as residential mental health, brain-injury case management, rehabilitation therapy, employment counseling, and psychotherapy, we have discovered consistent results that we have translated into goals or expectations for the program.

- Significant reduction in target behaviors identified by each participant
- An increase in prosocial behavior
- An increase in participant self-esteem and assertiveness and overall mental health
- A decrease in the use of aggression, violence, or abusive behavior
- A decrease in risk-taking behaviors (quick fixes, feelings fixing)
- A decrease in physical symptoms of stress or anger (headaches, stomach pain, nosebleeds, etc.)

I do not believe in a one-size-fits-all solution for anything, especially not for humans. We are all unique in our biological, neurochemical, and psychological makeup, so proposing one therapeutic solution for such unique experiences and problems seems foolish. To that end, *Anger Solutions* combines aspects of rational emotive behavior therapy, cognitive behavioral therapy, solution-focused therapy, reality therapy, and dialectical behavior therapy in what I call a *multimodal* approach to therapy. The content of the program includes psychoeducation about emotions and anger styles, knowledge about how anger develops through a choice theory lens, verbal and nonverbal assertiveness, problem resolution, listening skills, forgiveness/acceptance, and releasing the physical energy of anger. Using the psychiatric rehabilitation model of teach/practice/practice, participants are given ample opportunity to rehearse and acclimate to each aspect of communication and problem-solving skills. Role-playing is included as an essential component of skill rehearsal, but it is not the central focus of the teaching.

Every child should have counseling before they finish high school. If I could, I would shout this from the rooftops. The data bears this out. Consider the risk that ACEs pose to adult physical and mental health. Consider the degree to which middle- and high school students experience mental health distress and engage in risk-taking and antisocial behaviors. Consider that the wealth of CAMH's data was gathered prior to the single most impactful moment in history for our generation, the COVID-19 crisis. Imagine how much more severe student mental distress is now after two years of social isolation, virtual learning, too much screen time, and being fixated on their fear of the future.

If it were up to me, here's how I would do it. First, create a curriculum for elementary-school students beginning with the junior kindergarten (JK) students and based on their developmental stages. For the early-year students, focus on emotional regulation and mastering verbal expression of their emotional states. Make this curriculum mandatory for all students from JK through to grade 1. This initial learning represents the foundation for all the learning that will follow in years 2–8 in elementary school.

In addition to establishing and building on emotional regulation and expression skills, problem-resolution skills are then introduced in the second grade and built on every year to grade 6. In grades 6–8, prosocial learning skills are introduced so that during the years when bullying behaviors would typically reach their peak, students instead are actively learning how to increase prosocial behaviors and work through problems together toward a mutually desired end. Antisocial behaviors would be consequenced by school administrators, teachers would be supported in disciplining undesirable behaviors, and students would be rewarded for prosocial choices and actions.

Make counseling available to every student from JK to sixth grade. Make two hours of counseling per academic year from grades 7–12 a requirement for graduation, just as forty hours of volunteer or community work is mandatory for Ontario students. Give students a chance to work through the effects of their ACEs, to lock in healthy coping skills, and to master their problem-solving communication skills *before* they graduate high school and to ensure greater success for year one of university or college.

This is not to say that mental health supports should suddenly expire once a student begins their postsecondary journey. After normalizing counseling and therapy in the formative years, it follows that students will have stronger resiliency stores to enable their success in their first year of postsecondary education, and they will be more open to seeking out supports when they feel themselves struggling with their mental health.

This may sound a tad utopian to some of you, but think about it for moment. How might your life's trajectory have been changed had you had the opportunity to offload your ACEs and work through the effects of trauma before you started college or university or went out into the world of work? I know what it would have meant for me.

Remember that wherever you go, you take you with you. The trauma experienced in childhood and in high school will follow students wherever they go and whatever role they find themselves in, so it is advisable to put the monsters of the past to death and bury them firmly in the past, where they belong. Kill the monster when it's a baby. Then it won't grow up to eat you.

Summary

Bullying is repeated aggression with the intent to harm another, where a power imbalance exists between the bully and the target.

Every problem is, at its heart, a relationship problem. Bullying and other aspects of school violence are, at their heart, relationship problems.

With school violence on the rise, viable, actionable solutions are desperately needed to reverse this alarming trend. Mental distress in secondary and postsecondary students is also trending upward.

Wherever you go, you take you with you. Resolving ACEs early and normalizing therapy are ways to kill the monster while it's a baby.

Reflection

Do you believe your ACEs still influence your adult decisions? How might your coping and communication strategies be different had you experienced the opportunity to unpack and resolve the trauma associated with your ACEs when you were younger?

In your school years, were you a bully, a victim, or a bystander? If you could go back, what would you change about how you got your needs met?

Action Step

1. Document in your journal: with the knowledge and insight you have now, what can you begin to change today about how you express your anger and resolve problems?

8

THERE'S AN APP FOR THAT

CELL PHONES WERE invented in 1973. Back then, they were as big as your head, clunky, and inconvenient. They were also mainly available only to those who were rich and powerful. Although I was neither rich nor powerful, by the time the '90s rolled around, mobile phones were a little more accessible to Joe Public, and near the end of that decade, I was able to purchase one. My first mobile phone was just that—a *phone* that allowed me to communicate with people while on the go. It was attached to my landline and calls were forwarded to the cell for the convenience of both the caller and me.

Then I dropped it in the toilet. Even though the phone had few features outside of a regular landline, I had become attached to it, so much so that I did not even want to leave it unattended while I was taking care of necessities. Imagine my horror when my new toy that I had just paid off slid from the top of the toilet tank and into the drink. You know those movies where someone is screaming, "Nooooooo!" in slow motion as the thing falls in? That was me.

My second one was a basic mobile phone with even fewer features than the one that took a plunge in the porcelain pool. Text messaging came along. I traded up for a new phone with text capability and traded up again when phones got cameras. Then came the Blackberry. Insert nostalgic sigh here. Games. Data. Internet. Camera. SMS and email. Integrated and connected to my computer. The phone that US president Barack Obama said they would have to pry from his cold, dead hands.

When I went into the Telus store to purchase my first Blackberry, the store owner warned me of the dangers. "They don't call this a *Crackberry* for nothing," he said. "You have two choices. You can control your smartphone, or you let it control you."

I took those words to heart and imposed some rules for myself and the phone. I set it to power off each day at 11:00 p.m. and to power up at 6:00 a.m.

I eventually set all notifications to silent except for phone calls. Even now, all my notifications are set to silent. If I pick up when someone calls, it's because I see the call coming in on the screen. That is not because I'm rude or avoidant; it is because I'm working, and my focus needs to be on work. When I'm sitting with clients, my attention must be centered on them rather than on my phone. I trained my brain from day one of smartphone ownership to subject the device to my authority so I wouldn't become a Crackberry addict. Even with these preventive measures in place, from time to time, I was subject to phantom phone alerts and compulsive urges to check for the next incoming text message or email.

Dysregulated Brains, Dysregulated Bodies

What is emotional dysregulation? It is a lack of emotional awareness and clarity, perceived limited access to effective regulation strategies, and self-denial of emotions. People struggling with dysregulated emotions have trouble managing their emotional states, engaging in goal-directed behavior, and exhibiting impulse control. There are several factors that could contribute to poor emotional regulation including temperament, personality, neurodiversity, ADHD, congenital conditions such as fetal alcohol syndrome, and the effects of parental drug use or a traumatic experience by an expectant mother. Other factors are simply environmental or conditional on our immediate circumstances.

Have you ever been *hangry*? You know what I mean, right? Hangry— the blending of the words *hungry* and *angry*. That phenomenon that occurs when hungry people express their need for food with irritability, snappish behavior, and low frustration tolerance. *Hangry*. Well, surprise! New research confirms that feelings of hunger can indeed invoke emotions like anger and irritability and lower levels of pleasure.

The participants of the study recorded their levels of hunger and numerous ratings of their emotional well-being for twenty-one days, using a smartphone app. Records were documented five times a day, allowing for a variety of environments to be factored into the study, such as work and home. Even after considering demographic factors like sex, age, body mass index (BMI), diet, and personality, the data showed that hunger is linked to stronger feelings of irritability and anger and lower ratings of pleasure. While the researchers acknowledged that their study provided no solutions for negative hunger-induced emotional states, they noted that awareness of being hangry is a step in reducing negative emotions and corresponding behaviors.

Seems simple, doesn't it? You're feeling cranky and irritable, so you bring your *awareness* to your feeling state. You *acknowledge* that your emotions are directing your attention to a problem that needs to be solved. You *accept* this is the case, *assess* how you're feeling, and process what the problem might be. You look at the clock and see it is 2:00 p.m. and you haven't eaten. *A-ha!* You're feeling hangry. You immediately *adapt*—you stop working and head to the kitchen to hunt and gather some sustenance. After a few minutes, with your belly full and your body satiated, the hangry feelings disappear. Why? Because the problem that caused the feelings has been solved. This principle rings true for emotional regulation. Focusing only on the symptoms of irritability, anger, or low feelings of pleasure would rarely result in a full tummy for the hangry. Likewise, spending time on fixing feelings or on *symptoms management* is unlikely to result in solved problems.

The Word on the Street

New research in the *International Journal of Mental Health and Addiction* has emerged regarding psychological distress, emotional dysregulation, and coping behavior in relation to screen time. Emotion dysregulation facilitates the connection between psychological distress—depression, anxiety, and stress—and problematic smartphone use. Significant positive correlations were found between psychological distress, emotional regulation, and problematic smartphone use. These devices that were created for our convenience have now become a stumbling block to healthy emotional regulation.

As one of the most-used sources of information and communication, the smartphone has more than 6.5 billion users worldwide. Cell phones are used for content consumption and creation, meaning they are used for social media engagement, various forms of entertainment, communication, or study. Smartphones are used to track exercise and to monitor nutrition, sleep patterns, spending habits, and budgets. They are employed for money management, dating, investing, and creating content. It is no wonder, then, that overuse of these handheld devices and its impact on the mental and physical health of young adults is now in question.

Certainly, when used mindfully and with intention, smartphones have multiple benefits to their users; however, recent research suggests that excessive use of the device is a form of addiction and may have adverse effects on health and well-being. Studies have found smartphone overuse to be a predictor of depression in teens. Excessive smartphone usage in adults was linked to depression, anxiety, feelings of loneliness, and higher stress. A correlation between excessive cell phone use and obsessive-compulsive disorder behaviors was found along with symptoms associated with ADHD. There is a growing body of research about excessive smartphone use that substantiates the ill effects of problematic cell phone use as described above.

Another study of college students found a negative correlation between cell phone use and GPA, as well as a positive correlation to anxiety. Furthermore, it found a positive correlation between GPA and happiness, while the correlation between anxiety and happiness was a negative one. In effect, those college students who experienced excessive smartphone use would expect a lower-than-average GPA, higher anxiety, and lower feelings of happiness or satisfaction in comparison with their peers who spent less time glued to their devices.

Hangry for Hits

It is estimated that currently 72 percent of US adults use social media, a dramatic increase from 2005, when a mere 5 percent of US adults were found on at least one social media platform. In the United States, young and emerging adults account for the highest and most frequent participation in social media. Close to 95 percent of US youths have access to a smartphone, and 45 percent are reported as being online continually.

Mobile phone addiction is regulated by the same brain circuits that contribute to other addictions—including substance use, gambling, or compulsive sexual behavior—involving the brain circuitry implicated in reward and pleasure. Specifically, smartphone use results in hyperactivation of specific areas of the brain that are dedicated to cognition, motivation, and reward. According to emerging research, when social media users get comments, likes, follows, or shares, it activates the excitatory synapses in these areas of the brain.

Dopamine is one of the primary neurotransmitters involved in reward pathways. Memory, motivation, and movement are produced and received through dopamine receptors. With every like, follow, or share, the brain receives another dopamine hit, stimulating the areas of the brain responsible for pleasure, motivation, and reward. Note, too, that smartphone use activates areas of the brain associated with cognition. Problematic smartphone use influences how you think on a neurological level. The short-term, reward-based, dopamine-driven feedback loops convince users to return to the platform, creating a sense of emotional *hangriness* if they stay away from social media for too long.

As it does for successful in-person social interaction, the brain gets a dopamine hit after positive feedback is received in social networks. Social media platforms influence the same neural circuitry that addictive substances and gambling organizations employ to keep users hooked. The consequence of this ongoing excessive dopamine release is a neurological deficit: when users are not mindlessly scrolling their social media, they experience less pleasure because their levels of dopamine are pushed below baseline. It's like experiencing the crash after the high; the discomfort of the crash is what makes users want to stay online and continue interacting with their socials. In the short term, the dopamine deficit imitates symptoms like depression and anxiety.

The instant gratification and subsequent dopamine hit that comes from getting likes, shares, and follows contribute to emotional dysregulation in that we lose the ability to delay pleasure. The inability to employ patience, to wait for the next good thing, makes it challenging to focus on tasks that do not come with an inherently immediate reward. When you are unable to focus on tasks with long-term positive outcomes, you're more likely to choose behaviors and responses that lean toward quick fixes because your brain has become accustomed to accessing the dopamine high through simple repetitive actions like checking your socials.

Think about what this means for emotional regulation and expression. The advent of the smartphone has shifted the mindset and brain patterns of an entire generation. My younger clients get a kick out of my stories of my dating years. Rotary phones. Answering machines. No voicemail. No text messaging. No messages at all if the *tape* got tangled in the message player.

Waiting for hours until your love interest got home from school, work, or football practice. Trying to place a call at the right time so it wouldn't be intercepted by the parents. They have no clue.

It is unfathomable to conceive of a time when people were not so easily accessible. Can you imagine it now? I mean, what if the zombie apocalypse started today? What if a massive electromagnetic pulse (EMP) took out all our electricity and everything digital just fried and died? How many of us would survive? I suspect most of the folks who were born in the mid-'90s and afterward would be the first to go. Heck, some of them might even try to record their own demise, hoping that someday in the future when the world gets electricity back, someone might see their video and share it.

In all seriousness, social media is not a healthy coping mechanism to help divert our attentions from things happening in real life (*IRL*) nor should it be used as a self-soothing tool. It's a quick fix that offers little more than a passing yet addictive feel-good moment, and it draws our attention from all the beauty, enjoyment, and wonder of living life in the now instead of living for the next like.

Young Brains, Self-Regulation, and Addictive/Aggressive Behaviors

Chester was eight years old when he was referred to therapy. A precocious child with a sweet, endearing smile, Chester had been branded *the problem child* at home and at school. Chester was often oppositional, particularly at bedtime, when screen time had to be eschewed in favor of the nighttime rituals of putting on pajamas and brushing teeth. Behaviors at school included acting out in class, running away, and attempting to "discipline" other children who broke the rules; since he was always getting in trouble for breaking rules, he figured those rules should apply to everyone. Like many preadolescent boys, Chester loved playing video games, but when he lost, he also lost his temper. It was not uncommon for him to break controllers or toss them at the monitor screens and for other collateral damage to ensue. Mom and Dad had difficulty enforcing the termination of screen time, and the inconsistent messaging from his parents reinforced Chester's attempts at prolonging his periods of gaming. Things would escalate when the parents started yelling, and Chester would respond with more defiance or acting out.

Evidence suggests that children who receive a phone earlier than others have difficulty adjusting to its use, and hence age is an essential mediating factor in the impact of mobile devices. There has long been a lack of agreement among researchers regarding the effect of witnessing violence and vicarious learning. The debate rages on even today, with new studies coming out on both sides for and against limiting screen time for young children. Many would argue that children who witness violence on television, in the home, at school, or online are likely to behave more violently or aggressively. Others would say that while playing aggressive or violent video games may contribute to an increase in "agitation" in children, there is no clear positive correlation between playing violent games and choosing aggressive behavior.

Two such studies caught my attention. The first concluded that children aged eight to twelve who witnessed aggression or violence in real life or on a digital device were more aggressive. It was noted that observing aggression or being a victim of violence was a predictor of increased aggression compared with measures taken from the children six months earlier. The study concluded that the degree to which children were exposed to violence or aggression contributed to normalization of this behavior, in turn leading to more aggressive behavior by the subjects themselves.

The second study determined that children aged eight to eighteen who played games like *Call of Duty* or *Grand Theft Auto* were not significantly more violent than their peers who did not play violent games. Most interesting was the reporting by parents that children were more likely to destroy *things* after playing violent video games. The researchers concluded that violent video games might contribute to *agitation* but said agitation did not convert into violence against *people*. As video games are most often played at home, there are fewer opportunities to engage in violence, creating an "incapacitation effect."[1] Finally, the authors of the study noted that the incapacitation effect was particularly important for violence-prone boys as they are more drawn to violent video games.

To clarify this line of logic, boys who are prone to aggression are drawn to violent video games. When they are playing at home, there is less opportunity for them to act out violently toward people; however, they may become agitated and resort to destroying property. Here's the thing: if young boys are displaying dysregulation by acting out during or after playing violent games and the parents don't know how to help them self-correct, that disordered conduct can and will most likely escalate down the road, culminating in aggression against people rather than destruction of property.

Teach Your Children Well

Unsupervised or unregulated screen time in young children leads to dysregulated behavior. The human brain does not fully mature before the age of twenty; why do we assume that eight-year-olds can regulate their own screen time? They haven't matured enough to learn the kind of self-control required to manage playing against invisible opponents, trash talking online, and then losing to an invisible entity. They lack the emotional intelligence to effectively express their frustration with the game, so it is expressed by acting out behaviors. Nor do they know how to walk away from the game before they reach the frayed ends of their frustration tolerance.

Two-year-olds are so device-savvy that they know how to unlock their parents' phones, access games on their tablets, and efficiently use the television remotes to watch endless hours of their favorite children's shows. Have we set up the next generation for a lifetime of addictive behaviors coupled with emotional dysregulation linked to their electronic devices?

The challenge of mitigating the damaging effects of electronics overuse is a daunting one. Indeed, the Canadian Pediatric Society (CPS) has revised its guidelines around setting concrete limits on screen use in toddlers and preschool-aged children. Shifting the focus away from simple rules around how much screen time children should get each day, the priority is now on meaningful screen interaction with content that is educational and age appropriate. The society suggests screen time for children under two should continue to be limited to live interactions only, such as with grandparents. Passive screen use for toddlers and preschoolers should be limited. Instead, parents can sit with their children and interact with them and the media content while demonstrating appropriate behavior during the interaction.

The CPS noted that while the devices themselves may not be dangerous for children, the time spent interacting with them takes the place of key developmental activities, which can contribute to delayed language development and interference with prosocial behavior and executive function. There is a common thread here, and that is dysregulated use of screen time contributes to further emotional dysregulation.

Four principles for managing screen time are the emphasis of the CPS's new strategy: minimizing, mitigating, mindful usage, and modeling healthy use of screens. And there's the rub. To minimize unhealthy use of electronic devices, parents must be engaged with their children rather than relying on screens to babysit. Mitigating screen overuse means ensuring that there are screen-free zones in the house, that outdoor activities are encouraged, and that children are engaged in crafts, baking, or other activities that are educational and teach them how to self-regulate, problem-solve, and interact prosocially with others.

Mindful usage means parents and caregivers don't just hand kids the remote or the tablet and expect them to choose what is age appropriate and educational. They have got to have boundaries and hold those boundary lines. And modeling appropriate screen use means that adults must stop checking their social media to see if anyone has engaged since their last check-in two minutes ago. You see, it is difficult for kids to learn they can step away from their screens when Mom and Dad are having such a challenge staying away from theirs.

I Miss You, I Hate You

It would be convenient to think that excessive smartphone and electronic device usage is only a problem for immature humans with underdeveloped brains. Studies suggest that lurking your ex's social media after a breakup increases feelings of sadness and depression and makes it more difficult for you to let go. Scrolling through your social media newsfeed so you can see what your ex is up to is a compulsion unique to this digital age. Not only have social media platforms normalized the cyberstalking of exes but they also have built-in features that make it difficult for you to turn away. Consider features that prompt you with suggestions for new friends or followers. Or pictorial reminders from one, five, or fifteen years ago. These types of features make breaking up, letting go, and moving on much more of a challenge.

Now, I am a child of the '80s. We didn't have voicemail, AOL, instant messages, or MSN Messenger. When a relationship broke up, there was no Facebook or Instagram to check and see if they were feeling miserable or were back in the game, living their best life. Breakups were painful, but gaining distance from your lost love was a whole lot easier.

Now with reminders of happier days and prompts to connect with siblings, parents, friends, or colleagues of your ex, it is nearly impossible to completely disassociate from them. After unfriending, unfollowing, and blocking, social media can still remind you of your ex multiple times a day. Even worse, when your ex pops up in your feed with a new relationship status, it's another shot to the heart. It's hard to remember that much of what we see in social media posts is not real life; what we see is the highlight reel, the best of the best, people faking it until they make it. Still, it is all too easy to fall into the trap of believing that what you see is the truth and nothing but. Sadly, it's just one more way that compulsive use of social media contributes to negative emotional experiences.

Whether your poison of preference is dating, money management, science, meaningless hookups, or business meetups, your smartphone has you covered. Tumblr, Snapchat, TikTok, IG, FB, Bumble, Tinder—it doesn't matter what you're interested in; there's an app for that. Funny how almost fifty years after the cellular phone became mainstream, the last thing people want to use it for is the original purpose for which it was invented. People would rather video conferencing, text, or converse through a series of voice notes rather than place a phone call.

Do people become addicted to digital media because they are poorly regulated, or does digital addiction contribute to emotional dysregulation? It's a bit of a chicken-egg argument if you think about it. Here's what I know from the work I have done in different forms of addiction. The opposite of addiction is connection. *The opposite of addiction is connection.* Now consider that digital platforms like the now-defunct My Space, Facebook, Instagram, Pinterest, Snapchat, Twitter, Tinder, Bumble, Google Hangouts, Meetup, Zoom, and the plethora of others out there claim to exist so that we can find and connect with our tribes. The irony of this is that the algorithms built into these platforms to encourage their use mimic the pleasure achieved from social engagement in real life but lack in the lasting effect of that social engagement, thereby fostering addiction.

Gaming online with invisible players is not the same as engaging with family or friends in a game of SkipBo, Scrabble, or Battleship. In faceless online interactions, we have no body language to read, no facial expressions to interpret, no peer-to-peer feedback concerning socially acceptable responses, no recourse for acting out when a level is lost. While on the surface, it feels like we are connecting with others through our socials and various digital platforms, we are in fact becoming less connected, less satisfied, less regulated.

The Silent, Unspoken Epidemic

Humans of all ages are susceptible to the dangers of addiction. Alcohol. Nicotine. Illicit drugs. Prescription medications. Gambling. Gaming. These forms of addiction are readily discussed, and campaigns like MADD have publicized the need for moderation, temperance, and treatment. Using drugs, smoking, drinking, and even gambling are hard habits to break because they carry with them a social component. There is pleasure in being out with friends and tossing back a few drinks or passing around a joint. The social engagement becomes neurologically linked to the state induced by the substance, and users will associate one with the other: *I am going to a party; I will drink wine or my beverage of choice because parties with friends and alcohol consumption go together.*

There is another form of addiction that no one likes to talk about. It is not considered socially acceptable, nor is it something people gather to do in social settings. This addiction is one that is fed in the dark, in secret, and it is shrouded in shame and self-loathing. That is the silent addiction to pornography and compulsive sexual behavior. Whereas pornography was once only available if you were over eighteen and were able to go into the "special section" of the magazine aisle, with the prevalence of social media apps, even the innocuous ones like Pinterest, porn is now readily available to the whosoever will. Reports coming through my office are telling me that children are gaining access to pornographic images and GIFs as early as grade 6. It's as easy as opening an app and plugging in the right search criteria.

From 1997 to 2007, millions of websites dedicated to pornography appeared on the worldwide web. In the ten years that followed, those sites were amalgamated so that only three or four companies control most of the online pornography content. In 2016, Pornhub.com documented 3,110,400,000 GB of pornography had been streamed. That's 99 GB per second, 6 TB per minute. If you quantified that by USB drives, that would equate to 194 million USB sticks. The number of pornographic videos viewed in 2016 totaled 91,980,225,000, or 12.5 videos viewed for every person on earth. There were 23 billion visits to Pornhub. That's 64 million per day, 2.6 million per hour; 44,000 per minute, 729 per second. And that is just *one* website. The year 2016 was the tipping point for pornography use on smartphones; it was the first time porn consumption exceeded that of desktop, laptop, and tablet computer devices.

Did you know that for many popular video games, there is a pornography alternate? It's the same for movies. Whenever a popular movie is released, searches for the main characters increase on porn sites. These games are designed to attract young people early so they can create lifelong consumers of pornography. It is so easy to access pornographic imagery in the digital age, and there are very few, if any, checks and balances to ensure that young, impressionable minds are not ensnared. A simple button that asks "Are you over 18?" is not enough of a barrier. Anyone can click *yes* and have access.

When I was teaching at a local postsecondary institution, I cannot tell you how many young men I referred to counseling services or online support groups for erectile dysfunction because the only way they could achieve orgasm was by masturbating to pornography. I'm talking about eighteen-year-old boys, barely out of high school, who were unsure of how to foster healthy, intimate connections because they were too accustomed to self-induced orgasms. I'm talking about kids whose first exposure to porn occurred before their voices had begun to change. I'm talking about students who couldn't even submit a simple psychology assignment without littering it with pornographic imagery. That is how normal the consumption of pornographic content has become.

I'm not talking about people who turned to porn to normalize their trauma. That's another topic for another day. I'm talking about *contemporary* pornography users, not rooted in trauma or early exploitation—yes, that happens—folks who stumbled across it, found it titillating, and got sucked into consuming more and more even as the imagery and sensations shifted their brain patterns until their perceptions of self, others, and healthy sexual relationships were irrevocably altered.

Pornography is a multitrillion-dollar industry, and the stakes are high. Research on the effects of pornography on the developing and adult brain abounds; meanwhile, proponents of the porn industry are funding their own research. One side argues—and convincingly so—that exposure to pornographic content in youths is positively correlated with unrealistic sexual values, beliefs, and expectations; more permissive sexual attitudes; preoccupation with sex; and earlier onset of sexual activity.

Studies show that the use of pornography that depicts violence has been correlated with increased degrees of sexually aggressive behavior by adolescents. Pornography use appears to have a correlation to adolescent self-concept—as pornography use increases, positive self-image, self-perception of attractiveness in girls, and virility in boys decrease. Adolescents who use web-based pornography appear to be less socially integrated, have more conduct problems, engage in more delinquent behavior, exhibit more depressive symptoms, and appear less bonded to their caregivers.

The other side of the debate claims that pornography is not addicting at all. They say that high users of porn, the ones who might *appear* to be addicted, only seem that way because they have a higher libido. The proponents of "free porn" would suggest that having discussions about varying levels of sexual appetite and releasing judgment about porn use would be more helpful than attempting to restrict its use and availability. What we know for certain is that it is too late to stem the tide of pornography flooding our screens. All we can do is make good choices about what we consume and how.

Listen. The age of apps has contributed to us forgetting that we should be well informed before making any decisions, especially choices that will impact every aspect of our lives. Apps make it too easy. Click here. Submit there. Agree to cookies. Accept terms and conditions. Pay with your Apple or Google wallet. Set it and forget it. Perhaps it is time to step back and employ our critical-thinking skills once again and ask some key questions of ourselves and the ones entrusted to our care.

What is the motivation for consuming this content? How will this content serve you and the greater good? Is this content good for you beyond the immediate thrill of porn-induced orgasm? How will you feel afterward? If you are compelled to keep this activity a secret, if the practice is shrouded in shame, how good can it be for you?

At the end of the day, it all comes down to this. We must be mindful of how the content we interact with daily impacts both the upstairs and downstairs brains. The upstairs brain can be easily diverted away from tasks that lead to favorable long-term outcomes because of the conditioning toward immediate gratification incurred by the social media reward system. The downstairs brain is left to run amok when the upstairs brain is distracted and obsessed with the next ping, like, share, or other form of engagement. Overexposure to electronic devices, games, social media, or any digital media with a built-in reward system of its use puts us at risk of becoming subject to the device rather than master over it.

Choose Wisely

Society has reached and fallen over the tipping point regarding social media, virtual gaming, and its enmeshment with electronic devices. There is no way to turn back the tide of digital engagement that we have attained in the twenty-first century; however, we can make informed choices about how we use our devices and why we use them. I was an early adopter of many things—the cellular phone, the Blackberry, the Blackberry tablet, phablets, laptops, you name it. The adoption of these items was always for their utility, not for their entertainment value. I still believe in putting apps on my phone that serve a function that brings value to my quality of life or to the efficacy of my business. No matter how I try to add apps that have entertainment value, I always end up deleting them because one second, I'm looking at a video, and the next time I look up, I've lost two hours to mindless scrolling.

I love technology. Love it. It loves me too, but I realize that my relationship with tech could easily become toxic if I don't maintain healthy boundaries. My phone is equipped with apps dedicated to monitoring my health and fitness—and that includes mental health. I have financial and banking apps; apps that help me share content for my social media; my "connection" apps that are used to engage with family, friends, and followers; and apps that make it easy for me to work on the fly. There are few entertainment apps on my phone because I think they are massive time suckers. No streaming media, no games, no e-readers, no book clubs. Setting boundaries with my device enables me to maintain a healthy relationship with it.

Now before you go criticizing me for personalizing my device and talking about my relationship with it like it is a tangible thing, remember that every problem is, at its heart, a relationship problem! When toddlers throw a tantrum because they aren't allowed that one more episode of *Cocomelon* or *Paw Patrol*, it is because they don't know how to set boundaries for themselves. When young children destroy their controllers or their screens because of a lost online game, it is because their relationship with the AI or with their online friends is not moderated in the same way it would be if they were playing in the same room. When romances break up and people are feeling lonely and remorseful, it is easy to go to social media to lurk the ex's page, but that leads to feelings of deeper sadness and makes it difficult to let go. Influencers showcase a perfect life for the sake of likes, shares, and follows, but many are secretly hiding deep shame, depression, or addiction. The truth of their relationship with themselves and the real world is there if we care to look. Every problem is a relationship problem, even the problem of digital device overuse.

The solution to this problem is to go to the root. Limiting screen time is symptoms management. Medicating people for anxiety and depression caused by addictive use of smartphones is symptoms management. Chasing the next dopamine high for a short-term fix rather than setting long-term goals and pursuing them with determination and patience is symptoms management.

What do you want? Really? What is your desired long-term outcome? Would you like to find true love? Get in shape? Be more mindful? Excel in your business or your career? Whatever it is that you would like to achieve will require the setting of clear goals and carving out a path toward their achievement. You want to have healthier relationships? Spend more time with family? See the world? You could do that virtually for the quick dopamine hit, or you could foster real connections with real people in real life.

The solution to emotional dysregulation brought on by overuse of electronics is a simple but effective one. *The opposite of addiction is connection.* To be truly connected, we must eschew the semblance of connection for the real thing. Use your phone for the purpose it was intended. Place a call. Talk to someone for real. Listen to the intonation of their voice, the lilt of their laughter. Learn to read the nonverbal communication in their tone, pitch, and speed of speech. Get out of the house and hang out with people. Go to the mall and people-watch. Enjoy the sparkle in their eyes. Flirt. Date. Connect. *Engage.* Practice patience. Set a lofty goal and chip away at the steps to attaining it. Train your brain to appreciate the long game.

Summary

Having technology at our fingertips may contribute to lower impulse control, emotional dysregulation, problematic smartphone use, increased aggression, and desensitization to sex and violence.

The opposite of addiction is connection.

We can apply TSA and our critical-thinking skills to our relationship with technology.

Reflection

1. If your smartphone were a person, what would it be like? What would it look like? How would you describe your relationship with it? Is it a healthy relationship or a toxic one?

Action Step

Make a list of the strategies you could implement to set boundaries with your phone and ways to make your relationship with technology a healthier one.

9

CUT THE RED WIRE

THE BOSS STORMED into the main area of the building and called for an impromptu meeting. On the whiteboard, he drew a fish tank and some fish.

"What is this?" he demanded.

Someone raised a tentative hand. "A fish tank?"

"Yes!" he yelled. Then he drew a bottom-feeder fish. "What is this?"

Someone else raised a hand. "A bottom feeder?"

"Yes!" he yelled again. "That's what you all are—bottom feeders. All you do is float around and focus on sh*t!"

Aggression in the workplace can manifest like my boss's shouty object lesson; sometimes it shows up as microaggressions or passive-aggressive nonverbals such as eye-rolling, heavy sighing, backhanded compliments, or forgetting to send the memo. Yelling, screaming, verbal aggression and nonverbal aggression like standing too close, intimidating stance, closed-off body language, gritted teeth, or scowling faces are in some ways easier to deal with than the subtler behaviors. Passive-aggressive behaviors can often be missed by bystanders, but they strike the heart of the targets. Forgetting to send the memo could be misconstrued as an honest mistake; the target calling out microaggressions might lead to them being labeled as whiny.

No matter how you cut it, I do not love any form of aggression in the workplace, but when a diatribe like the one I described was followed by the statement "You teach people how to treat you," I decided he was right, and I decided it was time for me to put on my teacher's hat. The long and short of this story is that our "fearless leader" had made some key mistakes in leadership, which I pointed out to him as gently as I could, given my head was about to explode:

1) He forgot about the law of seed and harvest. The day you plant the seed is not the day you eat the fruit. You have to water, fertilize,

and nurture whatever you're growing, whether that is people, relationships, or sales. He assumed that because sales were not closing fast enough (i.e., immediately after the first contact) his team was lazy and uncommitted.

2) He believed his perception and interpretation of events: "If I don't see results, that *means* no one is working." He failed to see how hard his team was working to reach out to contacts and build relationships so that we could close the sales. My high school English teacher used to say, "When in doubt, check it out." If he had doubts about the work his team was putting in, all he had to do was ask. A simple check-in to see how many contacts had been made and the nature of the relationships in development would have set his mind at ease.

3) He let his expectations get the better of him and then responded to his disappointment in a way that was both inappropriate and unprofessional.

Berating staff is a surefire way to kill morale, douse the flames of passion, and ensure that people will do only the bare minimum to get paid. Twenty-first-century enlightened leaders know they can ignite passion and inspire loyalty by asking questions, providing answers when people need help, coaching and encouraging the team, and leading with empathy rather than anger or aggression. Failure to do so is, in my opinion, the number-one contributor to a long-standing phenomenon now dubbed *quiet quitting*.

Quiet Quitting

Quiet quitting is an updated iteration of work-to-rule marked by employees' refusal to work outside their defined work hours or to perform tasks not specified in their job descriptions. Remember when all job descriptions came with a clause "other duties as assigned"? Well, people are no longer feeling that vibe. The name belies the philosophy of quiet quitting, which is more about doing only what the job requires rather than quitting the job entirely.

Years ago, I found a statistic that noted 50 percent of employees were not engaged at work. Poor engagement contributed to higher rates of absenteeism and presenteeism—showing up in person but not getting much work done—a larger drain on employee health benefits, and of course, lower productivity. Guess what? That hasn't changed. A recent Gallup poll on workplace and well-being found that a large group of survey respondents were classified as "not engaged." These workers were the quiet quitters, those who admitted they would do the minimum required at work but not much else. Gallup further noted that approximately 50 percent of today's workforce is unmotivated to participate in so-called citizenship behaviors like working late or overtime or taking on additional roles or extra responsibilities for no additional remuneration.

The great resignation and the lack of engagement and commitment called quiet quitting is evidence that frustration with negative, toxic workplaces is at its tipping point. To get out in front of workplace negativity, employers and human resources (HR) departments need a plan and a strategy for implementing that plan. It takes courage and consistency to call out behaviors that erode trust, deplete morale, and irrevocably damage the bottom line.

Beneath the Mask

The 2020 COVID-19 crisis forced us all to hide our faces beneath surgical masks for the sake of our health. Now, with mask mandates lifting across the world, the mask of engagement remains firmly in place. This is the mask of smiles that don't reach one's eyes. The subdued voice disguising the low vibration of rage. The blank expressions masking frustration and fury. And the nonverbal tells that, when you're looking for them, demonstrate just how disengaged and fed-up people truly are.

Not gonna lie. I've been there. I did not hesitate to tell my fish-loving boss that when my contract was up, I would not be looking to renew it. I stopped doing extra work and just did what was required. My reasoning was simple: I had gone above and beyond for previous employers, taking on additional duties, working late, or working beyond the end of a contract. I even gave one employer a month's notice so they would have time to hire and train a new person when what I really wanted was to quit without notice and run screaming from the building. No amount of going above and beyond made a difference. The agency waited until my final day to post my position, making my gift of a month's notice a total waste. One supervisor justified the cancelation of our annual team celebration by saying that a job well done is its own reward. *Right.* So I understand the motivation behind quiet quitting.

Here's the thing. Since the dawn of time, people have searched for and applied methods to get more out of their slaves, servants, and employees than what they were paying for—if they were even paying at all. This postmodern generation of workers is not having it. Employers must adjust to the reality that, like in every other exchange of goods and services, the price is the price. In the case of employment contracts, the employee agrees to provide a set of services, tasks, assignments laid out in the contract in exchange for a certain level of remuneration. Asking the employee to do more with less, to take on additional tasks for no extra pay, or to stay late or put in overtime without fair compensation is akin to asking a car dealer if they can throw in a year of free fuel and service, free winter tires, a personal mechanic, their firstborn child, and an extended warranty for no additional charge. No dealer would agree to those terms, yet the expectation is that employees will continue to accept unfair working conditions without complaint.

Microaggressions and macroaggressions—racist or sexist practices like being passed over for a promotion due to being a woman, over forty, transgender, or a person of color when the one promoted is less mature, less educated, or less qualified—leave a sour taste in the affected employee's mouth. Bullying and harassment that go unchecked and unpunished, policies that have no teeth, and HR departments that do not care enough about their human resources contribute to employees feeling unsafe with their employers. Add to this frustration with the massive bonuses paid out to executives while frontline workers doing the grunt work can barely make a living wage, refusal to support workers who are struggling with physical or psychological workplace injuries, the desperate need for work/life balance—the list goes on. It is no surprise that employee engagement remains stuck at about 50 percent.

Every problem is, at its heart, a relationship problem, and communication is the key to solving every relationship problem. The levels of anger experienced individually and corporately in the workplace are a manifestation of violated boundaries, broken rules, unmet expectations, and thwarted goals.

The top-down communication style of old will no longer do.

"That was how my sales managers got me motivated" will no longer do. "You should be happy you have a job in this economy" will no longer do. "We're sorry you feel that way" is not an apology.

"I know it's late, but we need you" is a passive-aggressive way to guilt people into doing something they don't want to do.

"I won't be in all week because I'm working from home, but I need you to be in the office every day, all day" screams that you value the convenience of the hybrid workplace but only for yourself and not for your team.

"I'm going to need you to work through your lunch today" sends a message that your work product is more important than your employee's right to a healthy work/life balance.

Quiet quitting is a symptom of anger in the workplace, and the fact is, while the phenomenon has been around for a long time, these days, it is more about setting firm boundaries: *If you want me to do more work than is in my job description, then pay me for it. If you want me to take on these responsibilities that used to be handled by a whole other person, then pay me their salary on top of my own. If you expect me to work late, give me time off in lieu. If you're not allowing me to have flexible hours, don't expect me to be flexible for you.* This is the sound of clearly expressed boundaries, rules, and expectations. Likewise, employers either need to change their expectations of what work product should look like and what they will get from their employees, or they will need to shift with the times and begin to compensate their employees fairly. Quiet quitting is quite simply anger expressed.

What's Your Problem?

Imagine aggressive, abusive, or violent behavior as an incendiary device. There are four key components to bomb anatomy. First is the battery, the power supply, or the source of energy. That energy is directed to the second part, which is called an initiator, the thing that causes the bomb to explode (e.g., a blasting cap). The third component is the explosive material or the main charge. The main charge is divided into two categories: the high explosive consists of materials like C4 or TNT, which when detonated create supersonic shock waves that burn at a high rate of three thousand to nine thousand meters per second. The deflagrating explosive results in subsonic combustion—a huge blast that can throw shrapnel at a speed of one meter per second. The final component of the bomb is the switch, the thing that sets off the initiator. That could be a cell phone, a key fob, a trip wire, a pressure plate, or a timer.

Anger is initiated when rules are broken, boundaries are violated, expectations unmet, or goal attainment is thwarted or frustrated. If those are the triggers, what are the wires that connect the anger IED components? The red wire is the muddled mindset. To disable or reroute a muddled mindset, limiting beliefs must be challenged, and desired short- and long-term objectives must be clarified. You've got to be realistic and honest about what you really want. What are the long-term outcomes that feel good, are good for you, are good for others, and serve the greater good? What are the best options you have for achieving those outcomes? How do you stay focused on those outcomes even when someone or something is pressing the trigger to trip the red wire?

IED: Intermittent Explosive Disorder

When I first learned of intermittent explosive disorder (IED), I was a skeptic; however, over time, the nature of the diagnosis has been refined. IED is a disorder of behavior regulation, a subtype of impulse control disorder. Characterized by poor impulse control and unruly, volatile expressions of anger, aggression, and/or rage, IED may sometimes be accompanied by violence. The Diagnostic Systems Manual V classifies IED under the category of "Disruptive, Impulse Control, and Conduct Disorders." The low-intensity version of the disorder is marked by recurring impulsive outbursts consisting of either mild verbal or physical aggression not resulting in property damage or personal injury, which occurs two or more times per week for longer than three months. A more intense type of IED is characterized by three or more outbursts resulting in personal injury or destruction of property within a twelve-month stretch. While this type of IED may occur less frequently, the aftermath is more severe.

In all cases of IED, the verbal or physical aggression is far more severe than the occasion calls for; there is no premeditation—it is more a reaction than a response. Of course, these impulsive outbursts cause distress and may contribute to impaired functioning as well as dire natural, legal, social, and/or financial consequences. Other possible causes for recurring explosive expressions of anger must be ruled out (e.g., substance abuse, brain injury, cognitive disorder, or medical condition), and because preschool-aged children have not yet learned how to regulate their emotions, no one under the age of six can be diagnosed with IED.

Clearing the Killing Fields

It is no coincidence that this disorder of emotional regulation so closely tied to anger was cleverly named IED. In the Canadian military, field engineers are tasked with the delicate work of diffusing bombs, land mines, and improvised explosive devices (IEDs). There are six key tools used in the field for defusing explosive devices:

1. The wheelbarrow is a remote-controlled robot outfitted with tools that the controller can use to identify the materials that comprise the bomb. It then relays that information to the bomb disposal teams so they can decide how best to proceed.
2. The tanglefoot is an adjunct to the wheelbarrow, one of its most effective tools. The tanglefoot clears a path for army personnel, using a system to uncover trip wires attached to IEDs.
3. The bootbanger is a projected water disrupter that sends a directional water projectile-shaped charge into the IED.
4. The bottler is also a projected water disrupter, using an omnidirectional charge. Both the bootbanger's and the bottler's purpose is to destroy the IEDs by severing the detonation cord inside the device.
5. Pigsticks are percussion-actuated neutralizers. They fire propelled jets of water directly into the bomb or IED in the hopes of disrupting its circuitry. All the above systems or tools are meant to be used in close proximity to the explosive devices.
6. Lasers can be used to control explosions from a distance. Laser beams are used to heat the explosive fillers in bombs so that they burn slowly. What follows is a controlled explosion, effectively destroying the device while mitigating any collateral damage.

Up Close and Personal

In the *Anger Solutions* world, having tools and devices, such as the following, to defuse IED is invaluable.

1. Practice self-evaluation (wheelbarrow). Examine the situation objectively. Look inside to see which "materials" are comprising your impending explosion. Locate the red wire and determine the best course of action.

2. Clear a path between your downstairs brain and upstairs brain (tanglefoot). Deep breaths calm your central nervous system and reoxygenate the upstairs brain so it can reengage and get you thinking clearly. Focus your attention on the desired outcome, short and long terms. Do not allow yourself to be sidetracked by quick fixes or reactive behavior.

3. Sever the wire to flip the switch that would trigger the explosion. Sometimes a directional approach is best (bootbanger). Get straight to the point and begin the process of problem resolution with the person who can best help you solve it.

4. Other times, a multidirectional approach (bottler) is warranted, particularly when there are many moving parts and many contributors to the index problem. This may require a team or collaborative approach to problem-solving with a view to achieving the best possible outcome for all involved.

5. Scramble your circuitry (pigstick). The pigstick's aim is to disrupt IED or bomb circuits by flooding them. You can do the same for your brain by interrupting and disrupting old, useless, limiting, deeply ingrained thought patterns and belief systems, rendering them ineffective. Using humor, walking away, changing your communication strategy, or drastically shifting your perceptions and interpretations of events are all examples of how to "pigstick" your anger circuits.

6. Control your chaos. Sometimes the pigstick approach to scrambling circuits is not enough. There are times when a laser focus on the problem at hand, the optimum solution, and the best possible

strategy is what's needed. The more complex the problem, the more complex the solution.

Chaos Contained

When my boss called that impromptu meeting and started going on about bottom feeders and how he perceived us, I must say he tripped the red wire. It was not the first time that I had endured that kind of unwarranted unprofessional behavior in the workplace, but for me, it was the tipping point, as we all reach when we have had our fill of toxic workplaces. Conflict, negativity, and toxicity are corrosive agents to the workplace hoping for cohesion, collaboration, and maximum productivity. A 2022 Grammarly study found that while employees spend over two-thirds of their time connecting and collaborating, business leaders estimate their teams lose approximately 7.5 hours per week to poor communication. Of 251 business leaders surveyed, 86 percent of them estimate the value of lost business due to poor communication to be ten thousand dollars or higher. Prior to the COVID-19 pandemic, the cost of poor communication in the workplace was estimated at a whopping $400 billion per year. Nine out of ten business leaders expressed having experienced the adverse impact of poor communication at work. Poor communication contributes to conflict, workplace negativity and stress, staff turnover, poor customer relationships, and decreased productivity and profit.

Glasser says that every problem is, at its heart, a relationship problem. You got a money problem? It's a relationship issue—with yourself, with your bank account, or with your attitudes/beliefs about money. You got a problem with your partner? It's a relationship problem. Church/religious organization? *Relationship*. Faith? *Relationship*. Body image? Gender identity? *Relationship*.

Who before do, remember? You need to be clear on who you are—that means sifting out the truth of who you are versus all the things other people have said you are. It's all about relationship, first with yourself and then with others. Do you hate your job? That's a relationship problem with your passion and purpose, with your coworkers, clients/customers, the mission and vision of the company, the management or leadership of the company, or the corporate values that don't line up with who you believe you are.

Every problem is a relationship problem, and the number-one reason relationships fail is lack of communication. You've got to be willing to do the introspective and intrapersonal work to develop a healthy relationship with your sense of self as well as willing to be vulnerable enough to talk with others to help you strengthen those relationships that have lifetime value.

Thomas and Kilmann's Conflict Resolution Styles

In my seminar *Transforming Toxic Workplaces*, I share Thomas and Kilmann's model of conflict resolution, infusing it with a little *Anger Solutions* flavor. Thomas and Kilmann propose that there are five behavior styles or approaches to conflict and confrontation. I have lined them up beside my theory of conflict styles for easy reference.

Compete—take charge (aggress): This style is all about being "the boss." The competitive person speaks first and listens rarely. They tend to give orders, assuming they are the only ones who have a solution to the problem at hand. Because of this, they rarely understand or perceive that they might be part of the problem. Sometimes taking charge is exactly what is needed. In an emergency, when adrenaline is running high and the collective downstairs brains have taken over, someone must be the voice of reason to take charge, give orders, and ensure the situation is handled effectively and safely. That said, in most complex situations, the take-charge or aggressive style will only breed further conflicts, confrontation, and animosity.

Collaborate—share ideas (approach): The collaborative conflict resolution style focuses on the collective sharing of ideas. Consensus is king in the collaborative style, where everyone is given a voice, and the majority rule wins the day. Again, the collaborative style is not appropriate for every conflict situation. Sometimes there are too many cooks in the kitchen, and that creates chaos. So a good leader will be able to determine based on the need that's presenting as to whether the collaborative approach is the best way to solve the problem. When the larger collective all have a stake in the desired outcome, when they are all invested, they all have skin in the game, the collaborative approach engenders a sense of community, fosters trust, and deepens loyalty from the team.

Accommodate—give in (acquiesce): This style is also known as the fourth component in typical trauma responses or crisis responses: *fight*, *flight*, *freeze*, and *fawn*. I know right away that some of you, when looking at this accommodating style, will perceive it to mean that the person who accommodates is weak-willed. That they don't know how to think for themselves, or they're afraid to speak up. This may not be the case at all. In fact, sometimes the best thing you could do is to just give in. You know the saying: pick your battles. Sometimes you must concede the small battles so you can win the war. The accommodating style is about making a conscious decision as to whether your desired outcome is worth more than the outcome that is best for the collective. Is the desired outcome worth more than your relationship with your supervisor or your subordinates? Is the desired outcome worth more than your mental health? Sometimes we've just got to let things go.

I cannot stress enough the importance of understanding your long-term desired outcomes. When you know what's truly important, you will know what is worth fighting for and when it is okay to concede to someone else's point. Remember that just because you think it is a certain way doesn't mean that's the only way to look at a problem. Do not allow your mental set or functional fixedness to interfere with your ability to work with others to solve a shared problem. What matters is that if you choose to acquiesce, it is because it is for the greater good rather than an instinctual response to avoid trauma triggers or to make everyone else happy at your own expense.

Avoid—run away (avoid): My client lived his entire life in avoidance. Avoid conflict. Avoid difficult conversations. Avoid getting hurt. Avoid taking risks. Avoid offending his mother or his wife or his children. Avoid choosing for himself. Avoid, avoid, avoid. The day before he died, he came in for a session and told me he was ready to make bold moves and to do the things he had been avoiding or procrastinating. And then it was over. He passed never knowing the joy of meeting a challenge head on or the thrill of overcoming his fear. Avoidance may be self-rewarding in the short term, but it leads to nothing but long-term regret.

I heard a story the other day that I thought was fitting for an analogy of avoidance. Buffaloes hate storms. They hate water. So they have learned that when they see a storm coming, they should run toward it because doing so means they will spend less time inside the storm. If they run toward it, they can run through it and come out the other side to a place of comfort. But if they run away from the storm, the storm follows them. It will eventually catch up to them, and as they are running away from it, the storm stays with them; they end up being in that place of discomfort much longer.

Think about what this means for us. When we want to avoid that situation, that confrontation, that conversation that feels uncomfortable, the longer we run away from it, the longer it follows and stays with us, causing more frustration, more discomfort. But if we were to approach it instead, run toward it, we would work through the conflict and come out the other side to a place of comfort much sooner than we would if we chose avoidance.

Compromise—win-win or fair/fair (agree): The compromising style is a close cousin of the collaborative style; however, whereas the collaborative style pools ideas and proceeds with the majority vote, the compromising style gives a little and takes a little, to the point where no party has won all or lost all. The goal here is to arrive at a fair/fair solution.

Compromise is the language of negotiation, and we learn this skill surprisingly early. Imagine little Sara asking for a cookie before supper. She is relentless, and she won't give up. "Just one cookie, Mom, please!" Your position is that sweets before dinner will ruin her supper, but then again, if she chooses to have dessert first, what's the harm? So you say, "Okay, Sara. You may have one cookie before supper as long as you agree that you do not have any sweets after supper." Sara agrees but figures she can try for a little more. "Can I have two cookies then?"

Tough negotiator, right? Already toddlers have figured out that if Mom will concede one point, surely she might concede another. At the end of the day, a compromise is won if Mom feels like she is keeping her baby healthy, while her baby is happy with her one treat before supper. The win/win or fair/fair agreement will solve the problem at least temporarily, but as we have seen happening in every collective bargaining agreement, both parties may keep coming back to the table asking for more.

Now that we have clarity about the different styles of conflict resolution, let's talk about the language of conflict resolution. It is one thing to know what the strategies are; it is another to know how to implement them. Let's begin with engaging others in the process of conflict or problem resolution.

Strategy 1: State the problem. This is the work of *say* and *ask*. Understand that helping others meet their needs can help you meet your needs. Once you have said your piece and asked for input or feedback, allow the other party to state their problem. Good relationships are the priority. Work to build mutual respect. The language sounds like this: "Hey, I have a problem, and I need your help to solve it. This is how I perceive things to be going, and it is a problem because . . . I wonder if you have any thoughts on this, and if you would be willing to work with me to make this better."

Strategy 2: Listen. This comes after *ask*. I promise you, we've got a whole chapter devoted to listening. For now, here's what you need to know. When people do not feel seen or heard, they will check out of the conversation. It is paramount that once you have stated your problem and asked for input, you stop talking. Be present. Do not interrupt. Make eye contact. Stay open to feedback. The language of good listening sounds like this: "I hear what you're saying." "I can understand why you're upset." When presenting your problem or responding to what you have heard, avoid using *you* statements because they can often feel accusatory to the other party.

Believe in innocence. This is a great concept I learned from Richard Carlson. Instead of choosing to believe that everyone is out to get you and that this conflict was designed specifically to make you look bad, why not trust in the innocence of the other party and approach them with kindness and openness rather than with animosity or defensiveness? Engage yourself fully, using active listening skills. Stay focused and centered. When the other party feels truly seen and heard, they will become more invested in resolving the conflict because they feel *valued* in the relationship.

Strategy 3: Look for common ground. This is a tool of both the collaborative style and the compromising style. When you establish the facts of the case, explore options together, and eliminate the ones that just don't fit while remaining open to other ideas, you create an environment in which you can work toward that which is mutually acceptable. The language of this strategy sounds like this: "We seem to be clear on the problem or at least the different aspects of the problem. Why don't we take a moment and get clear on the overarching goals to which this problem poses a barrier? What do we want? Can we agree on what we all want? Then let's talk about the solutions we would like to apply and see if there is any common ground there." I guarantee you, every argument my husband and I ever had about our kids was about *how* to solve the problem as opposed to the nature of the problem or our desired outcomes. We both wanted—and still want—our children to be happy, healthy, productive members of society. We always agreed that our kids should be consequenced for their actions. We often disagreed on how we would get our kids to launch and how to administer discipline. At the end of the day, we recognized that we were on the same team with the same goals, and compromise most often won the day.

Strategy 4: Separate the person from the problem. Remember, we do not see things as they are; we see things as *we* are. If you really want to solve a problem or resolve conflict, you have got to separate the person from the problem. You see Alex spending a lot of time on the phone rather than interacting with customers in the store. You interpret that to mean he doesn't care about good customer service. You haven't decided to believe in his innocence, and you're the boss after all, so you choose to aggress. "Look, Alex. I am tired of your lack of interest in serving the customers. If I catch you on the phone once more, you will be fired."

Hang on! What if Alex's kid is sick, and he is getting regular updates from the hospital? What if his home alarm app keeps getting triggered, and he is afraid his house is being burgled? Now we could assume *you* are the problem because your behavior in aggressing demonstrates you don't care about your staff. Separating the person from the problem means you identify the behavior that is concerning and explain what it means to you. Get clarity on why the behavior is occurring and be compassionate in requesting changes in behavior only.

The formula I have for this is an adaptation of TSA. I call it ASC: ask, say, continue. In this scenario, you listen first and talk second. Ask, "What is going on with you? Are you struggling? Why? And how can I support you so you can be more successful?" Then say or explain your perspective: "This is what I see, and this is what it means to me." Let them know what your expectations are and state them clearly. Share some tips on how they can be successful at meeting your expectations and give some encouragement. Finally, continue to offer ongoing feedback. Performance should not be reviewed only once annually. When you see people doing things right, acknowledge it immediately. When you notice them doing things outside the parameters of your quality expectations, help them to correct right away. We should never allow people to practice mistakes.

The language of problem versus people looks like this:

- "You are the reason we are not achieving our monthly quotas" versus "I notice your numbers are low this month. Can we talk about why you think that might be happening and how we can support you in getting them back on track?"
- "You're more interested in your personal calls than our customers" versus "I know you have a lot going on, and you need to check your phone regularly. Perhaps we can work something out so that you can take a quick break every thirty minutes to check in on your son, and while you are on the floor, please ensure you are connecting with customers within the first few moments of their arrival."

When Conflict Has Passed—Defusing the Next Bomb before It Is Ignited

Recently after the shooting death of a local law enforcement official, grieving officers were told they couldn't sit around and mope forever. They were then instructed to get out there and get some traffic violations or DUIs. There was no time to debrief, no time to grieve, no time to process what the death of their colleague meant for how they would show up in the community, and there was no *empathy*. The message received was "So what that an officer died? Sure, it could have been you, but it wasn't. We don't care about you so much as we care about you getting work done." That, my friends, is adding kindling to a pile of slow-burning embers. That's going to get hot right quick!

After a conflict or crisis has passed, there must be a strategy to help people reconcile what happened so they do not carry the effects of that confrontation forward with them. One of the best strategies is to debrief those involved. In law enforcement and the world of first responders, this is called *critical incident stress management* or *debriefing*. At some point, people need to return to work as usual, but pretending the crisis never happened is fruitless, and it minimizes people's natural response to the event, causing them to feel like their emotional responses are invalid. Provide a safe environment for people to discuss the conflict or confrontation and to encapsulate what they learned and how they can use the lessons moving forward in the work environment. You may need to bring in a third-party mediator or someone who specializes in critical incident debriefing to support your team in this process. What is essential is that the team move forward with an understanding of how this conflict came to be, how it was resolved, and how they can continue to work together with a renewed collective purpose.

Initiate the Blue Wire

If we return to the analogy of anger as an incendiary device, and the red wire is the one that initiates the switch that triggers the bomb to explode, what, then, is the blue wire? The blue wire bypasses the communication between the switch and the initiator. Let's call it *anger inoculation*. The concept is derived from a psychotherapy method labeled *stress inoculation therapy* (SIT), which is used to assist clients in preparing to handle anticipated stressful events effectively. The notion of inoculation stems from the idea that the treatment builds a resistance to stressors much like how vaccinations work to make the recipients resistant to the effects of disease.

Stress inoculation has three phases. In the initial conceptualization phase, the therapist educates the patient about the general nature of stress, explains key concepts that play a key role in shaping stress responses, and shares the factors that contribute to good and poor coping. The second phase, skills acquisition and rehearsal, centers on the skills required to effectively manage stressful situations. The skill sets may include emotion regulation, relaxation, cognitive appraisal, problem-solving, communication, and socialization skills. The final phase, application and follow-through, provides the patient with opportunities to practice their coping skills using visualization, vicarious learning, role-playing of anxiety-inducing or stressful situations, and repeatedly practicing coping routines until they have been assimilated.

The *Anger Solutions* reimagining of anger inoculation has four components instead of three: (1) awareness (much like SIT conceptualization); (2) knowledge acquisition and skill acquisition; (3) skill and knowledge application, including rehearsal; and (4) assessment—measuring the success of the intervention. In the awareness phase, we help people to unlearn everything they thought they knew about anger—the lies, misconceptions, and ill-informed philosophies that inform the conceptualization of anger as behavior rather than emotion. Myths about anger are debunked and replaced with facts. In the knowledge and skill acquisition phase, the truths about anger, how it develops, and the ways in which we can enhance our problem-solving abilities are embedded. Those skills are rehearsed through various methods including in-vivo exposure to anger-inducing situations, role-playing, modeling, and vicarious learning, much as it is done in SIT. Finally, once the clients have fully integrated their new problem-resolution and communication skills, the efficacy of the intervention is assessed, and the clients are able to see for themselves the degree to which they have created radical positive change in their own development.

Anger inoculation builds resiliency. It enables people to think through potentially inflammatory or incendiary situations before they arise and reminds them of their long-term desired outcomes, whatever those might be. For some, it is the preservation of a reputation, the integrity of a brand, or being a positive influence and a light in dark places. For others, it is the restoration of relationships, healing of past hurts, or simply making others feel better about themselves. Having the ability to clearly and assertively express and resolve angry feelings is the key to cutting the red wire.

Summary

Failure to lead with compassion and empathy may be the impetus behind the phenomenon called quiet quitting, which is a symptom of anger in the workplace. Poor communication contributes to workplace toxicity.

Intermittent explosive disorder is a disorder of behavior regulation and is a subtype of impulse control disorder. To diffuse IED:

1. Practice self-regulation.
2. Clear a path between your upstairs and downstairs brain.

3. Cut the incendiary trigger (the red wire).
4. Scramble the angry circuitry.
5. Control your chaos.

We can apply conflict resolution tools and *Anger Solutions*-informed communication strategies to work through workplace conflict.

Anger inoculation includes four phases: awareness, knowledge and skill acquisition, knowledge and skill application, and assessment.

Reflection

When you are faced with conflict in the workplace, what is your go-to strategy for dealing with it? Do you choose avoidance, try to control the situation, compromise, or collaborate?

Action Step

1. Think of a situation happening in the workplace right now that holds the potential to become explosive. How might you apply the principles in this chapter to achieve a peaceful and agreeable resolution to the problem?

10

WE NEED TO TALK

HAVE YOU EVER had a problem or challenge so severe that it required—no, it demanded—to be addressed? Imagine processing TSA and getting clear on the nature of the problem, your desired outcome, and what you believe will be the best approach to solve the problem. Then you go to the person who can best help you solve that problem, and you communicate to them as assertively as you know how, and you ask them to work with you to resolve the issue. In response, all you get is a blank stare and crickets. I had one such situation. I had thought it through, said all the things, and got nothing in response. It was unnerving.

Here's the thing, and I'll be totally transparent with you: My desired outcome was for the relationship to be severed amicably, but truth be told, I also wanted an apology. I felt I was deserving of one. I *expected* the other party to be contrite, to be embarrassed by their behavior and its negative impact on my family's existence, and I expected them to acknowledge the inappropriate and inconsiderate nature of their choices.

Crickets.

For many years, I pondered that interaction. After I was done speaking to the brick wall that was the other party, I experienced an upset stomach of epic proportions, but then I went to sleep and slept well. I knew I had done my job by expressing myself assertively and that the ball was in the other person's court. It was up to them to decide if they would amend their behavior. I can also acknowledge now that I spent many years feeling disappointed that I did not get the *interim* outcome I desired of the contrite, apologetic response even though my ultimate desired outcome was achieved—the relationship ended amicably. My unmet expectation and the ensuing disappointment were the result of a common misconception about assertiveness. We think being assertive *should* result in us getting what we want, and this justifies us resorting to aggression or other tactics when we don't because, after all, isn't the goal to get *what we want*?

What You Want versus What Is Best

When my psychotherapy practice moved into a new office building, one of the other tenants made it her personal mission to make every day miserable for me and my team. She drove me to the point of wanting to take her out using the tactics of John Cena or the Rock. I. Was. Done. I wanted revenge. I wanted satisfaction. I wanted to make her pay. I wanted to punch her in the face. None of those outcomes was what was *best* for the situation.

I'll never forget the day she pushed me over the edge. Rather than taking her down with a martial art move worthy of any comic book character, I calmly collected my things, drove home, and immediately took my dog for a long walk. My neighbor came with me, and I vented to her all about the situation as we were walking. Once I had talked it out, I felt better, and I had a clear picture of my desired outcome as well as a plan of action—one that I felt would be *best* for me, my reputation, and the mental health and morale of my team.

My process included TSA, of course, but it was a two-part thing. I also worked my way through a variety of options using the following matrix. My immediate desire in reaction to my work neighbor's antics was to pursue immediate satisfaction by knocking her out. That would have been a wrong choice, yielding only a short-term satisfactory result followed by long-term negative consequences in the way of assault charges and the destruction of my reputation. No way was I interested in going down that dark road. My decision-making process required me to consider all the combinations and permutations of possible outcomes before pursuing a course of action.

The Choice Matrix

The choice matrix shows how our decisions and ensuing actions may impact our short- and long-term outcomes.

Wrong choice / Feels bad: As it was with my unfortunate situation with the office neighbor from Hades, we often know what the right choice is, but we don't want to make that choice because it doesn't feel good, or we *think* it won't feel good in the moment. When we make the wrong choice and it feels bad, we experience both short- and long-term pains. There is no gain in this scenario. The decision does not fix feelings, nor does it resolve a problem. So we go for what feels good instead.

Wrong choice / Feels good: Let me tell you, punching that woman in the face would have felt *awesome*, but choosing the quick fix is often the wrong choice because it brings us short-term gain—the temporary fixing of our feelings—but long-term pain. The emotional fix isn't lasting, and the problem that caused the feeling is often still there.

Right choice / Feels bad: Sometimes we make the right choice, or the best choice available, knowing it will not feel good in the moment. Examples of this might be apologizing, admitting you're wrong, paying for something now rather than buying it on credit, or getting your car serviced regularly rather than waiting for it to break down. Typically, the bad feeling only lasts for a short time—short-term pain. Your bank account might be low until your next paycheck, but in the long term, you have gain because you won't be paying 19 percent interest on the cost of your car repair. You might feel a little shame or embarrassment at having to apologize or admit you're wrong in the moment, but the repaired relationship is a long-term gain.

Right choice / Feels good: The last box indicates that when you make the right choice or the best choice for the situation *and* it feels good, you experience short-term gain—an immediate positive emotional response—as well as long-term gain. An example of this might be choosing between two job offers after weighing the options and deciding on the one that will provide you with more opportunity, better-extended health benefits, or an opportunity to travel or pursue your true passions. You've evaluated the decision well enough to know that taking the job is a good choice in both short and long terms—hence, no pain.

When it came to our neighbor, I talked it over with my team, and we agreed to kill her with kindness. Anything else would be a compromise of our individual and shared values; punching her in the face would be a direct hit to *my* reputation as an anger-resolution specialist, and we would not allow ourselves to sink to her level. As Michelle Obama advised, when she went low, we went high. Amazingly, only a few short months after we decided to just flood her and her staff with smiles, kind words, acknowledgments, and general politesse, she announced that she was moving out. We may have shouted a few *hallelujahs* when we saw the back of her. When we weighed what we wanted (satisfaction) against what was best, we ultimately obtained both desired outcomes—we frustrated her with our apparent indifference to her guerilla tactics so much that she moved out (our long-term desired outcome).

Every problem is a relationship problem, and the primary reason that relationships fail is a lack of communication. Thinking it through is good, but it isn't enough. Deciding on desired outcome is a step forward, but by itself, it isn't enough. You must be willing to work that problem out with the other party, and that requires communication. Sometimes communication feels uncomfortable. It's the right choice, but it feels bad. Sometimes we choose communication, but we choose our words poorly. Wrong choice / feels good or bad depending on the words you choose. It is not enough to just *say something*; we must be mindful and intentional about what we will say and how we will say it.

Words Have Power

Communication is key to getting our needs met. It is essential for giving and taking direction. Chaos ensues when messages are transmitted with no way of their content being interpreted. Whether we are driving down the street, navigating the high seas, passing through aisles in the grocery store, or flirting with strangers, communication is necessary for every activity. When my clients say they just want to live alone on a deserted island, I remind them of the main character in the movie *Castaway*, who developed a relationship with a soccer ball he named Wilson. As a human being, he craved communication, and the only available sources for communication were himself and Wilson. I'm constantly reminding my clients that even if they chose to be hermits, communication would still be required because wherever you go, you take you with you. And the relationship you have with yourself is just as important as any other.

There are many things that contribute to intrapersonal relationship damage—that is, damage to the relationships we have with ourselves—but the two that I hear about most in my practice are *guilt* and *shame*. Guilt typically accompanies clients who have been referred for problems stemming from emotional dysregulation. They are almost always faced with an impending consequence for their quick-fix reactions: potential breakup of a relationship, job loss, criminal charges, or the loss of access to their children. Guilt and remorse go hand in glove with poor decisions, as they should. Once clients take ownership of the error of their ways and begin taking steps to repair the harm that was done, in most cases, the guilt can be assuaged. Not so for shame.

You see, guilt is in response to what was done. Shame is more deeply tied to identity. Think of it this way. Someone violates one of your boundaries, and you respond by yelling at them and saying verbally abusive things. Once the heat of the moment has passed and you acknowledge that your reaction was a bit over the top, you feel guilty, and that remorse compels you to call that person and apologize for your behavior. Shame sticks around because while guilt is about what you did, shame is deeply tied to *who you are*. You might feel guilty because you did a bad thing, but feelings of shame come from believing you are a bad, an angry, or a verbally abusive person.

When people come into my office bearing deep shame, I am compelled to ask them to leave it at the door if they can. Shame does no one any good, especially not in the therapeutic process. *Shame* is another word that is entrenched in the language of unmet expectations—this time, about the self: "I should have responded differently. But I didn't because I am a horrible person. This is just who I am. I'll never be able to change. I'm stuck being this awful human and hating myself for the rest of my life."

Please don't think me overdramatic. You would be surprised how many people repeat some version of this narrative when they are shrouded in shame. Shame is paralyzing. Where guilt might compel someone to make amends, shame elicits a feeling of helplessness, one that impedes the ability to actively work toward positive change.

My clients who struggle with shame have learned from childhood that they are not enough as they are. That they are the sum of their actions and reactions. That meeting the expectations of others is more important than being their authentic selves. That their emotional states do not matter as much as the needs and expectations of the adults, authorities, or leaders in their lives. And because they are enveloped in shame, they do not know how to assert their ideas, wants, needs, or opinions. They don't feel *worthy* of that privilege.

Look, every time we are told we should be ashamed of ourselves, we are being deeply conditioned to house, harbor, and cultivate feelings of self-loathing. Words have power and can have a devastating effect on the human psyche. The things we say and the way we say them are part and parcel of the outcomes we can expect short and long terms when we are attempting to resolve anger.

When parents say things like "I'm disappointed in you" or "You should be ashamed of yourself," it may seem like it is the assertive thing to say in the moment, but it's a cop-out. Let's say your child has done something that was wrong; they lied, stole, used drugs, or assaulted someone. Why not ask them to go through the same process that we as parents should be going through, which is TSA? What if we encouraged them to think about what they did, why they did it, and what their desired outcome was? Why not ask if the cost of the behavior was worth their desired outcome? *"So you took drugs because you were sad or because you wanted to fit in with your peers. You fit in with your peers for the moment, but what are the long-term consequences of taking drugs?"*

Instead of gently walking our children through active use of this decision-making model, too many parents take the approach of *"I'm the parent. I'm the person who knows everything; my kid knows nothing."* Rather than teaching them what could help them in the future, how to make better decisions, parents cast judgment with statements like "I'm disappointed in you." I'm disappointed in *you*, the person, instead of "I'm disappointed in this *decision* you made." It would be more empowering to say, "I'm sorry you made that choice. I'm disappointed you made that choice. I'm sad you made that choice. Here's what I wish you would have done instead. Here's what I wish you would do in the future. Let's talk about it. Let's talk about what led you to making that decision in the first place."

I wonder if parents don't follow that process because, deep inside, they fear they might have contributed to their child's poor choices. And in that sense, they're not wrong because they have not equipped their kids with the information they need. Parents are often the worst hypocrites. They drink and smoke while telling their children they should do neither of those things. They roll joints at the kitchen table while warning their kids off drugs. They drone on about having integrity and a good moral code, but they cheat on their spouses and then lie outright when they are confronted with the truth. They withhold information that is necessary for their children to have to successfully navigate the world and then wonder why they fail.

Generational Trauma and the Legacy of Shame

My maternal grandmother overheard her parents talking about pregnancy. What she heard was "Wow, a boy only has to touch a girl on her shoulder, and she's knocked up." My grandmother was in her teens, yet she knew nothing of the facts of life. Immediately, she thought of the boy at school who was kind to her and always touched her lightly when they interacted. She thought, "If he has touched me like my mom said, I could already be pregnant." The next time she was with that boy, she allowed him to more than touch her—and wouldn't you know it? She got pregnant.

The people who were supposed to educate and equip their child with information she needed so that she could be a functioning, contributing member of society fell down on the job. Why? Because somebody taught *them* that it was shameful to talk about the facts of life. This is generational trauma at work. That unfortunate couple believed that talking about sex, the reproductive system, the natural body functions that God created in us was shameful. So they never talked about it. Then when their children came along and needed guidance, they had no resources with which to support them. Those children entered their adolescence sans guidance, without resources, feeling ill equipped to cope with their bodily functions and traumatized by the functions of their own body.

For millennia, people, systems, religions, organizations, governments, and corporations have harnessed and weaponized shame, using it to coerce conformity to their preferred doctrine, belief system, political agenda, whatever is at play. Shame leaves behind a stain of trauma that permeates generation after generation after generation.

In the 1880s, in concert with the government of Canada, four major churches—the Roman Catholic Church, Church of England, Methodist or United Church, and Presbyterian Church—forcibly removed Aboriginal children from their homes and communities and placed them in residential schools. The residential school program was designed to disrupt the Aboriginal way of life, with the ultimate objective to destroy the core of Aboriginal identity. The residential school system, in which the school administrators were granted legal guardianship of the children, was part of a broad set of assimilation efforts to destroy their precious culture and identities and to suppress their histories.

Students were forbidden to speak Native languages and punished for practicing their culture. One hundred and thirty-six Native residential schools were established across the country, and they operated for approximately one hundred years; the final schools only closed as recently as 1998. Canadian law made attendance at the schools mandatory for all Aboriginal children, and it is estimated that over 150,000 First Nation, Inuit, and Métis children were torn from their families and forced into deplorable living conditions. Even today, the unmarked graves of children who never saw their families again are still being uncovered.

Consider the generational impact of this. Three consecutive generations endured the theft of their children and the loss of their identity. Consider the loss of language, knowledge, culture, and life that was inflicted by the perpetrators of this great injustice. Consider the messaging that made this policy and its execution possible; somewhere deeply embedded in that message is shame.

Trauma destroys your identity and shatters the self. It steals your voice. Why is it that First Nations people, as part of the truth and reconciliation process, need to tell their story? Because their voice was stolen. They were not allowed to celebrate their culture; they lost the language of their people. The message the country received and what was delivered to the First Nations was that who they were was not good enough. They had to be ashamed of who they were, where they came from, their cultural identity, their religious practices. That was all coded in shame so they could be conquered. Shame was the weapon of the colonizer.

Throughout the seventeenth and eighteenth centuries, people were forcibly removed from the continent of Africa, compelled, and exploited as slaves in the American colonies. White slave owners held ultimate power financially, economically, and politically. Attempts to escape were punishable by whippings or lynchings. Physical punishments were dispensed for a great many infractions determined by the masters. Sickness or pregnancy was no excuse for missing work. New mothers were expected to return to work immediately while their babies were wet nursed. This practice ensured poor attachment between mothers and their children, making it easier for owners to sell off individual family members. Enslaved people were starved, hung on hooks, raped, beaten, lynched, tortured, and burned to death as ways to make examples of them to the larger groups. This level of cruelty ensured the complicity of those watching.

The prevailing mindset of white slave owners was that their chattel slaves were not human; rather, they were stupid, ignorant heathens—animals that did not even deserve life or liberty. The notion that all men were created equal did not apply to them because enslaved Africans were not men. This messaging, rooted in the propaganda of racism, is the language of shame: *You are not worth anything. You're not even a whole human. You're no better than a dog. That's why we can work you like this. That's why we can beat you. That's why we can whip you. That's why we can hang you. It's why we can burn you because you're not human.* That's the dehumanizing, demeaning language of shame. For hundreds of years, generations of people were covered in a stain they didn't earn and didn't deserve, but it was passed down to them.

Now consider how this messaging has been embedded in the DNA of a people. If we will ever be able to communicate in a way that asserts our individuality—asserts our wants or needs—or state our thoughts, opinions, dreams, hopes, or goals, if we're going to be able to communicate the problems we're having and ask people to help us solve those problems, what must first go is shame. Shame must go because if you're ashamed of who you are or what you are, you will never ask for what you want. You will never actively search to solve problems; you will fall into a state of learned helplessness and stay there, and you will comply with whoever or whatever has convinced you that you should be ashamed of yourself.

The alternative is to rage against the machine. Perpetuate the narrative of "the angry Black," "the unruly Native," or "the histrionic woman" because after generations of violated boundaries, broken rules regarding basic human decency, broken treaties, and decimated trust, it follows that people would go to extreme lengths to get their needs met.

Shame minimizes everything about you. Your feelings are not valid. Your boundaries are foolish. Your needs don't matter. Emerging from the shroud of shame is essential to effective problem-solving. You cannot ask for what you want, for your boundaries to be respected, or express your feelings effectively without first shedding the shame.

Healthy Relationships Begin and End with Assertive Communication

Psychologist Robert Sternberg suggested that love is made up of three key components: intimacy, passion, and commitment. Intimacy is about the *mind*. Do you have things in common? Do you like each other? Do you trust each other? Do you feel safe with each other? Passion is about the *physical* connection, the spark, the attraction you feel toward another person. Finally, commitment is about the *spirit*. It is that thing that makes you decide you want to remain engaged in the relationship, even to the point of forsaking all other relationships. Intimacy alone is just liking, passion alone is infatuation, and commitment alone is empty. But when you have all three components working together, you find the sweet spot that is consummate love.

The hallmarks of healthy relationships are assertive communication, healthy boundaries, forgiveness/acceptance, and intimacy. Consider these questions when evaluating your relationships: Do you like each other? Do you trust each other? Do you share common interests? Do you enjoy

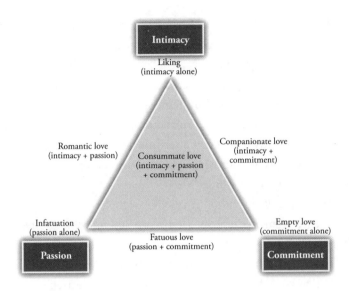

spending time together? Are you supportive of each other? Can you celebrate each other's wins? Can you be patient with each other? Can you be accepting of each other's differences? Are you able to set clear boundaries, and are they respected? Do you feel *safe* with each other?

Regardless of the type of "love" you find yourself in, you will find that intimacy is the lynchpin that holds love together. Where there is no intimacy, what you have is infatuation (passion alone, or just the sex), fatuous love (passion and commitment, which is almost impossible to achieve, by the way), or empty love (commitment alone—no passion, no intimacy). Where there is shame, all the elements of intimacy—safety, trust, acceptance of self and others, security, and healthy boundaries—will be compromised. There can be no intimacy without communication. Communication is more of a challenge when shame is present and intimacy is lacking.

The same can be said of self-esteem. Positive self-esteem makes assertiveness easy. Assertive practice leads to better short- and long-term outcomes, increasing self-esteem. Self-esteem levels have a direct correlation with how assertive, passive, passive-aggressive, or aggressive we will be. Even if we are making a concerted effort to make verbal communication assertive, when self-esteem is low, body language might sabotage the entire effort.

Body language or nonverbal communication can be a barrier to effective communication if assertive speech is overridden by "unfriendly" nonverbals such as looking stern, frowning, rarely smiling, or staring. If we communicate that we are constantly angry through speaking in a stern, firm tone of voice; tightening the lips; using a flat, final tone that excludes others' opinions, even if we are speaking very assertively, our words will be lost on the recipient. The hearer will only remember that we seemed to be quite angry about something or other. Furthermore, if we rarely make eye contact or speak too softly, it won't matter how assertively we speak. Eye rolling, smirks, sarcasm, or comments made under the breath are also telling. Actions speak louder than words.

How can a realistic and positive self-esteem help one to become more assertive? Self-esteem is the value you place on yourself, the feelings and thoughts you have about yourself and your sense of being a worthy person. It is related to and can affect the way you see yourself in the world, as well as your belief that you can achieve the goals you set for yourself.

If we believe we are valuable, if we like ourselves, if we are confident in our abilities and feel "worthy" of others' affection and friendship, it follows that we will portray that confidence and assuredness in our communication. We will not be afraid to ask for things because we won't feel unworthy of receiving them. If we are confident in our abilities, we won't be afraid of asking for that raise or disagreeing with the boss. If we like ourselves, then we will behave in ways that will reflect that self-liking. We will not allow others to run roughshod over us, nor will we treat others with a lack of respect. Having positive self-esteem makes being assertive easy.

How does assertive behavior increase one's self-esteem? Let's say someone is trying to break out of the mold of always using passive forms of communication. They begin by trying to be more assertive in expressing their wants, needs, or opinions. Let's say their first few attempts don't work due to lack of congruence between their verbal and nonverbal communication, but they decide to keep trying.

When they succeed at using an assertive technique, what will they feel? Relieved, pleased, perhaps even proud. Then as they experience the positive emotion of pride in their accomplishments, what happens? Self-esteem rises. Why? Because they feel more valuable, they feel good about themselves for achieving this new accomplishment, and they think the effort was worth it because they are worth it. They think perhaps this goal or desired outcome is attainable, so they continue with the assertive behavior. As self-esteem increases, they in turn become more assertive. This symbiosis between self-esteem and both verbal and nonverbal assertiveness is yet one more reason shame must go.

My nasty work neighbor did all she could to make me feel as though I did not belong in the building. Perhaps in her own way, she was attempting to impose a sense of shame on me, as though I was not worthy of being in that space. Rising above her petty tactics took some effort, but it was possible because I had done the work of breaking free from the shroud of shame that others had placed over me in my early years. By the time I was confronted with my neighbor, I had plumbed and reclaimed my lost identity, and I was secure in who I am. Sure, she made me angry, but she never once shook my sense of self. With my armor of positive self-esteem, secure identity, and healed trauma wounds securely in place, weaponized shame had no power to harm me.

Assertiveness is a complex skill that is acquired by making the right choice for the right reasons until it feels good. Sometimes it means sharing your heart even though you know the response will be crickets. Sometimes it means walking away in silence. Sometimes it means asking for what you want or setting firm boundaries. Sometimes it means asking for help. And sometimes it means asking for forgiveness. At the end of the day, assertiveness is about using your words and doing so wisely because words have power. It is about ensuring your body doesn't work against you by sending mixed messages. It is about shedding the shame that has been placed on you through generational trauma, propaganda, religious teachings, or parental discipline so that you can confidently use your voice.

Summary

Words have power. The language of shame is demoralizing and paralyzing. For generations, shame has been weaponized to rob people of their voice and their autonomy.

Assertiveness is the healthiest form of communication. Having a positive self-esteem makes one more assertive; gaining successful outcomes as a result of assertiveness grows one's self-esteem.

We always have a choice. The goal is to make the right choices, to feel good about those choices, and to enjoy both the short- and long-term pleasurable outcomes that result from those right choices.

Reflection

1. Have you personally experienced the weaponization of shame? Journal about the experience and what you learned about yourself and others as a result.
2. Does assertiveness come easy or hard for you? Why? What one thing about your communication style could you change today to be more assertive?

Action Step

Find the Choice Matrix Cheat Sheet and the Communication Style Cheat Sheet in your downloadable workbook. Take particular note of the positive characteristics of assertive communication.

II

TWO EARS, ONE MOUTH

MY CLIENT HAD a volatile temper. She was not an expert communicator, and she had difficulty expressing her feelings in ways that we might expect or be prepared for. This often led to frequent misunderstandings between herself and those who worked with her. When we decided to explore the root of her many outbursts, one of the things she repeated was that she didn't like it when she felt that people weren't listening. In her mind, she was making her best effort to communicate, and we were not *hearing* or *understanding* what she was saying. This caused her an immense amount of frustration, and she reacted by acting out using tantrums, yelling, and verbal aggression.

This was a real wake-up call for all of us who worked with her. We recognized that we had to beef up our own listening skills. We had certainly been hearing what she was saying but had often misunderstood the context or the meaning of what was said. When we took the time to study both her methods of communication and the ways in which she used her body to send nonverbal messages, we experienced more clarity in understanding her communication; thus, *she* experienced less frustration. We also found that by paying closer attention to her nonverbals, we could catch when her frustration was building toward an outburst. The conversation could then be redirected before her frustration built to the point of initiating an explosion. Because we improved our listening skills and responded to her body language, we were able to effectively cut the red wire, resulting in a significant reduction in her outbursts both with us and with other people.

I once saw a movie in which a psychiatrist was conversing with his patient.[1] She asked him how he did his job, and he responded, "I take the last two words of the client's sentence and turn it into a question . . . like this: 'Your mother?'" If that is all there is to listening, then how come we have so many misunderstandings in the world?

When people complain, it is only because they have an *ideal-world* picture of how it could or should be. They are holding an image in their mind of *something better*. How often do those who receive the complaint gaslight or dismiss the one complaining? *"That person just has a negative attitude. They are always unhappy about something. You can never satisfy that person."* How often do hearers of complaints use shame to shut the complaint down? *"Can't you just be satisfied with what you have? You should feel lucky you have a job in this economy. After all I've done for you, when will it be enough? You're so selfish; all you think about is yourself and your needs."* Do the shamers, gaslighters, and dismissers ever wonder if *they* are the reason they keep hearing complaints? To engage in real dialogue with the intent to resolve problems rather than avoiding the real issues, it is essential to develop the art of good listening.

If you attempt a dialogue or discussion to resolve your anger, you must be committed to seeing it through. It is unfair to everyone involved to think, say, ask, and then walk away because you don't like the answer. The goal is to stay put and listen, even when physiology, emotions, and thought processes are all crying out, "Attack! Then retreat."

We have established that when you are in a state of heightened awareness, your downstairs brain activates the physiological state of fight, flight, freeze, or fawn. It's hard to focus and concentrate when your heart races and adrenaline rushes while thousands of thoughts flow through your mind. Also, remember that when you experience fight or flight, your body restricts the flow of blood to your outer extremities. Breathing also becomes shallow, thus reducing the amount of oxygen available to the brain. This means the upstairs brain is effectively checked out from an individual in a heightened state of stress, thinking too much but not very clearly.

If you tend to focus on what your body is feeling and how angry you are, your thoughts will tend to flow in that direction. If you forget to monitor your breathing and do not make a conscious attempt to slow it down, you will perpetuate the cycle by maintaining low oxygen levels in your brain. You may even try to go through the process of resolution, but you will not be able to think clearly enough to follow through and attain the results you desire because of lack of engagement from the upstairs brain. Keeping the upstairs brain involved is essential to effective problem-solving.

I Don't Wike You

As a child, one of the things I hated most was the "parent lecture." Sadly, as a highly intelligent youngster with too much brain and too little maturity, mixed with a healthy dose of mischief, I often found myself on the receiving end of these talks. It wasn't that I did not believe I deserved the discipline or punishment. Most of the time, I was guilty as charged. The thing was that I only needed to be told I was wrong and for my parents to dispense the appropriate punishment. My mom often wanted to reason things out with me, but she had not mastered the art of two-way dialogue.

Honestly, I loved my mom to the ends of the earth, but her parent lectures often drove me to tears. Many times, she believed my tears were a manifestation of my remorse when, in fact, they were tears of frustration. I only wanted her to stop talking so I could "go to my room and think about what I had done." The frustration stemmed from the fact that I was expected to do all the listening, but I was never given an opportunity to respond. That lack of reciprocal communication made me feel unseen and unheard. It felt like I did not matter. Even though my mother's desperate attempts to talk me into being "good" implied that I mattered a great deal, her apparent lack of concern for my thoughts, feelings, and opinions in those moments negated the underlying message.

Not gonna lie. As a parent, I have been guilty of giving the parent lecture. That said, I have made a concerted effort to give my children the floor, even when they were saying things like "I don't wike you." The fact is that sometimes I didn't like them much either, and I didn't hesitate to tell them so! But I always followed up with "But I do love you, and that will never change." I learned the hard way how important it is to give children a voice, even if what they say is hard to hear.

Listening to Your Heart

Now let's talk more about the importance of listening in dialogue. One underrated aspect of good listening is the skill of responding to your inner wisdom, or your gut instinct. I once found myself caught between two sides of an issue. The proponent of one side was quite vocal, and his argument made sense to me; in fact, I found myself supporting his position. The other side also made perfect sense, and I supported certain points of that argument as well.

Amid all the commotion and confusion, I felt a little tugging somewhere deep inside of me, somewhat like a child who very quietly but persistently tugs on Mother's clothing to get her attention. Just as we moms often tend to ignore that consistent prompting, I failed to recognize the importance of paying attention to that tiny twinge of instinct. Had I been more mindful of that inner wisdom, I might have asked more pointed questions of both sides and made more of an effort to get a more complete picture of the real issue. Because of my oversight, it took me a couple of days to figure out where I really stood on the issue, when in fact it should have only taken me a few minutes or a couple of hours at best.

When we are amid an argument, a fight, or a debate, we must be able to detach ourselves from our emotions enough so that we can clearly analyze both the issue and what is being said about it. This means engaging your breath to oxygenate your brain. Stepping back and using TSA to keep the upstairs brain engaged in processing. It means *hearing* what people are saying as well as what your own internal instincts are telling you, *seeing and interpreting* body language to substantiate the verbal communication, and *reading* between the lines.

We must understand that many human beings have difficulty expressing themselves clearly and succinctly. When it comes to discussing our negative feelings, our vulnerabilities, and our insecurities, that difficulty becomes even more pronounced. We tend to trail off our sentences . . . you know what I mean? And we expect people to know what we mean! What we are saying is that we want people to be able to understand what we have said even though we haven't really said it. Whenever possible, we should try to make a concerted effort to be clear about what we are feeling, what we want or expect, and how we intend to see the dialogue through to resolution. Only through clarity and good use of our words and nonverbals can we communicate effectively to those around us.

Imagine what life would be like if you never really heard or understood what people said to you. If I said to you, "I'm so tired; I need to sit down and take a break," but you heard, "I am so tired of you; why don't you sit down and shut up?" what would your reaction be? You would likely react in anger or defensiveness. Then I would be wondering what I said to set you off. It stands to reason that if you misinterpret my verbal communication, it is because either you were not really listening, or I was not being clear in my communication.

A while back, my friend Dr. Jeremy Goldberg conducted a social experiment on his social media (Instagram: @longdistancelovebombs). He posted, "I believe in mandatory *vacations*. People who don't take *vacations* should be forced!" It was laughable how many people filtered his post through the lens of their senses, their values as they related to another word that starts with V, and their experiences in the context of the COVID-19 crisis. The vitriol that people spewed at Jeremy was unbelievable. If only they had moved beyond the Instagram square and read the caption—that is, if they had taken the time to be fully centered and to listen to what he was saying, they would have interacted differently with the post or not at all.

People saw the words *mandatory* and *forced*, they applied those words to the context of the COVID-19 pandemic, and they assumed that the V word was *vaccinations* instead of *vacations*. You know what they say about assuming, right? Never assume because it makes an *ass* out of *u* and *me*. Imagine how sheepish people must have felt when they realized Jeremy was not trying to be politically or socially divisive; he was simply making a point about how our perceptions inform our responses, which can be highly explosive, especially when we have already made up our minds about how things are or how they should be.

Dialogue is a two-way process. It involves both the giving and receiving of communication. It also requires a willingness to do more than receive information; one must receive, interpret, understand, and feedback the information received. This is a function of sensation, perception, meaning-making, and, to some extent, memory. The information must also be incorporated into the context of the dialogue as well as the feelings, needs, and wants of each party. Giving someone a lecture does not constitute dialogue. The domination of a conversation, either verbally or physically, by one party or another does not represent fair, two-way communication.

You may be asking why it is so important to have good listening skills in the process of dialogue, and what are these good listening skills anyway?

First, we all want to be heard and understood. No one likes to feel as though their opinions are worthless or that their feelings are insignificant. You call that certain someone when you have a problem because you know they will *really listen* to you. What is it about the way that person listens that differentiates them from your boss or the receptionist at work?

Beef Up Your Listening Skills

Effective listening involves creating an atmosphere that shows the other person you are involved and attentive. You can demonstrate this by making eye contact, maintaining a relaxed and open body posture, and keeping an appropriate physical distance. While the ideal physical manifestations of good listening vary somewhat from person to person—and often vary dramatically from culture to culture—we can usually tell if someone is really listening by their eye contact and body language.

In some situations, we might feel more comfortable to communicate with little or no eye contact. This could be interpreted as an attempt to avoid showing our true feelings about what we are hearing, or that we are intimidated by the other person, or even that we have something to hide. In Western culture, it is commonly believed that direct and frequent eye contact leads to a stronger and more effective message that the listener is both hearing and attempting to understand the message being relayed.

Test Your Listening Skills

Whenever I want to show my clients how easy it is to command the brain to be centered and focused, I encourage them to look around my office and spot everything that is red; there is a lot of red in my space. I then ask them to close their eyes and visualize the room, and I ask them to tell me everything in the room that is blue. Very few clients can correctly recall more than one item because their brains immediately filter out everything that is *irrelevant* to the current task of finding red things.

This principle applies to dialogue. We can, if we choose, filter out everything that is irrelevant to the interaction at hand. Smartphones. Television or computer screens. Ambient sound. The music on the radio. The kids chattering in the background. We can selectively listen; perhaps the problem is that sometimes we just don't want to.

Answer the following questions as truthfully as you can. Then perform some self-evaluation. Do you think you have the characteristics of a good listener? Do you have the will to listen with the intent to understand? If you need someone to talk to, would you turn to someone with your caliber of listening skills?

- Do you put what you are doing aside, ignore distractions, and look directly at the person who is talking?
- Are you sensitive to gestures, voice tone, and facial expressions? Does your own body language encourage conversation?
- Do you find yourself racing ahead to formulate a response before the other person has finished speaking?
- Do you have difficulty waiting until someone finishes speaking?
- Do you finish people's sentences for them?
- Do you give people equal floor time? Do you encourage others to talk?
- Do you give feedback to acknowledge your understanding of what has been said?
- If you do not understand something, do you ask the speaker to clarify?
- Is it obvious to the speaker that you respect every person's right to their opinion even though you disagree?
- Do you respond with judgmental statements, or can you remain open-minded and empathetic?

The following formula, which I call **FRIEND**, may be useful in helping you to use your attending skills more effectively.

Follow what people say with verbal prompts: "I see," "Tell me more about it."

Respect people's right to speak and be heard. Resist giving uninvited advice.

Invite people to speak. Create a safe, caring environment in which they are free to share.

Encourage the speaker to discover their own solutions by reflecting on their verbalizations.

Nodding, touching, smiling, making eye contact, and sitting or
standing in close proximity (eighteen inches of personal space) are
nonverbal indications that you are paying attention.

Defer judgment; don't give unwanted advice; don't interrupt; don't
doodle, distract, or fall asleep.

When you incorporate these behaviors into your dialogue, you show
the other participant(s) that you are willing to be a true FRIEND, to listen without judging, and to hear out the other side of the argument. Even
though you may not get exactly what you want in the long run, you will be
respected for demonstrating your willingness to listen.

But I Want What I Want When I Want It!

Many of us think that if we show our vulnerability or if we take a risk in
sharing our true feelings, that justifies our wanting a situation to be resolved
the way we want it to be resolved. Not so. The reason we share our true feelings is for our own sake, for *our* well-being. It is not about the other person
at all. You see, you share your feelings so that the other individual will *know*
what those feelings are. If you don't say something, they may never realize
they have hurt, insulted, compromised, undermined, or damaged you in any
way. So you tell them. Then you explain how that behavior has affected you
personally so it has some *meaning* for them.

Remember the Fallacy of Control

Search your motives. If you are sharing your heart with the hopes that the
hearer will suddenly fall at your feet and apologize, don't hold your breath.
Once the ball is in someone else's court, you have no control. You cannot
dictate, legislate, or control the behavior of others. You are responsible for
yourself and your behavior, and you are responsible for giving others the
information they need to make decisions about their behavior. Outside of
that, don't try to manipulate people with your feelings. That's not what you
were given them for.

The reason I say this now is that we often enter a dialogue with pre-
conceived notions about how it will or *should* turn out. We tell our partners
or exes how they have hurt us with the expectation that they will bow down

and kiss our feet and make it better. We try to mend a broken relationship by saying, "I want you back" and expect the same response. However, true dialogue is a process over which we have no control outside of ourselves.

It is true, as Proverbs 15:1 states, that "soft answers turn away wrath, but grievous words stir up anger," thus indicating we have some influence over the tone of a conversation. However, we cannot control what comes out of another person's mouth. What we can do is make sure our ears are attuned to what is truly being said and not what we want to hear.

When you say to your ex, "I want you back," you must be equally prepared for a negative response as you are for a positive one. Whatever the response is, you must be willing to hear the person out, ask questions, find out how they feel, and try to understand. Showing an unwillingness to listen will certainly not endear you to the heart of an estranged partner, sibling, parent, or friend.

To resolve larger issues, it will inevitably take more than one simple dialogue with simple statements and simple answers. Be prepared to hear, listen to, and understand all that is said. You will be better off regardless of the outcome.

Reading between the Lines

One of the finer skills of listening is reading between the lines. As a therapist, I know this is an essential skill to have because, as I have mentioned earlier, human beings seem to have trouble expressing their vulnerabilities and insecurities. People tend to make "thought" statements rather than "feeling" statements, expecting the listener to derive the hidden meaning in what was said.

The method I adhere to for sifting through hidden meanings is a psychiatric rehabilitation skill dubbed *demonstrating understanding*. There are four levels of response to an individual's verbal communication:

(1) responding to thoughts
(2) responding to feelings
(3) responding to feelings and thoughts
(4) responding to personal meaning

Demonstrating understanding is a simple but effective model for showing the speaker that we are fully engaged in the listening process. Echo what an individual says in different words that might more accurately express what they are trying to communicate. For example, if your girlfriend tells you about an incident that happened at work, and she says, "That woman is so vindictive," you might respond to that *thought* with, "You think she did this to you on purpose?" She might then affirm your assessment by saying, "Yes! She does this all the time, and it is always directed at me. I'm so tired of the office politics." This is more of a *feeling* statement, to which you could respond, "It sounds like you're feeling really frustrated."

She might come back with, "Frustrated doesn't even begin to describe it. I can't believe this woman does what she does and gets away with it every day." Your response to this statement will want to reflect both her feelings and her thoughts: "You are angry because you do not think justice is being served." You might not be surprised then to hear her say, "That's it exactly! It just makes me so furious that she can carry on however she pleases, and the management just ignores her behavior. If they only followed policy, she would have been fired long ago."

This last statement indicates that the source of her anger is not only the behavior of the "accused" but also the apparent lack of concern on the part of the management. You might want to clarify this by asking about the *personal meaning*: "It sounds like you're disappointed in the management because they are not playing by the rules. I guess it makes you wonder where you stand at work if people make up the rules as they play the game."

She may well respond, "You've got that right. I go into work every day wondering what's going on and whether I should abide by policy or play her game. What applies for her might not apply for me, and I don't want to lose my job."

Do you see how this formula works? You *must* pay attention to be able to hear and formulate responses to what another person is saying. People do not typically make statements that start with "I feel [feeling word]." They tend to say, "I feel like" and then interject verb statements or thought statements. This encourages the speaker to identify and *own* their feelings and to acknowledge *why* it is they feel that way. Your role as the listener is to clarify and acknowledge, and perhaps even validate, the speaker's feelings.

Notice what does not happen in the above conversation. The listener does not say, "I know how that feels; the same thing happened to me." Nor does he say, "Well, you should just do this." The listener only *feeds back* what the speaker said. Try this the next time someone calls you and begins to vent about their hard day at work.

1) Respond to their thoughts: "You think that . . ."
2) Respond to their feelings: "You feel [use a feeling word]."
3) Respond to feelings and thoughts: "You feel [feeling word] because [describe the thought process informing the feeling]."
4) Respond to personal meaning: "You feel [feeling word] because you [personal significance]."

The Case of Jax

Jax called after seeing a television interview I did about *Anger Solutions*. "I need this," he declared. "I am twenty-four years old, and I have been in jail, on bail, or on probation since I was fourteen." Jax shared that he was estranged from his wife and child, jobless, homeless and couch surfing, and had just been released from a seventy-two-hour detox program. Jax had hit his rock bottom, and he was ready to do the work to create radical, positive, lasting change.

We met once a week to work through each of the key components of the program, and right about when he was ready to acquire listening skills, his wife called. She was sick, and there was no one to look after their child. Would he come over and assist? By this time, Jax had unlearned all the unhealthy beliefs he'd had about anger. He had learned to identify and express his emotions, and he had leveraged the pain of his aggressive anger style into shifting toward healthier choices. He had begun using TSA, and he was actively rehearsing his assertiveness skills. Was he ready to put everything he had learned to the test?

The suggestion I made to Jax was simple. The best apology is changed behavior: show, don't tell. The best way to show that he had changed would be to demonstrate the shift in his attitude and behavior and to reestablish connection with his wife through listening. We discussed this, and he practiced the skill of demonstrating understanding with me. Then he went off to support his wife.

The following week, Jax came for his session, and he was brimming with excitement. "We had the deepest conversation. I did what you suggested, and I just listened using the skills I learned. We felt so connected to each other! We talked for hours." With a voice tinged with gratitude, he told me that she was open to dating him again with a view to reconciliation if everything went well. Jax applied his listening skills, ensuring that his wife felt seen and heard, resulting in a deep sense of connection. Had he walked into the room, performed his *duty* as a father, and launched into a lengthy, one-sided lecture about all the reasons she should take him back, nothing would have changed. Jax got the results he wanted because he had experienced true transformation, and it was clear that his behavior could be believed.

By the way, over a decade has passed, and Jax has maintained his transformation, never returning to the aggressive, abusive person he was before he embraced the *Anger Solutions* model.

The House Always Wins

Every time we speak, we're gambling on our relationships. When we speak out of anger, the odds are always against us. There is a reason I harp on about TSA. Thinking objectively and critically about our lives is no longer an option; it is essential. With the way we are bombarded with visual, auditory, and digital stimulation all day long, much of it fake news and the rest of it filled with inflammatory and emotionally triggering content, we need to have complete mastery over our thought life.

It would be foolish to walk into a casino and bet your life savings on a single game of blackjack, especially if you have no idea how to play the game. It would be even more foolish to expect to win by repeating this strategy without improving your skill at the tables. Likewise, it makes no sense to continue giving the downstairs brain free rein, allowing it to remain reactionary and/or refusing to think before speaking or to actively listen with a view to solving problems and deepening connection.

Beating the house requires skill, attention to detail, an understanding of the strategies being used to keep you in the game, and a knowledge of when to call it a day. You must be willing to listen with the intent to understand, be fully centered on the person with whom you are dialoguing, and resist the urge to launch into a full-blown lecture. Once you've said your piece, relinquish the floor. Stop talking and open your eyes, your ears, and your heart. That's when the magic will happen.

Summary

Lectures and monologues hinder collaborative problem-solving. Engagement in true dialogue means we listen to our internal and external perceptions and read between the lines. Dialogue is a two-way process involving the giving and receiving of information.

Reflection

Consider the FRIEND formula for active listening. Are you a strong listener? Do you tend to interrupt because you are listening with the intent to reply rather than the intent to understand? Which changes could you make to your facial expressions, body language, and focus so that you can be a better listener?

Action Steps

Find the FRIEND formula and Demonstrating Understanding Cheat Sheets in your workbook. Practice the steps in demonstrating understanding with a friend. Document the results.

12

MAYBE SWEARING WILL HELP

GROWING UP IN a strict household, words like *stupid*, *crap*, and *frig* were frowned on. I mean, using them would get you a swat across the butt or worse. God forbid any of us should escalate to the entry-level swear words, much less graduate to the truly profane. In my therapy space, I leave my conservative mom self at home. When my clients enter that safe, secure space, if they need to let fly, I generally give them the space to say what needs to be said. Swearing is a form of catharsis, and under the right conditions, it helps.

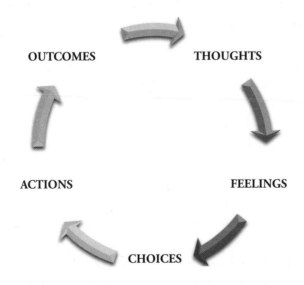

Do you remember the thought matrix? To recap, thoughts inform feelings, which then inform choices and actions. When we focus too heavily on our emotional state and the discomfort it brings, instinct will drive us to fix the feeling. This is where releasing residual anger comes in. The simple chart above demonstrates the requisite nature of looking forward to desired outcomes rather than finding a quick fix. When you focus only on fixing your feelings, you may feel a temporary sense of satisfaction; however, the problem that generated the uncomfortable feeling will remain unresolved. You will soon find yourself in a pattern of repeating behaviors that only provide a short-term gain but contribute to long-term pain.

Think of the choice matrix to which you were introduced earlier. The goal should always be to choose an informed response that leads to long-term gain, even if that response feels uncomfortable or painful in the short term. Releasing residual anger, or intentional catharsis, is about releasing the emotional energy that is left behind—the *residual* energy—after you have done all you can to resolve the anger-inciting problem.

Pain and Potty Mouth

Earlier we established that pain can be widely defined as a noxious or an undesirable emotional or physical response to a negative stimulus like touching a hot stove or being called a mean name. Research substantiates that swearing when one is in pain mitigates the severity of the pain experience— at least for those who don't swear on the regular. For those who only swear in extreme situations, swearing in response to pain proves to be up to four times more useful than it is for people who swear all the time.

The first group of subjects consisted of young adults who swear less than ten times per day. The second group swore upward of forty times a day or more. All seventy-one subjects were asked to submerge their hands into ice-cold water and hold the position for as long as possible. First, they were asked to keep their hands submerged while saying non-offensive words like *fudge* or *oh, my stars* and then again while vocalizing their choice epithet. The subjects who swear less often were able to withstand the icy water while swearing for up to forty-five seconds longer than when they used PG language. The folks with frequent potty mouths were only able to endure the cold for ten seconds longer compared with when they held back on swearing.

The results indicate that swearing can release endorphins, the body's natural painkillers. Swearing appears to instigate an emotional response to stress like the flight-or-fight response that is triggered in the downstairs brain. Somehow, swearing "nullifies the link between fear of pain and pain perception"[1] but only for those who do not overdo it with their day-to-day use of profanity.

What Is Catharsis?

When you think of catharsis, what comes to mind? Catharsis is defined by Oxford Languages as *"the process of releasing, and thereby providing relief from, strong or repressed emotions."*[2] One might think of catharsis in the context of punching a wall, driving a car erratically, primal screaming, grappling, boxing, or swearing. There are countless ways to engage catharsis to release residual anger or other uncomfortable emotions. Some more creative ways include writing in a journal, creative writing, playing a musical instrument, dancing, or stargazing. These could be seen as effective, intentional cathartic tools *if used correctly.*

Here is what we know for sure about catharsis. Whether it is punching a heavy bag, primal screaming, grappling, boxing, jamming out on your guitar or drum set, or swearing, as the recent research indicates, *none of these tools will be effective* if you have not yet identified and attempted to resolve the problem contributing to the emotion. If you only use the behavioral aspect of catharsis without addressing the underlying problem, it simply will become yet another quick fix for your feelings, and you will most likely feel angrier when you're done.

Remember that negative conductor behaviors can be detrimental to your physical and/or mental health. Activities like smoking, drinking, using banned substances, working overtime to avoid problems at home, self-harming behaviors, risk-taking, or thrill seeking are all forms of cathartic behaviors designed to release or provide relief from strong/repressed emotions, but they are negative conductors. The challenge with these behaviors is that they may provide short-term pleasure, but they contribute to long-term pain. Incidentally, that is what makes these types of behaviors difficult to quit—because the pain is deferred, we are less inclined to take the steps to deal with the pain fully to make more lasting change. The key to effective conducting is to:

1. Identify and address the problem and seek to resolve it.
2. Use healthy cathartic tools to expel or release any residual emotional energy.

Strategies for Effective Catharsis

Physical activity is an ideal strategy to apply when seeking to release residual anger *after* you have done what you can to resolve the underlying cause of the anger. You may spend time in a gym, whether that is circuit training, weight training, freshening up on defensive tactics, performing martial arts, or punching a heavy bag or a speed bag. Others cycle, run, or swim; some may prefer yoga, canoeing or kayaking, fishing, hunting, or other outdoor activities. Any of these strategies and many others not listed here would be appropriate ways to expel unwanted energy.

When in doubt, check the nature of the activity against the choice matrix. Does the activity feel good now? Is it good for you? Will you feel good later? Will you be healthier in the long term by choosing this activity? Your best choice will most often deliver short-term pleasure and long-term gain.

In traditional anger management, the preferred form of catharsis is to take a deep breath, count to ten, and walk away. Follow up that immediate response with some form of energetic release, and you should be fine. Of course, we now understand that doing these things alone without attempting to resolve the problem that ignited the anger in the first place means the anger is likely to return—and with greater intensity each time. The truth is you must talk things through and then release what's left in angry energy.

Whereas *thinking without acting* (the more passive anger response) leads to mental and physical health problems, *acting without thinking* (the more aggressive anger response) creates its own kind of negative consequences, especially for those who swear with more frequency daily. Yes, swearing might help but not as much as if you kept the potty mouth at bay most of the time. Swearing also becomes a problem if it presents as verbal aggression or verbal abuse toward others. If swearing is a tool for releasing negative energy to cope with intense emotional or physical pain, okay, but directing abuse at others is never a good idea.

Catharsis for Healing

My client had experienced a great deal of loss in her young life and was emotionally unprepared for the effects of those losses on her psyche. As part of the grieving process, she experienced anger for the losses but had never examined the anger nor come to terms with it. Now she understood that she was angry, and she understood *why* she was angry. She simply had no idea *what to do* about it.

Due to the circumstances in my client's life before she came to me, she admitted that her self-esteem was very low. She divulged that she had created for herself a hard exterior and that she found it hard to cry. She further admitted that the only time she found herself able to cry was when someone paid her a compliment. She engaged in behaviors that bordered on being self-abusive and frequently found herself entangled in relationships that were either illicit or otherwise unhealthy. Clearly, her anger was turning inward as she had no means for expressing her feelings to those who had hurt her.

For this young lady, releasing her residual anger was paramount to her having the ability to move on and to desist from repeating the negative patterns she was establishing in her life. Once she found and established healthier ways to release the negative energy of residual anger and developed communication skills that helped her to express herself more assertively, she was able to make better quality decisions and to break the habits that were contributing to, rather than decreasing, her pain.

One of the first things I established with my client was that she write things down. She frequently had vivid dreams, which often held some sort of personal significance. I encouraged her to describe these dreams as fully as she could in writing before she forgot the important details. We reviewed the dreams together; sometimes she would draw the images she saw in her dreams, and we discussed the colors, shapes, and faces. What significance did those colors hold for her? Who did she believe those faces to represent? Much of the anger she felt at her losses was exhibited in her dreams. If we cannot express ourselves consciously, often our subconscious mind works overtime at attempting to show us where our difficulties lie. Even when hurts are not fresh, open, or bleeding wounds, they still exist. Those hurts must find an outlet—dreams are as good a vehicle of expression as any other.

I had my client write about how she experienced the initial losses. Many of her hurts were compounded on by those losses that followed, so she had much for which to grieve over a short period of time. The writing process takes thought, intellectual examination, and the ability to organize events and effectively describe those events through the written word. This all takes *time*. Time is what my client desperately needed to experience each painful event as a single entity rather than as part of the unmanageable whole.

As she wrote about each event, she was able to grieve for that single occurrence, to put it in perspective, and to let it go. Often, as she wrote, she was able to draw conclusions, to see the situation through the eyes of others involved, which she had been unable to do previously. She also found it easier to cry as she relived the memories both in her mind and on paper. In fact, as she went through the process of describing her life in writing, there was a period in which she cried for days. In her words, it was as though she had experienced a "cleansing" of her memories. Those open and festering wounds from her past finally began to heal.

Expressive Writing *(Suggested length of activity: 10-15 minutes daily)*

As it did for my client, expressive writing may help you find meaning and resolution of traumatic experiences, past hurts, or current stressors. Many of my clients are first responders, retired military, lawyers, doctors, nurses, or even paralegals, who are regularly exposed to traumatic content either directly or indirectly. There must be a way to release the residual anger that results from answering call after call, reading victim statements, typing up eyewitness testimony, or sewing up stab wounds in the emergency department. After being exposed to events with truly tragic outcomes and feeling the sense of helplessness, frustration, and anger that accompanies those calls, people need an outlet. Through the writing process, you may find that your emotional reactions to the trauma become more manageable, and you might be less disturbed by uninvited ruminations.

Expressive writing is not a quick fix. Be aware that the benefits of expressive writing only emerge over time. In fact, as is true for any type of cathartic exercise, directly after expressing, participants typically report feeling worse and are more physiologically aroused. You should plan and prepare for some time to engage in a physical activity like walking, running, or working out after a session of expressive writing. Here are some things to consider if you decide to try this exercise.

- Write about the *emotional* aspects of an event rather than the *factual* aspects.
- Remember that the goal of writing is not to find a culprit or to punish yourself. The idea is to connect to one's feelings and thoughts and write them down with the intention to express what is happening emotionally and to better understand what is going on. When feelings stay locked up, they can have detrimental effects on well-being in the long run.
- Talking about difficult emotions in an open forum (e.g., group therapy, with a therapist, or with coworkers) is challenging as this action often runs counter to the workplace culture, contributing to feelings of embarrassment and vulnerability. Expressive writing can be a powerful way for you to free your emotions in a non-threatening way.
- Take care in the storage of your writings at home. Many clients are hesitant to write for fear of others discovering and reading their journals. Feel free to dispose of your writings after you have written the day's entry. No one need ever see what you have written. The process of self-expression is beneficial even if the text is immediately destroyed.
- Typically, this exercise is done in four consecutive days. However, you may wish to proceed for a longer period. In any case, it is important to reflect on the experience. You can reflect privately or with someone you trust.
- Be careful that writing does not turn into another form of rumination. If you have not found the task helpful after three writing sessions, try something else.

Creative Writing

Much like the previous exercise, spending some time writing creatively may prove a wonderful way to express and resolve "unsolvable" problems and the emotions that accompany them. By fictionalizing the experience, you can separate yourself from the emotional responses, assigning them to your fictional characters rather than yourself. Creative writing allows you the opportunity to view and examine the problems or the anger-inducing situation through a different lens and may prove an effective tool for gaining insight, resolution of your emotional state, and relief from the repression of those uncomfortable emotions.

Relationship Strategies

Remember the question about lifetime value. When the problem or anger-inducing situation involves someone you care about, your approach to problem-solving may shift. Likewise, the ways in which you release the residual negative energy from those encounters may also need to be adapted to suit the situation. In occurrences where there is a lifetime value associated with the relationship challenges, you must apply TSA and use your assertiveness skills to the best of your ability.

You may be working on resolving a relationship problem and finding that doing so is a bit of a process. Not all problems can be solved in one fell swoop. The love letter is a tool I use often. I learned this strategy from Jack Canfield way back in the day from his program *Self-Esteem and Peak Performance*. It helps me to process my feelings so it is easier to talk about them when I feel ready to do so. Sometimes, I even rewrite the letter several times until it is fit to share with the other party. Using the letter ensures my true feelings are expressed, that the real problem is identified with clarity, and that my ideas for how we can solve the problem are outlined without any pesky emotional, accusatory, or hurtful language getting in the way.

This process helps you to come to terms with exactly why you are feeling angry and helps you take responsibility for your part in the problem. There is no expectation that you would deliver this letter to the person to whom it is addressed; it simply serves as a tool to help you clarify your thoughts and feelings about the problem so you can better express yourself when you're ready to talk about it.

The love letter consists of sharing your feelings using this template.

- Anger—How angry are you? Why?
- Hurt—What about the situation hurt you?
- Fear—What were you afraid of? What are you still afraid of?
- Sorry For—Are you a total victim? How did you contribute to the situation?

- Forgiveness—Please forgive me. I forgive you.
- What's Next?—What do you need moving forward to make the relationship better?

In chapter 15, Taking Response-ability, you will see an example of what the love letter looks like in the context of a failed relationship.

Gestalt: The Empty Chair

When addressing the target of your anger is not safe or appropriate, or the source of your anger has died or moved away, sometimes engaging with an imaginary version of that person can help to resolve residual feelings. There is much evidence that the brain doesn't know the difference between real and imagined; this means that even an exercise in imaginal exposure may have similar benefits to being there in actuality.

In group sessions as well as in private therapy, I often call on a gestalt exercise in imaginal exposure dubbed "The Empty Chair." It offers people an opportunity to express themselves and release their painful memories, directing them to the person who perpetrated the harm but in a safe, protected space.

Imagine yourself in a safe space of your own design and making. Close that space in with four windowless walls and one door. The room is empty except for you and an empty chair. Imagine the person who caused you harm or who contributes to your problem is standing outside that door. You have complete control in this space; nothing can harm you here. When you are ready, give that person access to your safe space and set them in the empty chair. Remember that nothing can harm you, but you may feel better imagining them with their hands and feet secured and their mouth and eyes covered.

When you feel safe to continue, you can take a minute or three to tell them everything you have kept pent up inside. There is no need to adhere to TSA here—this is catharsis, remember? And sometimes swearing helps. So let it fly. All of it. Once you have released all that yuckiness, take a deep breath, hold it, and let it go. Do that again. Release the person from the chair and give them permission to go. Take a few more cleansing breaths. Release them. Release the pain. Release the hurt. Release the person. Let it all go.

I know it is hard to do this exercise while you are reading, so I have made the audio version of this exercise available to you on the reader's-only section of my website. Visit the resource section on the website which will take you to the resource section on my website, which includes the Releasing Residual Anger audio exercise. To prepare for participating in this exercise, I recommend you find a comfortable place to sit or lie down, someplace that is quiet and where you can go through the whole exercise undisturbed. You may want to put on headphones so you are not distracted. The first audio file will provide you a very brief overview of the *Anger Solutions* model. The second audio file will take you through the exercise itself. Do this as often as needed. Be sure to have some tissues handy!

Cry It Out

We're all familiar with the clichés.

> Big boys don't cry.
> Real men don't cry.
> Crying means you're weak.
> Pull up your big-girl panties.

If we are to be completely honest, we might also admit these clichés are just pithy statements with no basis in science or fact that serve to shame us for experiencing or expressing our emotions. The truth is that *crying is good for you*. Research reveals eight benefits of shedding a few tears: crying has a soothing effect, helps people to calm down, reduces their distress levels, and self-regulates through activation of the parasympathetic nervous system, which aids in relaxation. People who cry attract others who can offer support. Crying releases endorphins, which support pain relief. Crying jags release oxytocin along with endorphins, which is why we often feel better after shedding a few tears. Toxins are released, and stress is relieved when we cry. A good cry often results in a good night's sleep. Crying helps to kill bacteria and keeps the eyes clean. Finally, crying may help to improve vision by keeping eye membranes moist. That settles it: when in doubt, cry it out.

After any of these exercises, particularly the physical or behavioral ones, it is paramount that you cool down just as you would after a physical workout. This is the time that you can take to empty your mind of the negative thoughts, just as you have emptied your body of the negative energy of your anger. Deep breathing and allowing some time for quiet meditation will help you bring a complete balance to catharsis. The cooling-down period is imperative for successfully re-attaining your baseline for stress.

The Power of Ritual

Rituals are a wonderful strategy to help release emotions such as unresolved grief, guilt, or anger, particularly when they are associated with those "unsolvable" problems that can cause vicarious trauma (trauma that occurs by listening to, seeing, or hearing about trauma experienced by another person). For example, first responders who have been called to a situation where vital signs are absent, a motor vehicle collision resulting in death, or even a domestic abuse call know these kinds of calls can stay with them long after their shift is over—for hours, days, or even years. Taking part in existing rituals or creating one's own could be helpful in expressing and releasing the emotions associated with these events. Here are a few examples:

- Go to a local church and light a candle for the victim(s).
- Write a poem or a letter to the victim.
- Make a memory vault, where you can store your letter, poem, expressive writing, or creative writings.
- Take something that is a poignant reminder of the situation and bury it. Hold a ceremony (e.g., speak some words over the spot where it is buried, leave a marker, send off a floating candle on a body of water, light a sky lantern) to commemorate the release of the situation and the associated emotions.

Nothing a Little Massage Therapy Can't Fix

Many of my clients and close friends have a benefits plan through their workplace that includes between three hundred and ten thousand dollars per year for paramedical services, including massage therapy. It amazes me how many are aware of this service but do not take advantage of it. Massage therapy is one of the best ways I know to reduce stress and keep its physiological effects from ravaging one's body. When I began receiving massage therapy in the mid-1990s, I sneaked a peek at my chart while the therapist was out of the room. The statement that struck me most was this: "*Walks stiff.*" The muscles in my back were so knotted and tight that I walked on a tilt to accommodate the spasming and pain I experienced. I had become so accustomed to the pain and tension in my body that I had simply adjusted for it.

My first massage session felt like some form of ancient torture. I was certain my entire back was black and blue. It hurt so much that I could not sit back against a chair for a couple of days. Not long after, though, I found that the spring was back in my step. I learned to relax *through* the therapies and eventually just fell asleep as soon as the therapist started. It was money well spent by my benefit plan! Massage therapy calms the nervous system and releases both superficial and deep muscle tension. Toxins are also released from soft tissue during massage, which is an added benefit.

Some of the tools used to work the stiff muscles in arthritic hands are also quite effective for releasing tension from tight shoulder and neck muscles. This is due to the "ripple" effect of flexing and unflexing your hands with resistance—the muscles will become tense all the way up your arm and into your shoulder and neck. As you release the stress ball or any other such device, you will feel the tension flowing out of your shoulders and arms, down into the ball. These types of exercises are wonderful because they can be done anywhere and unobtrusively. Just think of the uses for these little silent partners: driving in rush-hour traffic, while attending those tense staff meetings, waiting for your doctor's appointment to start. The joy of these little tools is that they do the job without high levels of exertion. Doing these muscle-relaxing exercises will not attract attention, nor will they disrupt anything going on around you.

It has been known for years that certain scents can stimulate pleasure and relaxation, lessen stress, or activate other areas of the brain associated with visual or declarative memory. The smell of apple pie reminds most people of happy days, grandmothers, Christmas dinners, and all that wonderful stuff. It sends a subconscious message to the brain that this is a homey, happy environment in which to live or work. It is the number-one scent to have permeating a home one is trying to sell.

Research supports the use of essential oils as an aide to healing or reducing physical and psychological symptoms. Studies have shown that the scent of orange oil significantly reduces anxiety in males. Some oils like oil of oregano and eucalyptus or tea tree oil have great efficacy as anti-fungals in the treatment of athlete's foot or thrush. Others are indicated for pain management such as peppermint, menthol, wintergreen, and blue tansy, and they work wonders on aching, spastic muscles. Lavender and lily of the valley are often used for relaxation and sleep. Oils with antioxidant properties may help to defer or prevent the onset of disease. Long before the advent of modern Western medicine, essential oils were used to promote good health and manage symptoms. Something as simple as diffusing the right blend of essential oils in your home or office may help to reduce your stress or anxiety symptoms associated with the presenting problem.

When the Time for Confrontation Has Passed

You feel angry for no reason, and you lash out at people around you. You are irritable and easily bothered. You turn your anger inward. Your eating habits change. You knowingly do little things that are self-destructive, but you just don't seem to care anymore. You really don't know *why* you feel angry, but it's there, and because there's no reason for it, you just stuff it inside, and you start having physical health problems like ulcers, irritable bowel, spastic colon, insomnia, or migraines. Can these techniques we've discussed help you in situations like these?

One of my former clients had been sexually abused by her grandfather. By the time I started working with her, he had already passed away, leaving her with scarred memories that long outlived her painful childhood. She was prone to self-abuse and would do just about anything to cause herself pain. She pierced her own nose with a safety pin sterilized by the flame from her cigarette lighter. It hurt her so much that she almost lost consciousness. As soon as she could get some money together, she started getting tattoos. She had slashed her wrists several times and bore the scars to prove it.

This young woman desperately needed an outlet for her anger, but the source of her emotional pain was dead. In her mind, it was unfair for her to project her anger onto the innocents in her life, and of course, she must have been to blame for the abuse anyway—that's what he had always told her. She deserved it. So she directed her anger inward, abusing her body with physical mutilation and substance use and tormenting her mind with deprecating, shame-inducing self-talk. Releasing her anger through alternative means wasn't just an option for my client. She had to find a way to do it or risk being unable to progress in other areas of her therapy and rehabilitation. Along with the rehabilitative support services she received, she was also enrolled in an intensive sexual assault survivor's group that required discontinuation of her medications. The group felt that usage of medications to dampen her emotions would only hinder the healing process. She needed to be able to *feel* to *heal.*

My role in this process was simply to help her find ways to cope with the intensity of her feelings. Anger was the most intense emotion that my client experienced. She hated the man for what he had done and resented him for dying before he received fair punishment. The angrier she became, the more she turned on herself.

To break the cycle of lasting self-abuse and do it quickly, she needed an alternative. We introduced rubber bands to satisfy the compulsion to induce pain by cutting her wrists. Instead of slashing, she could simply snap the band, thereby satisfying the urge without risking her life or creating fresh wounds. I encouraged her, as I had my other clients, to write in her journal so she could take more time to get in touch with her emotions as opposed to just reacting to them.

Finally, I involved her in the empty chair exercise, in which she visualized her grandfather and spoke out loud about all the things that she felt inside—the pain, hurt, loss, shame, and regret. She told him how much she had loved him and how she hated him now. She told him about her life and how it had been irrevocably changed.

Then something shifted. She began to describe to him what a strong person she was and how she had survived. He would not, could not, hurt her anymore. No one would ever hurt her like that again. Somewhere amid expressing her pain to a visualized image of her grandfather, my client experienced a pivotal shift in her consciousness. She crossed the line from "victim" to "survivor."

Just because the person who caused you pain has died doesn't mean you must be left holding the bag. Just because the time for confrontation has passed doesn't mean you must carry that anger with you everywhere you go. You *can* find a way to let the hurts of the past go if you look hard enough.

The key to releasing residual anger is to find a tool or a style of release that best suits you and fits your budget. Not everyone wants a one-year membership at the gym, and not everyone can afford it. Some folks will be happy with long walks on the beach or writing letters they can burn or dispose of later. Others may need a bit of both: a punching bag in the basement and a trusty journal. Make a commitment to yourself that you will at least explore the possibilities and see where they take you.

Remember that when we are experiencing fight or flight, our hearts beat faster, our blood pressure increases, the flow of oxygen is diverted from our extremities to our major organs, and the upstairs brain takes a hike. Often, resolving an anger-inducing issue through talking or problem-solving is not enough to bring our bodies back to our stress baseline. If we allow ourselves to remain in a state of heightened awareness, we put our bodies at risk for high blood pressure, high cholesterol, heart problems, and a multitude of other physical ailments—thus, the value of releasing residual anger. Do not wait until residual anger rises to a crescendo before doing something about it. It is much more sensible to be proactive than reactive when dealing with anger. If you know you have some unresolved issues, it is better to plan to ensure that when they surface, you won't do something you'll regret.

Summary

Sometimes swearing, a form of catharsis, helps to reduce the physical and emotional pain experience. Swearing about a situation is different than hurling verbal abuse at a person.

Catharsis can be used in the *Anger Solutions* process to expel or release any residual emotional energy. Residual anger can be released through catharsis using physical, emotional, ritualistic, or creative forms of expression. Without effective verbal processing of the problem, catharsis may prove less effective.

Reflection

Have you ever felt like you would just explode if you didn't find an outlet for your emotions or your pain? What did you do to find relief?

Action Step

Go to the website to access the ***Anger Solutions Releasing Residual Anger*** audio recording. Document or journal your experience of releasing your emotions using the empty chair technique.

13

LET IT GO

MY CLIENT HAD reached maximum recovery. There was *no way* she was ever going back to work. Her injuries were too severe, the trauma too deep, the impairments too far gone for her to return to full-time employment.

Out of the blue, she reached out for an appointment. She told me how she had been talking with her ex, who had been abusive throughout their marriage. He had turned his life around and apologized for the way he treated her while they were together. She told me that she forgave him for all the harm he had caused her, and when she did, a funny thing happened. All her pain went away. She regained a lost range of motion in her head and neck. Her memory impairments decreased. Her depression lifted. And she was returning to work full time. No gradual return to work was necessary.

I was flabbergasted, even though I am well acquainted with the power of forgiveness to heal physical and emotional hurts. When she learned to forgive and to let go of her past hurts, her body released the disease that prevented her from functioning at her peak potential.

In 2002, while writing the original *Anger Solutions* manuscript, I watched a portion of a television program in which Dr. Everett Worthington told the story about how he'd lost his mother. He recalled that his mother was asleep in bed when two young offenders broke into her house and began stealing its contents. From what police could reconstruct of the crime, it appeared that the woman woke up and confronted the thieves. One of them used a crowbar to bludgeon the poor elderly woman to death. When the police arrived on the scene, every item in the house with a reflecting surface had been smashed.

Worthington went on to tell of how he was filled with rage and hatred for the perpetrator of this heinous crime. He found that as he held on to his grief and anger, bitterness took root in his heart; it began to wither and shrivel, and he stopped growing. It was as though the weed of bitterness choked away whatever life he had inside and left him an angry shell of his former self. He recognized that he had to learn to forgive this youth for what he had done, or else his crime would claim yet another victim.

The turning point for Worthington happened when he placed himself in the shoes of the young man who killed his mother. Using the notes of the crime reconstructors, he imagined himself as a seventeen-year-old boy breaking into a house on New Year's Eve, believing no one would be home. He retraced the steps of the young man, climbing through the jimmied window, wandering in the darkness around the living areas of the house, and looking for good stuff to lift.

Then he imagined his alarm and shock at being caught in the act by an elderly woman who was brave enough to confront them. Worthington said that while envisioning the whole encounter, he could feel the sense of panic that the young man must have been overcome with. He could see the natural response in that intense state of fight or flight—he was still holding the crowbar, and it made sense to hit the old lady before she could get to the phone and call 911.

He could feel the confusion and the terror of the young man as he realized he had hit her one time too many and that she was soon to die. Finally, the teenager came to the knowledge that he was to blame for the death of another human being. As he was confronted by the consequences of his actions, he looked up into a hallway mirror and could not bear to see his own reflection—for in the glass, he saw the face of a monster that had once been a boy. So he smashed it—smashed everything that reflected that awful, terrible image of a boy killer.

In tears, Worthington then recounted the point at which his empathy enabled him to feel that young man's guilt and suffering for his crime. Empathy was the catalyst that enabled him to forgive.

One of my clients, a quiet, young, single mother of two small children, told me something that truly struck me. She said, "I carry my anger with me everywhere. I don't want to let go of it. It has been with me so long; it is like a friend to me." Anger was indeed her friend. It was the source from which she garnered strength to fight for what was important to her. She used her anger as her stabilizer because she did not believe she had the strength to stand on her own without it.

The problem with making anger your friend is that, like it did for Everett Worthington, bitterness takes over. My client struggled in relationships and made friends with people whom she knew would take advantage of her. She allowed herself to return to abusive situations because it fed her anger. She pushed away those who would show her real love and compassion because it was easier to do it herself than to suffer the loss at their hands later. Bitterness colored her view of life, love, and all those other mysteries. Although she longed to be loved and to love her children, that kind of unconditional love eluded her because she continued to nurture her anger.

The sad truth is that many of us don't want to forgive others because we think that forgiveness somehow means we condone what was done to us. People think those who forgive are weak and that forgiveness is a sign of giving in: "*If I forgive, then I must forget; at least that is how the old saying goes. And I don't want to forget. If I forget, I leave myself open to being hurt in the same way once again.*"

To see the ability to forgive as a sign of weakness is to deprive oneself of a world of freedom. In all reality, it takes courage, strength, and a willing heart to forgive others. I have alluded to bitterness as an uncontrollable weed. If left untended, it will continue to grow and wind around all the chambers of one's heart until the heart finally dies for lack of room to grow. To experience true forgiveness—either as the giver or the recipient—is to find real liberation.

I Remember You

In her book *Picking Cotton*, Jennifer Thompson tells the harrowing story of being raped in her apartment by an armed Black male who threatened to kill her if she cried out for help. During her ordeal, she did what she could to memorize his features so she could pick him out of a lineup should she survive. She committed everything to memory—his face, his clothing, even his shoes.

When she called the police and described her attacker, the police sketch artist rendered a drawing. Based on that drawing, they brought in Ron Cotton, a nineteen-year-old man, for the lineup. They questioned him, and his alibi didn't hold up. He matched the description she had provided the police, right down to the shoes. Ron Cotton walked into the police station a free man. He never left. Charged with rape and sexual assault with a weapon, Cotton was remanded until his trial. When Thompson was asked if she recognized the man who brutalized her, she pointed straight to Cotton. But she was wrong.

The Misinformation Effect

How did Jennifer Thompson get it wrong? Elizabeth Loftus, a leading expert in memory and eyewitness testimony, researched the phenomenon of faulty memory, and here is what she found. Memory is elastic, not static. Memories do not play back like a video; rather, memory is malleable, it changes and shifts, and it may be easily influenced by suggestion, leading questions, or positive reinforcement.

Loftus noted that when research subjects were shown video of motor vehicle collisions, their memories of what they witnessed were altered by leading questions such as "Did you *see* the broken headlight?" or "How fast were the vehicles moving when they *smashed* into each other?" Questions like the first resulted in a higher number of people recalling nonexistent objects such as broken glass. Questions like the second, with an emphasis on the word *smashed*, resulted in higher estimations of speed than provided by those who were not asked leading questions. Other research has shown that young children desire to be pleasing to adults, causing them to be highly susceptible to suggestion, resulting in them providing the answers they *think* the adults want to hear rather than the truth.

Loftus conducted an experiment in which people were asked if they had ever been to Disney. Some of those who replied in the affirmative were then asked to review an advertisement for Disney and to comment on the design and content of the ad, which, incidentally, featured a graphic of the Warner Bros. character Bugs Bunny. Later, when people were asked to recall their Disney experience, they were asked which characters they saw. Many recalled seeing Bugs Bunny at Disney, even though as a WB character, that was an impossibility. Loftus successfully proved how easily memory can be altered. This phenomenon is called *the misinformation effect*.

All my life, I replayed a narrative in my head about my father's absence from the milestone events in my life. As a first-generation immigrant to

Canada, my dad had to work triply hard to make ends meet and to give us the lifestyle similar to what we once had in our native Jamaica. For him, that meant having to choose between attending school functions or special events and collecting a paycheck. Still, I felt his absence at my track-and-field events, eighth-grade graduation, and other key events. He didn't miss them *all*, mind you, but it *felt* like he was more absent than present. I rehearsed that narrative until I believed it.

Every so often, I would pull out that story when I wanted to feel sorry for myself or I was missing my dad. One day, I was bemoaning my father's absence from all my big life events when my husband, to whom I have been connected since the age of sixteen, argued, "Your dad was at your high-school graduation." We debated this for longer than was necessary until he stated emphatically, "Julie. Your dad was there. I remember we went to Wendy's afterward, and you spilled Diet Coke all over him at the restaurant."

Suddenly, the memory of the spilled drink came flooding back. Many years later, I came across photographic proof of my father's presence at my graduation on my class of '87 social media page. How could I have forgotten? How much unnecessary bitterness had I harbored against my father because of a damaged memory?

The Role of Memory in Forgiveness

Flaws in memory have many contributors. There are three key functions of memory: the first is *attending*. We must pay attention to something and make sense of it before we can choose to store it in our memory. Some things we see or hear are just fleeting. We notice them, but they are meaningless; therefore, we do not choose to store the memory. The second function is *encoding* or storage. We choose to file what we have attended to, and if we store it well, it makes the third function of *retrieval* that much easier. If something goes awry in the attending stage, the meaning of what we have perceived could be skewed, or we may have poor recall. If we are distracted during the encoding stage, we may have trouble retrieving the memory later. If we feed ourselves a narrative that is contradictory to the memory, or we leave ourselves open to suggestion, or we allow others to superimpose a meaning that is different from the one we assigned, the memory will have shifted and altered at the point of retrieval.

This was the case for Jennifer Thompson. When she was brought in to identify Cotton in a lineup, she felt compelled to give *a correct answer*. When she identified Cotton in the lineup, she was rewarded with confirmation from the investigator that he was the same person she had seen in a photo lineup. All along, she had been picking Cotton, but he was never the culprit; rather, he was the victim of a false memory that had been reinforced multiple times. For this, he spent eleven years in jail for a crime he did not commit until he was exonerated by DNA evidence.

Pay Attention

Have you noticed that one of the common threads in most crime shows is the part where the detective declares they are certain they know who the perpetrator is? They latch on to a hunch or a couple of pieces of evidence, and they apply faulty heuristics to arrive at the conclusion, "They did it!" Once they are convinced of that so-called truth, they ignore any evidence that does not inform the narrative of guilt for their preferred suspect. This is a form of *inattentional blindness*.

What also happens in several of my favorite crime serials is the phenomenon of *change blindness*. Several shows and films capitalize on this failure of inattention. Think of any high-stakes heist movie in which sleight of hand or quick switches are involved, and you will see the exploitation of change blindness at work.

Both inattentional blindness and change blindness are malfunctions of visual awareness or the first task of memory: attending. While change blindness is a function of the failure or inability to notice an evident change, inattentional blindness occurs when one does not notice the existence of an unexpected stimulus. In each case, once we are made aware of the existence of the stimulus, it becomes clearly visible.

Have you heard of or seen the experiment of the dancing gorilla? This famous experiment encourages observers to count the number of times a basketball is passed from one player to another. While onlookers are focused on watching the passes, a person wearing a gorilla costume dances through the crowd. Nearly 40 percent of viewers failed to see the gorilla pass through the players. Once they were alerted to the presence of the gorilla, everyone saw it with ease. This is inattentional blindness at work.

I use exercises like this in my seminars. I encourage people to practice their listening skills and to become fully centered in the process. While they are engaged in conversation, I wander the room, stacking glasses and markers and moving things around. I have even changed my suit jacket to a sweater. No one notices until I draw their attention to it. In another exercise that often shows up in therapy, I encourage folks to look around the room and find all the things that are, say, green. When they have noted all the green things in the room, I ask them to close their eyes and see all the green things, but then I ask them to recall everything that is red. For most, this is a daunting task. You see, when we are focused too carefully on one thing, we become blind to all the stimuli we deem irrelevant.

These flaws in visual awareness and attending contribute to faulty heuristics, which in turn inform sustained blindness. When you hold rigid expectations that things should be a certain way, you will often miss it when they change. Change blindness is simply another mental set that takes the joy out of subtle shifts in language, tone, or behavior. This was the mental set that, when combined with my distorted memory of my father's absence from my significant life events, caused me to miss out on the memory of his presence at my graduation. This mental set reinforced feelings of unworthiness, rejection, and low self-esteem that were unfounded at their base.

Jennifer Thompson's memories of the night she was violated became irrevocably linked to Ron Cotton's face. She nursed a healthy grudge, praying that he, too, would be violated and that he would die in prison. With her traumatic somatic memories tied to a face and a name, she had a target at which she could laser focus her anger. Even when the real rapist was found and presented in court, Jennifer's memories of Ron Cotton's face were so entrenched that not only did she not recognize the rapist, Bobby Poole, but she felt even more anger at the defense for trying to claim she had identified the wrong man. When DNA evidence was finally presented that proved Cotton's innocence and Poole's guilt, Thompson was devastated. All that righteous anger went flying out the window when she realized her faulty memories had stolen eleven years from an innocent man.

Forgiveness Is a Choice

The story of Jennifer Thompson and Ron Cotton took a major turn when she asked to meet with him after his exoneration. Crumbling under the weight of remorse for having put him in prison, she begged him for forgiveness. Three simple words changed the direction of the narrative for both Jennifer and Ron: *I forgive you.*

I think of how my client's forgiveness set her body and mind free to heal and enabled her to return to the job she loved. I think of how much healthier my relationship with my father is now that I have let go of the thoughts and feelings I had about his interest—or lack of it—in my accomplishments. I think of the redemption, healing, and restoration that took place on the day Ron Cotton chose to forgive his accuser. I think of the wealth of knowledge we have about forgiveness today because of Everett Worthington's lived experience.

The Campaign for Forgiveness Research was Worthington's project, facilitating over seven million dollars of funding for research on forgiveness. The key findings about forgiveness were astonishing. In Worthington's words, "Emotional forgiveness occurs through the emotional replacement of negative unforgiving emotions with positive other-oriented emotions like empathy, sympathy, compassion, or love for the offender."[1] Let me break that down for you. Choosing to forgive has several measurable health benefits.

1. Reduce the risk of cardiovascular disease: Positive emotions—usually associated with forgiveness—reduce the hostility and negative stress a person feels, which in turn reduces that person's risk of heart problems.
2. Boost the immune system: Chronic stress has also been found to weaken the immune system, so reducing stress through forgiveness can give your immune system a boost.
3. Better relationships: People who forgive are also more likely to have stable romantic and platonic relationships.
4. Live longer: Studies have found that people with large social circles and support systems seem to be healthier, live longer, and recover more quickly from illness than their lonelier peers.

Following on the heels of Worthington's project came the Stanford Forgiveness Project, one of the foremost research projects dedicated to understanding the benefits of forgiveness. A 2005 study demonstrated that forgiveness is something we can learn to do, and by "practicing" forgiveness, we may increase our feelings of forgiveness toward those who have offended us. Furthermore, practicing forgiveness helps us to decrease hurt and angry feelings and will also decrease feelings of malice and estrangement. Treatment group participants also saw significant decreases in the symptoms of stress. A 2006 study found that the experience and expression of state and trait[2] anger decreased with the application of forgiveness. Studies further show that people with elevated anger expression scores were able to achieve significant reductions in blood pressure, indicating that forgiveness training may be a useful tool to help some hypertensive patients who also have elevated levels of anger.

These findings are consistent with and validate the conclusions of Worthington's research. The thing about trauma and hurt is this: whenever you think about the *index event*, the incident in which you were harmed physically or emotionally, and you have not practiced forgiveness, your body returns to the physiological state it was in at the time the event happened (fight, flight, freeze, or fawn). Your heart rate, blood pressure, diastasis of the liver, sugar and insulin production, cholesterol, cortisol, epinephrine, and noradrenaline production mirrors what occurred during the index event. It is this unnecessary, repeated revisitation of downstairs brain activity and the subsequent physiological aftermath that contribute to increased stress symptoms, cardiovascular problems, increased risk of diabetes, hypertension, and even some forms of cancer. Forgiveness literally has the power to reverse illness and to heal more than the wounds of the heart.

What It Means to Forgive

Look at these definitions according to Webster.

Forgive: (v) to pardon, to cease to bear resentment against, to cancel (as a debt), to exercise clemency, or to grant pardon.

Forget: (v) to lose remembrance of, to neglect inadvertently, or to disregard.

In one of my early groups, a couple was talking about how tricky this whole forgiveness thing can be. We were discussing the popular concept of forgive and forget. The husband noted that he tried to forgive and forget, except that whenever they got into a fight, he found himself calling up things that his wife said or did five, ten, or fifteen years prior. I asked him why he did this. He replied, "Well, I bring those things up because I need ammunition." My response to him was "I thought you were *on the same side.*"

What this gentleman said holds a great deal of truth. We hold on to events from the past because we need ammunition for the next fight. Why do we need ammunition to use against our partners? My theory is that nobody likes to be proven wrong in an argument. When you can't prove you're right, you lower yourself to intimidation tactics—if you can intimidate the other person, they will back away from the argument. If the other party doesn't back down, you need more leverage. Since by now you already know you are wrong, you start digging for memories of times when *they* were wrong, and you bring it into this argument. If you succeed, the person takes the bait and goes on the defensive. Now you are back in control because you have successfully diverted their attention from the issue at hand to one that died several months, maybe even years, ago.

A few problems exist with this tactic. The first is that it often works; however, the feelings conjured up by this chain of events typically consist of more bitterness, resentment, and frustration for both parties. Each time you revive a negative or painful memory, you relive it. Calling up old transgressions inflicts new hurt on the other party, and each time you bring up something the other party thought was resolved, you will inadvertently dwindle their trust in you. When you say you've forgiven someone but you bring up the old transgression every chance you get, it's hard for them to trust that you've truly let it go. Your actions will speak louder than your words.

In the early chapters of this book, you learned that belief is the basis of action. In other words, what you believe determines how you behave. Therefore, what you believe about forgiveness will determine what you do about it. If you believe that forgiveness is for the weak, and you do not want to be perceived as weak, then you will choose not to forgive others. In effect, you will choose to let bitterness control your heart. You will choose to let love die. You will choose to stop growing. If you believe that you will only find the closure you need through forgiveness, then you will choose to forgive. It's that simple. Does that mean you will forget? Perhaps, perhaps not. Part of getting past one's past means forgetting the things that happened in the past. But we should never forget what we learned from the events of our past.

When we talk of forgiveness, often people believe that we must "cancel" the transgression and behave as though it never happened. That may work well for financial debts but not so for emotional ones. The fact of the matter is that transgressions against one's feelings inflict much more pain than financial indiscretions or irresponsibility. So expecting someone to pretend you never hurt them is asking too much.

What we really want when we ask for forgiveness is *pardon*. We want to know that the anger has dissipated, perhaps that there is some understanding, and that the individual of whom we seek forgiveness will free us from ongoing punishment.

When we talk of forgetting, what we mean is not to entirely lose remembrance of what happened. Instead, we choose to disregard what has happened to the point that it no longer pops up every time we experience negative emotions. To *disregard* means to not give attention to something. In other words, we choose not to look at those events of our past for the purpose of using them against others. One of my favorite sayings applies here: *forget your past; remember only what it taught you.*

The Road to Forgiveness

Forgiveness is a process; it isn't something that *just happens*. You've got to be clear about what happened, and you must be willing to let go of the secondary advantages that come from holding on to the hurt—attention, pity, permission to behave badly, the ability to guilt others into doing your bidding. Come on now . . . you know what I'm talking about. You must find a way to separate the visceral emotional response to the index event from your memories of that event so that you can move on without constantly being triggered. How do we get there? To the place where you can remember only the lesson without recalling and reliving the pain of the lesson? Here is a five-step process that can help you take your first steps down the road to forgiveness.

1. Tell Your Story. What happened to you? How did you feel when it happened? What had you hoped would be the outcome? What was the actual outcome? Why do you find it hard to forgive now?

2. Reframe Your Story. What happened to you? How do you think the other person felt at the time of the incident? How do you think they feel now? Do you think they would do the same thing again? What have you learned from this—about yourself, about the other party, about relationships in general? How have you grown, changed, or matured? How has this helped you to become stronger?

3. Take a Break from Your Pain. What's good about your life? Focus on who loves you and whom you love. How can you use what you have learned to make life better for yourself and those around you?

4. Revise Your Expectations. We don't expect dogs to behave in any way that is out of keeping with what dogs do; why should we expect jerks to behave in a way that is not in keeping with what jerks do? Maya Angelou's quote applies here: *"When people show you who they are, believe them."* Realize that forgiving is not always an open door to renewed friendship or the same relationship that existed before. Just because you forgive someone does not mean you should allow them to hurt you in the same way again. When you revise your expectations to be more realistic, you will also revise your boundaries.

5. Make Forgiveness a Habit: Forgiveness is a choice. Remember that when you forgive, you do it for your sake as much as for the one asking forgiveness. By choosing to let go of the little things, it becomes easier to forgive the big things when they come along. Choose to learn from the past and then let the rest go.

There is one common word that is woven throughout this section—that word is *choose*. Forgiveness is a matter of choice. When you say you can't forgive someone, you are really saying that you choose not to. At least be honest about it and say it like it really is. Just remember that when you choose not to forgive, you are in effect choosing to choke love out of your life. The choice is yours.

Summary

Forgiveness is essential to healing. It doesn't mean you approve or sanction what was done, but forgiveness means to offer pardon, to no longer allow the harm to take up emotional real estate in your head and heart.

Flaws in memory may contribute to us embracing a false narrative that stokes the flames of unforgiveness.

There are a host of emotional and physical health benefits to forgiveness. The road to forgiveness includes telling and reframing your story, taking breaks from the pain, revising expectations, and making forgiveness a habit. Forgiveness is a choice.

Reflection

Whom in your life do you need to forgive? When you think of the harm that was done, how does your body respond (e.g., Can you feel your heart racing? Does your head ache? Does your body become tense?)? Imagine what it would feel like to be able to think of the index event and feel no pain, no hurt, no anger, no tension. Write your thoughts in your journal.

Action Step

Practice the steps on the road to forgiveness by applying them to the index event identified in your reflection. Document the results or your learnings along the way.

14

YOU DON'T HAVE TO LIKE IT, BUT
YOU HAVE TO ACCEPT IT

FOR MY CLIENTS who have been victims of a motor vehicle collision—particularly those who struggle with physical impairments or chronic pain—anger, anxiety, and distress are commonplace emotions. I cannot tell you how many times I have heard someone say, "I just want to be myself, the person I was *before* the accident." The sad truth for many is that returning to the person they were prior to their collision is an impossibility.

You see, everything in life changes you. From the day the egg with your name on it was fertilized by a sperm, you have been growing, shifting, changing, evolving. Leaving your parent for the first time to attend pre-school or daycare changes you. Puberty changes you. Falling in love for the first time changes you. Falling in love for the last time changes you too. That first kiss, that walk down the aisle, that miscarriage, that first child, that horrible thirty-eight-hour labor that ended in a C-section, that amazing mentor you had in your first job, the bully who tormented you in your third job, bankruptcy, failure, success—everything that happens in your life results in some measure of change.

While accident victims might one day achieve 100 percent of their physical functioning, and they may attain maximum psychological recovery, the reality of the collision having happened and all the consequences that followed will remain as part of their story. They may have learned some things about the fragility of life, about the importance of choosing a healthy lifestyle, about the value of safe driving habits, or about the importance of critical incident health insurance. There will be lingering effects, lasting lessons, or visual reminders by way of scars or a limp that document the accident as having happened. No matter what, there is no way to turn back time and pretend the accident never took place.

When folks in my practice are stuck in the place of wishing things were the way they once were, I direct them to *positive acceptance*, a concept made popular by Dr. Graham Price. Price suggests that the reason people feel uncomfortable emotions like distress, stress, anxiety, or anger is that when something occurs that triggers their frustration signal, their immediate thought response is to wish things were "already different."

Imagine you have a severe tension headache. It feels like a vice grip has been placed on your temples, and the hand of God is squeezing it so tight that soon your brain matter will begin to leak out of your ears. Now imagine that you sit in a dark room with your head in your hands, wishing your headache were already gone. Would wishing cause the headache to disappear? No. In fact, by wishing your headache were already gone, you are making certain that your distress over the headache will be prolonged because *now is now*. You're wishing the headache were gone now. But the now of the wish will have already passed by the time you check to see if the headache is still there. Then that now moment will also pass while you are wishing for the headache to be gone now. Wishing things were already different guarantees that you will be disappointed, thereby adding to your overall distress or anger.

Price notes that in Western culture, acceptance is more associated with resignation or defeatism, in which we suffer through it, suck it up, or make no effort to change our circumstances because it is what it is. Positive acceptance is quite a different concept. Positive acceptance means that you stop wishing things were already different because that is an impossible wish. Rather, positive acceptance acknowledges that it is what it is, but it *will be* what you make of it. Accepting the headache in the moment relieves you of the anxiety that comes from wishing it were gone. It opens your brain bandwidth to process which steps you might take to make certain the headache doesn't become a five-day headbanger. When you apply positive acceptance to your circumstances, you allow your brain to tune in to what can be done to resolve the current problem or to improve things in the future. Positive acceptance, in effect, helps to unmuddle your mindset.

Consider our gal pal Ella for a moment. Imagine if after her barracuda of a stepmother and her two harpy stepsisters left for the ball without her, she hadn't cried out, "Oh, but I do wish I could go to the ball!" What if she had sat quietly and applied TSA with a dash of REBT, overlaying her thought process with positive acceptance? Her thoughts might have run like this.

What's happening? Those horrible people are finally gone. I have the house to myself. I am not going with them to the ball. I do wish I could have gone. I notice that I have a wish to go, but as I am not already on my way there, I need to relinquish that thought because it is irrational to believe things could be already different than what they are.

What does this mean? It means I need to shift my focus away from wishing I were already on my way to the ball to how I would like the rest of my night to go.

How do I feel? Now that I've stopped wishing for the impossible, I don't feel so bad. I kind of feel hopeful that maybe this night won't be a complete train wreck.

What do I want? What is my desired outcome? I would very much like to go to the ball.

What can I do to achieve that outcome? What is the best thing / worst thing that could happen? Well, there are all these dresses, hair doodads, and fancy shoes lying about. I could do my hair and makeup and borrow one of these dresses. I could hitch the horse to the wagon and drive myself to the ball. The best thing that could happen is that the prince or some other eligible bachelor notices me and courts me away from my poor excuse of a family. The worst thing that could happen is I have a few hours of fun before I end up back in the kitchen masquerading as a scullery maid for my wicked stepmother.

Did you notice the turning point for Ella? It was between her thoughts and her feelings. She turned her *awareness* to what was happening and how it was impacting her. *Acknowledging* that she was engaged in an unhealthy thought loop of wishing things were already different, she chose to *accept* her reality rather than resist it. She then *assessed* how she felt, making note of the hopefulness that came with accepting reality. She further assessed what she truly wanted and the steps she could take to achieve her desired outcome. Then she *adapted* her behaviors, choosing to get dressed, hitch the wagon, and take herself to the ball.

Positive acceptance unmuddles the mindset, enables functional fixedness to be repaired, and frees the brain to focus on problem resolution rather than the feelings elicited by those problems. Remember, when you are fixed on how things should be instead of how they are, you will always feel distressed. It sucks if you expect people to be kind or considerate, but they aren't. It isn't fun when you expect people to care about your problems, and they don't. It is highly distressing to feel constant excruciating pain when all you want is just one single pain-free day. Wishing it were already different amplifies that pain. Acceptance is the key to reducing the distress of unmet expectations.

Change Your Expectations

A relationship is not a relationship without Give and Take. Expectations are a natural component of any relationship. Think about it. Every relationship is in effect a contract of sorts. I offer you my friendship. You offer me your friendship in return. I send you a text message; you send a reply. When three days pass without a reply, I might send another text checking in if you got the last one. Why? Because I have an expectation of a reply because I believe that is what friends do.

What happens when you have expectations within a relationship that are not consistent with the temperament, personality, or motivations of the other party? What if you have healthy boundaries, but the other party has diffuse or distant boundaries? What if one of you has an insecure attachment style? What if one of you is experiencing depression and low motivation so they are not as communicative as you would like? How do you navigate these differences in relationships? It's simple. Change. Your. Expectations.

Look, you already know there is very little you can control. Distress is born of unmet expectations, fueled by believing in the fallacy of control and resisting reality instead of accepting it. Acceptance is in part about shifting away from the need to control what you simply cannot. I often tell my clients, "Hey, you don't have to like what is happening, but you do have to accept it." Why would I say something that sounds so harsh? Because acceptance is the first step in the journey to radical, positive, lasting change. It is the key that opens the door to forgiveness. How can you forgive the driver who struck you while you were crossing the street if you cannot even accept that the accident happened or accept that you have physical limitations because of it?

Changing your expectations frees you of the burden of waiting for the fairy godmother to arrive. I hate to tell you this, but she isn't coming. Changing your expectations means that you examine what is truly happening and what that means, and you adjust your expectations accordingly. That boss who is a bully? They are likely to continue being one. Change your mindset and expect them to be a bully. I mean, why are you continually surprised and disappointed by the behavior of someone who has established themselves as toxic?

You know that guy who promises to call you tomorrow but ghosts you for weeks and then shows up for a booty call? He is telling you who he is. Believe him. Change your expectations. Recently, I saw a video on social media of a woman who slaved all day to host a Thanksgiving dinner, only to be excluded from the table she had laid out because her friend *needed a chair for her purse*. This poor lady needs to change her expectations of her friends. Time to recognize that anyone who would come and eat at your table and deny you a seat *in your own house* is not your friend. Change those expectations and show those spoiled, selfish cows the door! When people show you who they are, believe them.

Here's why you don't need a fairy godmother. The magic happens all by itself when you change your expectations. Suddenly, miraculously, you no longer feel angry, sad, hurt, disappointed, anxious, rejected, abandoned, or minimized because your expectations—when matched with reality—will be met more often, if not always. Just like that— *bippity boppity boo*—your perspective of life will be different. The other beautiful miracle that happens when you change your expectations is that when people *exceed* your expectations, it becomes easier to notice the subtle positive shifts in their behavior, and you will enjoy the relationship more.

That person who only ever talks about themselves when they call you? Change your expectations to reflect the truth of who they are. Then when they stop to take a breath and ask you about your life ("*What's new with you?*"), rather than bubbling over with anger ("See, I knew they had it in them to ask about me. Why can't they be like that all the time?"), you will react with a pleasant surprise: ("Wow, thank you for asking. Let me tell you what's happening."), and you will enjoy the conversation much more because you won't waste the interaction on wishing they would *already always* be considerate.

Total Behavior

William Glasser's suggestion that "all behavior is purposeful" means every aspect of behavior is one's best attempt to meet one's needs in the moment given the skills, knowledge, or material resources available at the time. In other words, all behavior is an effort to conform the perceived world to the images in the quality or ideal world. There are four coexisting components that make up the way we conduct ourselves, known as *total behavior.*

1. Actions or physical movements—doing
2. Thinking—self-talk and beliefs
3. Feeling—the action of emoting
4. Physiology—body talk / body language

All four components work simultaneously and are always operating in concert. Another way to understand total behavior is to think of yourself as a car. Actions and thoughts represent the front wheels, and feelings and physiology represent the back wheels. To operate effectively, all four wheels must be used at the same time. We have the most control over our front wheels—actions and thoughts—and it is these that enable us to steer our vehicle. We can indirectly control our rear wheels—feelings and physiology—by the direction in which we choose to steer the front wheels. We can control our feelings and physiology by what we choose to think and do.

Thinking consists of beliefs, meaning-making, values, and attitudes, and it comprises both conscious and unconscious thoughts. It is said that 80 percent of our thinking is under our active control. Acting encompasses conscious muscle control, muscle action, talking, emoting, and conscious and unconscious body language. As you know, emotions and feeling states are informed by thoughts, learned responses garnered from past experiences, values, and meaning-making, and they are expressed by universally recognized facial expressions as well as verbal and behavioral manifestations of emotion, which is *acting behavior.*

Finally, physiology is the internal response to sensory input; it is the felt experience of every stimulus and event. Autonomic responses such as fight or flight, stress, survival, anger, rest, and relaxation are all the purview of physiology. We would love to think that we act and think in certain ways because of what we are experiencing internally—our physiology—and what we feel emotionally, but it is truer that our physiology and emotions are informed by our thoughts. Our actions may well be informed by physiology and emotions, but those, too, are guided by our thought processes. Therefore, thinking is at the core of total behavior.

Remember locus of control? It is how you think about your circumstances, your worldview, and your perception of the activating stimuli that will determine how you feel about it and respond to it. Those with an external locus of control will tend to attribute their circumstances to outside sources, abdicating ownership when things go well and laying blame when things go poorly. Those with an internal locus of control will take ownership of positive outcomes by acknowledging their own hard work, and when things go poorly, they will carefully consider how they could act differently.

Imagine we were to take the analogy of the car even further and consider how the various functions of sensation, perception, memory, thinking, feeling, emoting, and acting coalesce to comprise total behavior.

Windows: Windows are the lens through which you view the world—aka your perceived world. Windows let air flow through, but they also keep bugs and birds, snow and rain out of your vehicle. Windows can be a barrier that allows others to see into your vehicle. You can tint them to manage how much people can see while allowing you to see out without obstruction. Our external and internal perceptions function in much the same way. We can hide our feelings and our interpretation of our perceived world from others while trying to take in as much visual or sensory stimuli as possible. Sometimes we see things incorrectly, or we miscalculate distance or the intentions of other drivers, and our corresponding choices result in accidents. We've got to keep our windows clean so we can see out of them. We must sometimes shift how we're looking at things to make sure we don't inadvertently make wrong choices due to misinformation.

Rearview Mirror: Hindsight. When we spend too much time looking behind us, we are likely to develop a pessimistic mindset. Being past-focused means you spend much of your time in regret, all the while creating more problems as you move forward because you are paying attention to the stuff behind you rather than the things ahead of you. It is appropriate to look back every now and again to ensure you have proper perspective and that you are safe, but overusing the rearview mirror is likely to result in a collision up the road, which you will add to your mounting list of regrets unless you shift your focus.

Lights: These babies help you see in times of low vision. They alert other people to your presence on the road. They give people a heads-up when you're making a move. Have you ever been on the road behind someone who refuses to use their signal lights? Isn't it fun to play the guessing game with their driving behavior? Make no mistake, when the prize to be won is arriving alive, the game isn't that enjoyable. Signals have a purpose. They are a form of nonverbal communication that allow others to perceive and understand our intentions. Use your lights. Communicate when necessary. Don't be that driver who forces people to guess—they may guess wrong.

Hazard lights are another form of communication that alerts others to the fact that you're in trouble and need assistance. It's okay to ask for help. Stubbornly refusing to put on your hazard lights when you are stranded on the side of the road puts you and other drivers at risk. The same is true for verbal communication when you're in crisis. Why endanger yourself and others when a simple call for assistance could minimize the risk for all involved?

Bumpers and Crumple Zones: These are your boundaries. Your bubbles. Your buffer zones. Bumpers exist for your protection from minor injury, and crumple zones act as a buffer against major injury. In life, your defense mechanisms may be useful in protecting against minor boundary infractions, but when the big hits happen, it is your mindset, your certainty about who you are, and your confidence in your resiliency and your ability to rise above the current challenge that will preserve you. A pretty exterior is no good if there is no strength in the vehicle's structure. Work on strengthening your crumple zones so you can survive the big hits.

Engine: The power that propels your vehicle is your engine. The fuel for your engine could be any emotion, but the more powerful the emotion, the more powerful your engine. Passion, fear, anger, or joy could easily propel your vehicle.

Steering Wheel: If emotion fuels your engine, your motivations and intentions steer your vehicle in the direction you want it to go. Avoiding quick fixes means steering with intention with your eyes set clearly on your end destination, your desired long-term outcome.

Glove Box: Typically, the glove box is for the resources you need to be easily accessible while you travel the road of life. Maps. User manuals. License and insurance. Weapon—sorry . . . . that was my outside voice. In truth, there are resources that help us stay on track—tools, items, or behaviors that demonstrate to others that we know what we're doing and that we are safe to be around. These should be easily accessible. If you have to dig deep to show someone that you're safe to be around, you are probably not safe to be around. Just saying.

Dashboard: Your dashboard represents your levels of self-awareness. Self-evaluation provides internal feedback and sends early warnings like "check engine" or "check tire pressure." In this context, your dashboard not only keeps you apprised of all the various mental and physical functions that are co-occurring in your body but it also alerts you to your frustration signals, indicating there is a problem that requires solving.

Trunk: This is where you hide the body, right? Indeed, the trunk is where we keep our tools, spare tire, emergency supplies—the *resources* we may need to help us along the journey. It is also where we place our baggage. Now, have you ever thought about this: When you get home from a journey, what do you do with your baggage? Do you leave all your stuff packed into the bags, or do you empty it out?

I went on a shopping trip with a friend, and we each took one suitcase with not very much stuff in it, hoping we would find some great buys to fill our bags. Sure enough, we found most of what we were looking for and got the items at a great bargain. After two days away, we packed up and made the journey home.

When we arrived home, I immediately took my baggage and my shopping items out of her vehicle. It wouldn't have made any sense to leave them in her car. After all, they belong to me. When I got into the house, I took out my new things, and after showing them off to my family, I put them away until I would be ready to wear them. I then removed the dirty clothes and put them in the laundry. I unpacked my toiletries and hair products and returned them to the bathroom. I have a special bag with toiletries that I save just for traveling; I put that away so that I would have no trouble finding it the next time I had to pack for a trip. Even my passport went back to its rightful place.

That all seems to make sense, doesn't it? Suppose I told you that I put my luggage in the trunk of my car and carried it with me everywhere I went from then on. Wouldn't you think me a bit strange? Sure, but the fact is that many of us are wandering through the journey of life dragging useless baggage with us everywhere we go. Contrary to some teachings, I don't believe that all excess baggage is useless—it is just excess. On my shopping trip, I had no intentions of doing any business, so I did not bring any business attire—no suits, no dress shoes. I brought my laptop only so that I could stay in touch with my family via emails and video conferencing.

The next trip I planned to take was purely for business. How successful would I be on the next trip if I took with me only what was already in the bag from my shopping trip? The dirty clothes would be useless to me for certain, and the other items would serve no purpose either. For each leg of my journey in business, leisure, and family life, I need to take what fits—and nothing else.

You wouldn't take a parka and skis to the beach. Nor would you bring sunscreen for a mining expedition. Yet you and I and millions of other people around the world drag around bags and bags of stuff that is not fitting for the journey. Things like repressed memories; bitterness, guilt, or shame from past failed relationships; unresolved grief; and that tiara from the year you were crowned prom queen that you think still defines you are weighing you down. Here's the thing. When you are laden down with unnecessary luggage, it is much more difficult to deal with additional anger-inducing problems. Do you really need that excess baggage?

Change Yourself

I expect that much of the challenge in practicing acceptance is caused by the baggage we lug around. Remember, our perceived world is informed by our senses, our values, and our *experiences*. Of course, we carry our experiences with us as we grow and evolve. The weight of those experiences can get heavy, especially if they were painful or traumatic. If we haven't healed through forgiveness, or at the very least reached a point of acceptance, all that dirty laundry will begin to stink and fester, eventually permeating all the good, clean stuff that we've crammed into the trunk alongside the junk.

If your focus is locked in your rearview mirror, remember this: You have the capacity to shift away from an external locus of control so you can take more responsibility for your outcomes. You have the choice to look at your life through a lens of positivity or negativity. A past-focused mindset is often more afraid, more pessimistic, less able to foresee and circumvent challenges on the road ahead because one is too busy looking back instead of planning forward. A future-focused mindset is intent on creating positive outcomes, avoiding the mistakes of the past, prolonging the peace of the present. You will take your eyes off the rearview mirror when you realize that the past is only important as it informs our present and future decisions.

Feelings of helplessness are exacerbated by trying to change your *circumstances*. We fall into the trap of learned helplessness because of the tendency to believe the fallacy that we can control things that we cannot. The truth is that we have only two options when faced with circumstances outside of our control: we can either (a) change our expectations or (b) change our behavior. No matter how you spin it, you can control *nothing* except for these two things. My former supervisor used to put it like this: "If you can't accept it, change it. If you can't change it, accept it."

We cannot change people. We may inspire them to change—I would not be writing this book otherwise—we might influence them to change, or we might even incentivize them to change, but at the end of the day, the change will come from within them. Likewise, we cannot change our immediate circumstances—hence the need for positive acceptance. What we do have the potential to shift is how things shape up in the future, and that change originates with us.

Summary

Everything that happens in life changes you. Rather than wishing something had never happened, embracing positive acceptance allows you to stop clinging to the fallacy of control.

Acceptance is not resignation or defeatism; rather, it is a choice to stop wishing things were already different.

Choice theory posits that actions, thoughts, emotions, and physiological responses are the four components that comprise total behavior.

When faced with seemingly impossible problems, we can either change our expectations or change ourselves.

Reflection

When you consider the car analogy in the total behavior model, what aspects of your car require an overhaul?

1. Do you need to clean your windows for clearer vision?
2. Do you spend too much time looking to the past in your rearview mirror?
3. Do your lights need to shine brighter so you have better insight? Are your hazard lights working?
4. How are your boundaries and buffer zones? Do you need to create healthier boundaries?
5. How's your energy? When was the last time you checked your engine lights and your dashboard?
6. What baggage needs to be removed from your trunk?

Action Step

Review the notes you made in your reflection. Outline three steps you will take this week to begin to tune up your behavior (e.g., get more sleep so I will be less irritable during the day, eat more water-based foods for better energy, and set boundaries with that coworker who is always asking me to do their work).

15

TAKING RESPONSE-ABILITY

I Don't Care

IT WAS MY first community workshop for the Learning Disabilities Association of Niagara, and I was presenting *Anger Solutions* to a parent group. Not knowing what to expect, I arrived at the venue early and began setting up for my talk. As the parents filed in, there was a palpable energy in the room. The space quickly filled until it was a standing room only. The introductory comments had barely ceased when the room erupted with parents talking over each other, complaining about the challenges of parenting kids with learning disabilities. "You have no idea what it took for us to get here," yelled one flustered mother. "My kid was screaming bloody murder the whole time I was trying to get ready." Another parent hollered about how their child wouldn't listen. Another complained about oppositional behavior. One after the other, parents voiced their complaints; I could hardly get a word in edgewise.

Finally, I shouted as loudly as I could, "I don't care!" That statement shocked the crowd into silence. "Listen," I ventured calmly and purposefully, "I really don't care what made you angry tonight because I could spend all evening helping each of you individually to come up with strategies to solve the problem that ticked you off today. Tomorrow something else will make you angry, and the next day, and the next day something else will trigger your rage. I'm here to talk with you about how to resolve anger safely and appropriately—not just for you but for your kids too. So how about everyone take a deep breath and exhale the stress of the day, and let's talk about *Anger Solutions* and how we can apply that to *every* problem in your life, not just the one you're facing right now?"

The truth? For a few moments, I saw my life flash before my eyes before I had the epiphany that saved the evening. It wasn't until I faced the threat of an angry mob that the solution became clear to me. Thank God it came when it did, and I was able to rescue a presentation that was about to run off the rails. When applied with intention, the principles and tools in *Anger Solutions* can be transferred to just about any situation, good or bad. Have you been offered a new job? That's great. Not sure if you should accept? Run it through the lens of TSA. Are you feeling unloved or even abused in your relationship? Apply TSA to the situation, determine your desired outcome, and act accordingly. Is your child being oppositional? Think about your desired outcome, check your options against the choice matrix, and choose the best response for both positive short- and long-term outcomes. Did someone call you the C-word? Before you punch them in the face, use TSA. It will keep you out of jail for assault. This is called *taking response-ability*, and that is what that parent group needed to learn.

When Friendship Dies

We had been friends for several years. I trusted her like a sister; our families were close. I stood by her while she went through some seriously dark times, and she had done the same for me. I thought we would be BFFs for life. Then suddenly, over the course of about two weeks, the whole thing began to disintegrate until what seemed a solid friendship imploded, and we were done. I'm not gonna lie: it took me several weeks to recover from the agony of that loss.

We had been such a key part of each other's lives. Then just like that, it was over. Had I paid attention, I might have noticed red flags popping up. But I was too invested in the friendship and lacked the self-confidence to do anything about the warning signs that the relationship was becoming toxic. I noticed several boundary violations, but I ignored them. I reasoned away the unacceptable behavior because she was my friend. I said nothing when she did things that were hurtful. By the time I'd had enough and was ready to reinforce my boundaries, it was too late. I had taught her how to treat me, and she was not interested in learning to do things differently.

I cried for days. Pleaded with her to talk things through with me so that we could redefine our friendship. Her response was that she was moving forward with the mindset that she once had a good friend but that she had died. In other words, I was dead to her. *'Nuff said.* The truth is that some people come into your life for a reason, some for a season, and others for a lifetime. When those reasons no longer exist, and those seasons change, it hurts. A lot. Platonic friendships break up, too, and the pain and heartache are as real as any other loss.

Fences Make Good Neighbors: The Value of Healthy Boundaries

There are different types of boundaries. Physical boundaries are in reference to personal space and physical touch. If someone touches you or remains in your personal space when you don't want them to, that would be a physical boundary violation. For example, approaching a pregnant woman and touching her swollen tummy without asking for permission is a boundary violation.

Intellectual boundaries are about thoughts and ideas. Dismissing someone's ideas or belittling them is an example of an intellectual boundary violation. Plagiarism is an intellectual boundary violation. Emotional boundaries are all about feelings. A way to express an emotional boundary might be choosing when, where, and how much personal information you share. A violation of an emotional boundary would be minimizing someone's feelings, trying to manipulate them through shame or blame, or discounting their emotional state.

Sexual boundaries are about the emotional, intellectual, and physical aspects of sexuality. Mutual understanding and respect of limitations around sex is healthy, including wanting to wait until marriage. Sexual boundary violations include unwanted sexual touching, pressure to engage in sexual behaviors, acting without consent, leering, and sexual comments.

Material boundaries are about the things you own or your finances. You get to choose how and with whom you share your material possessions. A material boundary violation might be someone borrowing something of yours and not returning it, pressuring you to give or loan things out, or stealing your money or possessions.

Time boundaries refer to how you use your time. You need to be able to budget your time, and you have the right to set limits about how much time you give to work, relationships, hobbies, or community. A time violation might look like making too many demands on a person's time or ignoring the hint when your hosts suggest it's time for your visit to be over.

I disregarded the many boundary violations that had been occurring over the years in my friendship. Emotional boundary violations, material boundary violations, time boundary violations, even intellectual boundary violations. Part of why I was loathe to call out the several violations of my boundaries was my own insecurity and low self-worth. I placed more value on the friendship than I did on my own personal needs.

It Begins with You

Remember that every problem is, at its heart, a relationship problem. The foundation of all relationships that will determine if they stand the test of time or fail is communication. How do you talk to yourself? The things you say to yourself matter. How do the people in your life talk to you? Remember that words have power. With that in mind, let's do a quick recap of TSA.

Think: What is happening? What does it mean? How do I feel about it? What is my desired outcome? What can I do to obtain that outcome without causing myself any long-term pain? What action will I settle on? What is the lifetime value of this event?

Say: Sometimes you need extra time and a little extra help to work through the right words to say. One of the tools I have used over the years to do this is letter writing. Letter writing is my go-to method of communication if the lifetime value of an event is significantly high. It allows me to process my thoughts, to read and reread my words, and to edit them deeply before ever sharing my thoughts with anyone else. See, I'm good with words. And when I feel deeply hurt or I am filled with rage—yes, it happens—I could do serious damage with my tongue. Now, I am aware of the power that resides in words, and I'm not about destroying anyone emotionally with mine. Don't need that on my conscience. So one of my personal boundaries is to shut my pie hole when my frustration signal is activated. I hold that boundary as much for myself as I do for others. This is a non-negotiable for me.

Ask: Engage the other party in a dialogue where possible and appropriate. Ask, "How can we work together to ensure this doesn't happen again?" Be ready to listen and collaborate as you negotiate a way forward together.

Taking Ownership

One way to sort through your thoughts and take deeper ownership of your feelings about any painful event is to write a letter to process your thoughts using this template I borrowed from Jack Canfield's *Self-Esteem and Peak Performance*, with a little add-on I learned in my *Rise and Shine* coaching sessions with Lisa Nichols.

- Hurt
- Anger
- Fear
- Sorry for . . .
- I forgive you for . . .
- Thank you for giving me . . . (This is the part I learned from Lisa.)

I introduced this template in chapter 12, promising an example of the love letter. Here it is within the context of the demise of my ten-year friendship.

Dear Jane,*

I felt hurt when you implied that I was only your friend for selfish reasons. I was angry because the way you spun our argument was unfair, and the things you said are not true. I'm also angry that you just kept talking over me, and you refused to listen to my side. I am afraid that our friendship might never recover from this—at the very least, it won't ever be like it was.

I'm sorry for not being clearer on my boundaries sooner. That is on me. I'm also sorry for not being clearer in my communication with you and that I wasn't better at showing you how important your friendship is to me. Please forgive me for that. I forgive you, too, for the things in our friendship that frustrated me that I recognize were boundary violations.

I forgive you for the hurtful words you said. Thank you for giving me the chance to recognize my mistakes in our friendship and to realize that I need to be true to myself and my non-negotiables.

Moving forward, I'd like us to think about what we want from our friendship. Perhaps when we have both had time to reflect and consider things objectively, we'll be able to talk about where we go from here. What I do know is that I'd like to remain friends, but we need to renegotiate the terms of our friendship.

Define Your Non-negotiables[1]

Struggling parents. Oppositional children. Disengaged partners. Abusive spouses. Micromanaging or bullying bosses. Frenemies. Fair-weather friends. Social loafers. Microaggressors. Macroaggressors. You might have some of these people in your life. If you don't, consider yourself fortunate and brace yourself because you're likely to meet them if you haven't already.

How do you get clear about your boundaries so you can cultivate healthy relationships of all kinds? Realize that you are surrounded by people, places, and things all bombarding you with requests, needs, ideas, and problems. They are vying for whatever energy you have available, and they won't take no for an answer. They most certainly won't until you fully grasp that you teach people how to treat you. Once you get comfortable with teaching the right lessons, those in your circle will begin to respect you and your needs.

Boundary-setting in relationships, especially in the early stages, is essential to killing the monster while it is a baby. Even when the monster begins to grow, it is never too late to begin setting down firm boundaries. Think of a relationship in which one party is aggressive and the other is passive. This will work for as long as both parties are happy in their roles. Should the passive party decide they have had enough and they do the self-work to grow and flex their assertiveness muscles, it will tip the balance of the relationship scales. The aggressive party may escalate, hoping they can intimidate or pressure the passive party into resuming their traditional role, thereby returning the relationship to its comfort zone. If the formerly passive party holds the new boundary, the aggressive party will have no choice but to either change their expectations or change themselves.

Teach People How to Treat You

Remember the principle of who before do? Before you can begin setting healthy and firm boundaries or asking for what you want in your relationships, you must deepen and strengthen your relationship with yourself. Get to know who you are; get clear on your identity, your passion, and your purpose. A therapist or a coach can help you to clarify your values and your needs and support you in this journey. Having clarified and solidified your identity and properly measured your self-worth, you will be ready to establish your non-negotiables.

Non-negotiables are your lines in the sand. My non-negotiables are more like a brick wall—the end of the line. There is a lot I will put up with, but when you push me to the end of the line, I am D.O.N.E., *done*. I have clear non-negotiables, and I won't compromise them for anyone. Here's how you can identify your non-negotiables. First, clarify the things you value. What and/or who is most important to you? That may be people, things, memories, or your mental health. Consider the different types of choices we are expected to make. If you had to choose between making that sale and compromising your values, what is more important? Are your relationships with the most precious people in your life worth risking for that financial gamble or that alcohol, drug, gaming, or pornography addiction? If you compromise your values to get your short-term goal, will you still feel good over the passage of time?

Consider the power of heuristics and how they may cause you to arrive at the wrong conclusion due to misinformation. Asking the right questions and applying your critical-thinking skills to every situation that requires you to set boundaries are essential. A muddled mindset may cause you to choose diffuse boundaries rather than holding to a firm non-negotiable. Sometimes the boundaries you must set are with yourself! Will you still respect yourself if you choose to do something that is outside the borders of your values?

Remember that you are the ringmaster of your own circus. If you don't want the monkeys to run the show, you must decide what is acceptable to you in terms of your own behavior, what is acceptable to you in terms of other people's behavior, and what is not acceptable for you or for others. When your expectations are not met, a frustration signal is sure to follow. You cannot forget that when you are not consciously aware of your ideal-world pictures, you may not realize that an expectation is unmet, a rule is broken, a boundary violated, or a goal thwarted until it happens and you feel upset about it. Thus, it behooves you to get clear on what you need from other people by way of communication, nonverbal interaction, honesty, timely responses, and other boundaries.

Assertive language is vital to communicating your non-negotiables. Shame has no place in this conversation. We know that trauma shatters the self and silences your voice. Reclaiming your identity, embracing your passion and purpose, and deciding on your non-negotiables are a renouncing of shame and a reclamation of your voice.

Use proper phrasing to express your non-negotiables to others. Let people know that you are setting these boundaries because you want to have a healthy relationship with them and let them know what to expect when the boundaries are violated. Let people know what you want, need, or won't allow. Communicate openly when people do or say something that you don't appreciate but be sure to express yourself assertively using language that states your feelings about what was said or done. Follow that with sharing your ideal-world picture or your desired outcome *("Ideally, I would love it if in the future we could resolve this issue in this way")* and ask a power question to engage the other party *("What could we both do differently so that this doesn't happen again? How could we work together to ensure our relationship is more open and trusting?")*. You have the right to set boundaries. Let people know what you will or will not permit. Inform them what they can expect of you—the things you will not say or do because they interfere with your non-negotiables.

Finally, do your best to keep yourself baggage-free. This means that you aim to leave every encounter with nothing unsaid, nothing stepped over, nothing unrequested, and nothing not acknowledged or appreciated. You say what there is to say immediately when you sense it. This is important because what is left unsaid may interfere with a relationship down the road. Any request unasked is a missed opportunity. When anger is allowed to fester, corrosion of the heart, mind, and spirit results. There is a reason the Bible instructs us to not let the sun go down on our anger. The longer we hold it, the more bitter we become.

Do you recall my boss whom I had to school on the law of seed and harvest? The day he decided to call us all "bottom feeders" because all we did was focus on the poop in life, I realized he was right about one thing. We had been teaching him how to treat us, and I decided it was time for a new lesson. Drawing from my defined non-negotiables, I set out to correct him as gently as I could in the moment—because you must know I was ripping mad—about why it was inappropriate to talk to his team that way. He acknowledged that his tirade was out of line, and he even attempted to appease me by placing me in charge of developing standards for professional workplace conduct.

I know from experience what happens when bottling pain results in too many words unspoken and too many hurts unchallenged. Hearts get broken, trust is irrevocably damaged, and bitterness and resentment grow, choking out love. No matter the circumstance, you must find the strength, the confidence, and the self-esteem that is necessary to educate those around you about what is permissible in your life. Let me be clear—the learning must begin and end with you. You must first unlearn destructive habits, reframe your interpretations of events through self-evaluation, and decide what you will allow to produce stress, anger, and fear or peace, joy, and passion in your life.

Three Perspectives

One of the tools I use in therapy and in the *Anger Solutions* program to help people find the sweet spot of response-ability is to tell their story in different ways. This is an expansion on what you learned about the journey to forgiveness; the first two steps are telling your story and reframing the story.

Begin with telling the story from a perspective of being a victim. Share the details of what happened to you, how it felt, and how awful it was. Pay attention to how your body feels, how raw your emotions are, the tenor of your voice as you relate the tale. Tell the story again but from the perspective of a non-invested third party like a reporter or a law clerk, just stating the facts. Notice how your body language shifts. Your voice is stronger. You don't feel the physical effects that you experienced when you were in the victim mindset. *Interesting.* Last, relate the story one more time from a place of response-ability. This is not about laying blame. It is not about assigning guilt or shame. It is about learning from the experience, taking what you've learned, and leaving the rest behind, much like I had to do when my friendship died. Looking back, I realized that I had not set firm boundaries. I had not valued my own self-worth, so I compromised on things that I should have held as non-negotiables. I believe that we should forget the past; remember only what it taught us. Passing the painful stories of your lived experience through these three lenses will help you to arrive at a place where you can distance yourself from the past while holding tight to the lesson.

Lessons Learned

If you want to know how to successfully tame the dino brooding dragon that lives inside of you, there are some things you must be.

Be teachable. Your way of thinking is not the only way. We learned this when examining the muddled mindset. If you are fixated on a single solution, you'll be oblivious to all others. Shifting from functional fixedness into a more flexible mindset requires humility and acceptance. Accept that you cannot always be right; it's a statistical impossibility. Allow for the fact that you might be wrong, and be open to receiving feedback. I cannot tell you how many relationships fall apart because one party desperately attempted to communicate their needs, wants, desires, and expectations, while the other party stood firm in their functional fixedness. If your answer to saving your relationship is for the other party to do all the changing because you're already perfect, you might just be a broken clock. Shiny and pretty on the outside, looking perfect for all the world to see, but still broken and dysfunctional on the inside. Get thee to a horologist, my friend! The greatest teachers were not always so. They were students first, and the greatest of these remain teachable throughout their lifetimes. Be teachable.

Be flexible. I promise you, if you want your relationships to succeed, you need sex appeal. Inflexibility and intractability are not sexy. Understanding that you have two ears and only one mouth, which means you should listen at least twice as much as you speak, is sexy. Seeking first to understand and then to be understood is sexy. Showing your partner that you both hear and understand their needs is more attractive than David Hasselhoff or Pamela Anderson running in slow motion, wearing nothing but a swimsuit and copious amounts of suntan oil. The key to intimacy is knowing you are safe with someone. Liking them. Trusting them. Feeling secure enough to be vulnerable with them. Having a solid connection. Do you want to foster connection? Listen. Respond. Then listen again.

Let me tell you what else is sexy as all get-out. Apologies. I said what I said! Apologies are sexy. I'm not talking about the fake apology: "I'm sorry you feel that way" or "If I said or did anything to offend you, I apologize." Come on! A real apology acknowledges the harm that was done, accepts responsibility for inflicting that harm without blaming or shaming the other party, and shares how they are working at making amends.

The day after the slap heard around the world, Will Smith published his apology on social media.[2] It read in part,

> *My behavior at last night's Academy Awards was unacceptable and inexcusable . . . I reacted emotionally. I would like to publicly apologize to you, Chris. I was out of line, and I was wrong. I am embarrassed and my actions are not indicative of the man I want to be . . . I would also like to apologize to the Academy, the producers of the show, all the attendees and everyone watching around the world. I would like to apologize to the Williams family and my* King Richard *family. I deeply regret that my behavior has stained what has been an otherwise gorgeous journey for all of us. I am a work in progress.*

This was a heartfelt, carefully considered apology, one that acknowledges the gravity of the harm, takes ownership, and indicates that he will continue to work on his self-growth and improvement.

Consider how this apology differs from the one delivered by Donald Trump after his lewd comments about how he treats women were exposed during his campaign for office. In part, the video-recorded apology stated,

> *I've never said I'm a perfect person nor pretended to be someone that I'm not. I've said and done things I regret, and the words released today on this more than a decade-old video are one of them. . . . Anyone who knows me knows these words don't reflect who I am. I said it, I was wrong, and I apologize . . . I have gotten to know the great people of our country, and I've been humbled by the faith they've placed in me. I pledge to be a better man tomorrow and will*

never, ever let you down. Let's be honest—we're living in the real
world. This is nothing more than a distraction from the important
issues we're facing today. We are losing our jobs, we're less safe than
we were eight years ago, and Washington is totally broken. Hillary
Clinton and her kind have run our country into the ground. I've
said some foolish things, but there's a big difference between the
words and actions of other people.[3]

This self-aggrandizing non-apology first implies that the infraction is so old it isn't even deserving of an apology. Second, Trump glosses over the issue for which he was called to task. Third, he makes an unattainable promise by saying he will never let people down. That is an unrealistic expectation, one that will surely be unmet. He then claims that the resurgence of this "old news" story was brought forward by his political opponents to distract the American people from the "bigger issues" of the day. The "apology" is opportunistically positioned as a campaign stump that could be used to divert attention from his misogynistic comments and shift shame to Trump's political opponents.

Assertive people with a strong, secure sense of self will have little issue with admitting when they're wrong. Those who are struggling with their self-worth and are amid their growth process must find the will to apologize with grace. I think people resist saying they're sorry because it feels like in so doing, they are surrendering a part of themselves. Perhaps they are right in that they would have to choose being vulnerable for the sake of maintaining intimacy and connection in the relationship. Isn't that a fair trade?

Be connected. Remember that the opposite of addiction is connection. Train your brain and the brains of your little ones to abstain from mindless scrolling, gaming, or engaging in meaningless online entertainment. Seek out true connections. Make eye contact, make conversation with real people, and ask people out on dates using your voice instead of Tinder, Bumble, or Match. Have conversations that matter; don't let the only interactions you have all week be with your online gaming buddies where you just trash talk each other for hours. Seek out true intimacy and pursue real passion rather than emulating what you see on your favorite pornography site. If there is anything you should avoid, it is the easy out. Train your brain to appreciate the long game and cultivate decisions and choices that are right for you, right for others, and right for the greater good—choices that feel good and bring you both short- and long-term pleasure or gain. The opposite of addiction is connection. Be connected.

Be mindful. Of your thoughts, your locus of control, and your choices. Determine if they are just quick fixes or intentional toward your desired outcomes. When situations arise that trigger your frustration signal, draw your awareness to how you feel, assess the situation, accept it, and then adjust your expectations or adapt within yourself.

Event plus response equals outcome. Unmet expectations are at the root of every frustration signal. When you find yourself overloaded by a charge of emotions, and you feel ready to combust, you've got to have the presence of mind to remember which wire to cut. Having the willingness and the commitment to do what is necessary to engage your upstairs brain so you can make right choices is at the heart of taking response-ability.

Summary

Boundaries can be physical, intellectual, emotional, financial, time-based, or sexual. Boundary violations are rooted in relationship problems, and the foundation of all relationship problems is poor communication.

E + R = O. Taking response-ability is about owning your choices and actions without taking on those things that are not yours.

Remember, you teach people how to treat you. Defining your non-negotiables is essential to maintaining healthy boundaries. To process past hurts, pass your index event through three lenses or perspectives: the lens of the victim, the "simply facts" lens, and the lens of responsibility.

Action Step

You have made it to the end of *Rise of Rage*! You may be wondering what's next.

1. If you have not already completed the reflection exercises and the supplementary work in the action steps that follow each chapter, now would be a good time to go back and do that. The reflections

and action steps will help you solidify what you have learned and will help you move further down that road to transformation.

2. Perhaps you would like to delve deeper into the *Anger Solutions* process. If you are a social worker, psychotherapist, psychologist, or another professional in the mental health / addictions / corrections space, and you would like to receive training in *Anger Solutions*, visit my website, www.angersolution.com, to learn more about how you can get certified as a facilitator or trainer. For those of you who would like additional assistance in your personal or professional transformation process, I'm happy to offer you a 40 percent discount on my virtual course "Triggering the Dragon," which is perfect for you to go through on your own or to present to your workplace team to explore together.

3. Perhaps you'd like me to speak at your next event. I'm happy to do that too! Reach out to me through my website: www.angersolution.com.

ACKNOWLEDGMENTS

I FIRST AND foremost must give honor to God, who blessed me with wisdom and talent and the ability to communicate effectively through words. Without Him, I am nothing.

I am infinitely grateful to several people who have contributed to the culmination of this work, and I will do my best to name them all here.

My parents, Delroy and the late Gloria (Blossom) Grant, taught me the value of hard work, encouraged my creative abilities, and always pushed me to do my level best no matter the task. Mom, I hope you realize now that becoming a doctor was not my path. At the first sight of blood, it would have been over for me, and it would have surely gone badly for my patients! I am so happy I can continue your legacy of influencing others through the written word, and I hope this makes you proud. Dad, I'm sorry I forgot the times you were present, and I'm grateful for the opportunities we have now to connect and establish a new kind of relationship. I love you so very much.

Elizabeth Eagles, my grade-6 teacher, was one of the first adults outside of my immediate family to recognize and nurture my writing ability. Other teachers of note include the late Peter Wale, David Gamble, and Rosemarie Hoey, who, to this day, I hold in the highest esteem.

Thank you to my beta readers—Barbara, Al, Jared, Stephanie, Melissa, Paul, Sonia, Shari, and Michele—for taking the first crack at this manuscript, for your thoughtful and focused feedback, for your friendship, and for your support. Thank you for helping me to perfect the thoughts, the messages, and the flow of this work! A special shout-out to author, coach, podcaster, and all-around amazing human Erin Skye Kelly. I would not likely be in the position I am right now without your selfless intervention.

Julie Gwinn, my agent at the Seymour Agency, you have tirelessly worked on my behalf from the moment we met. I will be forever grateful that ESK put us in each other's paths, even though you are on team cat, and I am on team dog. Thank you for believing in me and my work and for holding my hand while I take this journey. Jarrod Harrison and the team at Broadleaf Books, what an absolute joy it has been to work with you on this project. I couldn't have chosen a better team to bring this book to life. Jarrod, in your gentle, unassuming way, you pushed me to do more, to dig deeper, and to produce a book in a style that I have never used before, but I am so proud of this work, and I have you to thank for it.

My team at Spa for the Soul, you have been patient and supportive as I took time away from the office so I could work on this project. Our discussions helped to clarify my thoughts and often brought me different perspectives, which enriched the content immensely. I'm blessed to have you in my circle.

Shari Reimer, my right—and often my left—hand, I don't know how I survived before you entered my life. Thank you for being the Jill of all trades and propping me up in both businesses while I laser focus on one thing or the other. Thank you for all the reminders, the butt kicks, and the words of affirmation that always came just at the right time, but more I thank you for creating a space for me to work smarter instead of harder. Tracey Turavani also deserves my thanks for keeping me on track with administrative tasks and taking them on so that I don't have to. Thanks, Trace, for your loyalty and ongoing admin support over the years.

To my tribe at GroYourBiz, you have cheered me on, spurred me to aim higher, and often you have shaken your heads and told me to slow down. You have reminded me that faster is not always better and that it is okay to enjoy the process. You have made me better at business, and I'm proud to call you my friends. To my mentors and my friends who believed in me even when I didn't believe in myself, I owe a debt of thanks.

My kiddos—Cayla, Dylan, Thomas, Jon, and little Nova, and Finn—I have done my best to show you that hard work pays off, that good work is rewarded, and that you should find that thing you love, that thing that fuels your passion, and do it with all your heart, and the money will follow. My desire for you all is that you find that thing that sets your heart on fire and you pursue that passion and purpose wholeheartedly. I hope my example to you has been a good one. Bee Tee Dub, the stories I could have told! But I promise you that I worked really hard to ensure not to embarrass any of you in the writing of this book.

Stevan A. Christiansen, my heart. You have spent many a night on your own, watching reruns of your favorite shows or riffing on your guitars, while I clacked away on the keyboard you bought for me so I could *feel* like a true writer. *Best gift ever, baby!* That magical combination of you making music and the clicking of my keys was what enabled me to complete the manuscript three months ahead of the deadline. Your love and support and your willingness to continue cultivating passion, intimacy, and commitment in our relationship mean the world to me. In over thirty-five years of marriage, you have been my rock, my constant, my true North. Thank you for your stalwart support and belief in my ability to fly. I love you!

Lastly, I want to send a huge shout-out to my *Anger Solutions* community of facilitators, trainers, master trainers, and coaches. Your belief in this program and your loyalty over the years have not gone unnoticed. That you support each other and this process with such passion is one of the reasons I get up every day. Your commitment to serving your clients at the highest level to ensure they experience the radical, lasting, positive change that is promised to them through *Anger Solutions* stokes my fire. I am grateful for each of you and your amazing contribution to this community. Thank you for making *Anger Solutions* the best and the only evidence-based alternative to traditional anger management in the world.

GLOSSARY OF TERMS

ABCs: Antecedent, behavior, and consequence; activating event, belief, consequence; antecedent, belief, behavior, and consequences.

ACEs: Adverse childhood experiences include but are not limited to abuse, neglect, household challenges, bullying, witnessing violence, poverty, and racism.

Anger as basic emotion: A theory embraced by Dr. Paul Ekman and others that anger is a universally experienced and recognized emotion.

Anger inoculation: Includes four stages—awareness, acquisition, application, and assessment.

Anger myths: Anger is behavior, anger is bad, anger should not be expressed, anger and aggression are the same things, women and children should not express anger, expressing anger leads to negative outcomes.

Anger solutions: choices for conflict: Approach, avoid, aggress, or acquiesce.

Anger styles: Bottler, Controlled Blaster, Chronic Venter, Iceberg, Scrapper, ACME Poster Child, Captain Criticize, Snake, Give and Take, and Conductor.

Anger valence: A range of emotional states that differ in intensity but fall on the spectrum of anger (e.g., irritation, frustration, rage, or fury).

Bias: An inclination or prejudice for or against a person, a group, situations, or things.

BMI: Body mass index.

Boundaries: A line that delineates a limit.

Bullying: Repeated aggression characterized by the intent to cause harm where there is a power imbalance between the bully and the victim.

CAMH: Centre for Addiction and Mental Health.

Catharsis: The act of intentionally releasing negative energy from strong repressed emotions.

C4 and TNT: Explosive materials used in the making of incendiary devices.

Choice theory: Posits that all human behavior is driven by the pursuit of basic human needs. All behavior is the result of choices, which are the sole responsibility of the one making those choices.

Choice theory hierarchy of needs: Survival, love and belonging, power, freedom, and fun.

Conflict of choices: There are three types of choices we can make when we are faced with a problem—avoid/avoid, approach/avoid, and approach/approach.

Crooked thinking: A concept developed by Albert Ellis defined by distorted or illogical thoughts that impede efforts to achieve quality of life. There are four types: demandingness, awfulizing or catastrophizing, I can't stand it-itis, generalized negative ratings of self and others.

Demonstrating understanding: A psychosocial rehabilitation concept for listening that consists of four parts: responding to thoughts, responding to feelings, responding to feelings and thoughts, and responding to personal meaning.

Dopamine: One of the primary neurotransmitters in the brain's reward pathways.

Emotional dysregulation: Lack of emotional awareness and clarity, limited access to behavior regulation strategies, and self-denial of emotions.

$E + R = O$: Event plus response equals outcome.

(The) Exodus: A story found in the self-same titled second book of the Holy Bible, which describes the deliverance of Hebrew slaves from their Egyptian taskmasters.

Four factors that contribute to anger: Unmet needs or expectations, broken rules, violated boundaries, or thwarted goals.

Fallacy of control: Believing one can control outcomes, situations, or people by acting a certain way; by saying the right things; or by wishing or dreaming of the ideal result.

Functional fixedness: A cognitive bias that limits a person from using an object for anything but its traditional purpose.

Ghost riding: Directing a riderless bicycle into oncoming traffic or in a parking lot.

GPA: Grade point average.

Guilt: Remorse for something that was done, which was known to be wrongful in nature.

Hangry: The phenomenon that occurs when people are irritable because of hunger.

Heuristics: Shortcuts in thinking.

HR: Human resources.

IED: Acronym for both intermittent explosive disorder and improvised explosive device.

IRL: In real life.

Locus of control: The degree to which one perceives outcomes as related to internal characteristics versus external factors.

Macroaggressions: Large-scale or overt aggression toward those of a certain race, culture, gender, or otherwise marginalized group.

Maslow's hierarchy of needs: A pyramid of needs with physiological needs as the base; followed by safety, love and belonging, esteem; and peaked by self-actualization.

Mental set: A specific way of looking at a problem; a framework of beliefs one uses to help identify, process, and solve problems.

Microaggressions: Everyday actions or behaviors that are harmful toward marginalized groups.

(The) Misinformation effect: Demonstrates that memory is malleable, and it can be easily altered by implanting erroneous information.

OTT: Over the top.

Positive acceptance: Suggests that we feel uncomfortable feelings because we focus on wishing things were already different.

Quiet quitting: Emotionally/intellectually checking out of a job by doing only the bare minimum and resisting any additional tasks or engagement with the employer beyond what is absolutely necessary.

Scaffolding: Structured programming and support that is provided to targets of bullying.

Shame: Feelings of deeply rooted self-loathing tied to one's identity.

Six human needs (Tony Robins): Needs of the personality: certainty, variety, love, and belonging and uniqueness; needs of the spirit: growth and contribution.

Stress inoculation: Three parts: education, skill acquisition, and skill application.

Thomas and Kilmann's model of conflict resolution: Compete, collaborate, accommodate, avoid, or compromise.

Total behavior: This choice theory concept suggests that all behavior—including thinking, acting, emoting, and even our autonomous responses—is purposeful.

Triarchic theory of love: A concept developed by Dr. Robert K. Sternberg that posits a consummate love requires intimacy, passion, and commitment.

TSA: Think, say, ask.

Theoretical models:

    REBT—Rational emotive behavior therapy

    CBT—Cognitive behavioral therapy

    SFT—Solution-focused therapy

    RT—Reality therapy

    DBT—Dialectical behavior therapy

    MBSR—Mindfulness-based stress reduction

NOTES

Introduction

1 CBT is a type of psychotherapy in which negative patterns of thought about the self and the world are challenged to alter unwanted behavior patterns (Oxford dictionaries).

2 DBT is a type of talk therapy based on CBT for people who experience emotions intensely (https://my.clevelandclinic.org/health/treatments/22838-dialectical-behavior-therapy-dbt).

3 REBT is the foundation of all cognitive therapies, identifying negative thought patterns and shifting them to alter negative emotions and maladaptive behaviors.

4 Solution-focused brief therapy is future-focused and goal-directed. It focuses on solutions rather than on the problems that brought clients to seek therapy.

5 MBSR is a method of using meditation and yoga to cultivate awareness and reduce stress.

6 Psychosocial or psychiatric rehabilitation is a form of life skills training that enables people with serious mental illnesses to acquire and assimilate practical, intrapersonal, and interpersonal skills, which help them remain integrated into society.

1. The Rise of Rage

1 Michael Potegal and Raymond W. Novaco, "A Brief History of Anger," in *International Handbook of Anger*, ed. M. Potegal, G. Stemmler, and C. Spielberger (New York: Springer, 2009), 9–24, https://doi.org/0.1007/978-0-387-89676-2_2.

2. What We Don't See

1 Star Trek reference: drive plasma is a byproduct of fuel used in star ships, highly volatile, and dangerous to a ship when it becomes unstable.

2 Novaco, "Brief History of Anger."

3 BrainyQuote, "Helen Keller Quotes," BrainyMedia Inc, 2023, https://
www.brainyquote.com/quotes/helen_keller_383771 (accessed April
10, 2023).

3. I'm a Believer

1 Stanton Peele, "The Human Side of Addiction," *U.S. Journal of Drug
and Alcohol Dependence*, April 1982, p. 7.
2 Peele, "Human Side of Addiction."
3 Tony Robbins, *Personal Power II* (San Diego: Robbins Research International, 1997).
4 Novaco, "Brief History of Anger."
5 S. E. Taylor et al., "Biobehavioral Responses to Stress in Females: Tend-
and-Befriend, Not Fight-or-Flight," *Psychological Review* 107, no. 3
(2000): 411–29, https://doi.org/10.1037/0033-295x.107.3.411.
6 Freud, pleasure unpleasure principle. Sigmund Freud, *The Unconscious*
(London: Penguin, 2005).

5. Your Circus, Your Monkeys

1 Definition of bias (http://www.oxforddictionaries.com).
2 https://yndrc.tirf.ca/issues/aggressive_driving.php.

7. Kill the Monster When It's a Baby

1 Laurie Flasko and Julie Christiansen, *Bullying Is Not a Game: A Parents'
Survival Guide* (St. Catharines: Leverage U Press, 2012).
2 Utterly Global Youth Empowerment is an organization dedicated to
anti-bullying.

8. There's an App for That

1 City University London, "Just a Game? Study Shows No Evidence
That Violent Video Games Lead to Real-Life Violence," Science-
Daily, www.sciencedaily.com/releases/2021/11/211105084110.htm
(accessed April 22, 2023).

11. Two Ears, One Mouth

1 Final Analysis, 1992.

12. Maybe Swearing Will Help

1 R. Dobson, "Swearing Could Raise Tolerance to Pain: Study Finds People Who Use Four-Letter Words Can Stand Discomfort for TWICE as Long as Those Who Stay Polite," *Daily Mail*, August 26, 2017.

2 Catharsis, www.oxfordreference.com/view/10.1093/oi/authority.2011 0803095555720.

13. Let It Go

1 Everett Worthington Jr., "The Effects of Forgiveness and Resentment on the Heart," The Table, Biola University Center for Christian Thought.

2 A state is a temporary way of being (i.e., thinking, feeling, behaving, and relating) while a trait tends to be a more stable and enduring characteristic or pattern of behavior. www.psychologytoday.com/us/blog /think-well/201710/do-you-confuse-peoples-states-their-traits.

15. Taking Response-ability

1 The concept of defining one's non-negotiables is a concept I learned from the late Thomas Leonard, the founder of the online coaching community, Coachville.

2 https://www.instagram.com/willsmith.

3 "Donald J. Trump Apology," https://www.nytimes.com/2016/10/08 /us/politics/donald-trump-apology.html.

BIBLIOGRAPHY

Ackerman, C. E. 2017. "Reality Therapy: Techniques, Choice Theory & WDEP Model." Positive Psychology. https://positivepsychology.com /reality-therapy/#theory-reality-therapy.

American Psychological Association Task Force on Aggression. 2022. "Violence Directed against Educators and School Personnel: Crisis during COVID-19." American Psychological Association, May 2022. https:// apa.org/education-career/k12/violence-educators.

Ammirati, Rachel, and Stephen Nowicki. n.d. "Locus of Control." Accessed April 23, 2023. https://www.oxfordbibliographies.com/view/document /obo-9780199828340/obo-9780199828340-0168.xml.

Bauman, S., and A. Del Rio. 2006. "Preservice Teachers' Responses to Bullying Scenarios: Comparing Physical, Verbal, and Relational Bullying." *Journal of Educational Psychology* 98 (1): 219–223.

Burt, I. 2014. "Identifying Gender Differences in Male and Female Anger Among an Adolescent Population." *Professional Counsellor* 4:5. https:// tpcjournal.nbcc.org/identifying-gender-differences-in-male-and -female-anger-among-an-adolescent-population.

Candelaria, A., A. Fedewa, and S. Ahn. 2012. "The Effects of Anger Management on Children's Social and Emotional Outcomes: A Meta-Analysis." *School Psychology International* 33:596. https://doi .org/10.1177014303431245436 0.

Carton, J. S., M. Ries, and S. Nowicki Jr. 2021. "Parental Antecedents of Locus of Control of Reinforcement: A Qualitative Review." *Frontiers in Psychology* 12:565883. https://doi.org/10.3389/fpsyg.2021.565883.

Christiansen, J. 2003. *Anger Solutions: Proven Strategies for Effectively Resolving Anger and Taking Control of Your Emotions.* St. Catharines: Leverage U Press.

Christiansen, J. 2022. "Anger Solutions for Resolving Emotional Dysregulation in Youth." *International Journal of Technology and Inclusive Education* 11 (1): 1761–1765.

Ciciarelli, S., J. N. White, and G. E. Meyer. 2014. *Psychology, Canadian Ed.* Toronto: Pearson Education Canada.

City University London. n.d. "Just a Game? Study Shows No Evidence That Violent Video Games Lead to Real-Life Violence."

ScienceDaily. Accessed April 23, 2023. www.sciencedaily.com/releases /2021/11/211105084110.htm.

Covey, S. 2020. *The 7 Habits of Highly Successful People: 30th Anniversary Edition*. New York: Simon and Shuster.

Daily Mail Reporter. 2011. "Didn't Spot the Dancing Gorilla in Famous Video? Why People Suffer from 'Inattention Blindness.'" https://www .dailymail.co.uk/sciencetech/article-1378228/Didnt-spot-dancing -gorilla-famous-YouTube-video.html.

Daugherty, G. 2023. "What Is Quiet Quitting—and Is It a Real Trend?" *Investopedia*. https://www.investopedia.com/whqat-is-quiet-quitting67 43910.

Dobson, R. 2017. "Swearing Could Raise Tolerance to Pain: Study Finds People Who Use Four-Letter Words Can Stand Discomfort for TWICE as Long as Those Who Stay Polite." *Daily Mail*, August 26, 2017.

Fernandez, Valentina. 2022. "Social Media, Dopamine, and Stress: Converging Pathways." *Neuroscience* 22X. https://sites.dartmouth.edu/dujs/2022 /08/20/social-media-dopamine-and-stress-converging-pathways/.

Flasko, L., and J. Christiansen. 2012. *Bullying Is Not a Game: A Parent's Survival Guide*. St. Catharines: Leverage U Press.

"Forget." n.d. Dictionary Unabridged. Accessed July 13, 2012. http:// dictionary.reference.com/browse/forget.

"Forgive." n.d. Dictionary Unabridged. Accessed July 13, 2012. http:// dictionary.reference.com/browse/forgive.

Glasser, W. 1999. *Choice Theory: A New Psychology of Personal Freedom*. New York: Harper Collins.

Haberman, M. 2016. "Trump's Apology That Wasn't." *New York Times*. https://www.nytimes.com/2016/10/08/us/p9olitics/donald-trump -apology.html.

Harris, A. H., F. M. Luskin, S. V. Benisovich, S. Standard, J. Bruning, S. Evans, and C. Thoresen. 2006. "Effects of a Group Forgiveness Intervention on Forgiveness, Perceived Stress and Trait Anger: A Randomized Trial." *Journal of Clinical Psychology* 62 (6): 715–733.

Harris, Holly. 2021. "Understanding the Mental Health Needs of Post-Secondary Students." Ontario Shores Centre for Mental Health Sciences.

Hawkins, D. L., D. Pepler, and W. Craig. 2001. "Peer Interventions in Playground Bullying." *Journal of Social Development* 10:512–527.

Health Research Funding. n.d. "Elizabeth Loftus Theory Explained." Accessed July 13, 2012. https://healthresearchfunding.org/elizabeth-loftus-theory -explained.

Koletić, G. 2017. "Longitudinal Associations Between the Use of Sexually |Explicit Material and Adolescents' Attitudes and Behaviors: A Narrative Review of Studies." *Journal of Adolescence* 57:119–133. https://www.sciencedirect.com/science/article/abs/pii/S014019 7117300544?via%3Dihub.

Krippner, S., and D. Barrett. 2022. "Transgenerational Trauma Effects: The Role of Epigenetics." *International Journal of Communal and Trans-generational Trauma* 1. https://cttjournal.org/transgenerational-trauma -effects-the-role-of-epigenetics/.

Kubik, R. 2020. "Mental Health of Post-Secondary Students on the Decline." Lethbridge Campus Media.

Lepore, S. J., and J. M. Smyth, eds. 2002. *The Writing Cure: How Expressive Writing Promotes Health and Emotional Well-Being.* Washington, DC: American Psychological Association.

Ley, D. 2013. "Your Brain on Porn: It's Not Addictive." *Psychology Today.* https://Psychologytoday.com/us/blog/women-who-stray/201307your -brain-porn-its-not-addictive.

Lidell, C. 2022. "What Is Functional Fixedness?" *Study.* https://study.com /learn/lesson/what-is-functional-fixedness-psychology.html.

"A List of Some Past Canadian School Shootings." Canadian Press. Posted February 15, 2022. https://globalnews.ca/news/8621977/list -canadian-school-shootings/.

Lloyd, D. 2012. "What Happens When Bullies Become Adults?" Michi-gan State University School of Journalism. https://news.jrn.msu.edu /bullying/2012/04/01/bullies-as-adults/.

Loftus, E. 2003. "Make Believe Memories." *American Psychologist* 58 (11): 867–873.

Luskin, F. M., K. Ginzburg, and C. E. Thoresen. 2005. "The Effect of For-giveness Training on Psychosocial Factors in College Age Adults." *Humboldt Journal of Social Relations. Special Issue: Altruism, Intergroup Apology and Forgiveness: Antidote for a Divided World* 29 (2): 163–184.

Medical News Today. 2017. "Eight Benefits of Crying: Why It's Good to Shed a Few Tears." http://www.medicalnewstoday.com/articles/319631.

National Scientific Council on the Developing Child. 2004. "Young Chil-dren Develop in an Environment of Relationships." Working Paper no. 1. https://www.developingchild.net.

Owens, E. W., R. J. Behun, J. C. Manning, and R. C. Reid. 2012. "The Impact of Internet Pornography on Adolescents: A Review of the Research." *Journal of Treatment & Prevention* 19 (1–2): 99–122. https:// doi.org/10.1080/10720162.2012.660431.

Peele, S. 1982. "The Human Side of Addiction: What Caused John Belushi's Death?" *U.S. Journal of Drug and Alcohol Dependence*, April 1982, p. 7.

Pennebaker, J. W. 1997. *Opening Up: The Healing Power of Expressing Emotions*. New York: Guilford.

Pennebaker, J. W. 1999. "Health Effects of Expressing Emotions through Writing." *Biofeedback* 27:6–9, 14.

Pennebaker, J. W. 2004. *Writing to Heal: A Guided Journal for Recovering from Trauma and Emotional Upheaval*. Oakland, CA: New Harbinger Press.

Peter, J., and P. M. Valkenburg. 2016. "Adolescents and Pornography: A Review of 20 Years of Research." *Journal of Sex Research* 53 (4–5): 509–531. https://doi.org/10.1080/00224499.2016.1143441.

Pinter, A. P., J. A. Jiang, K. Z. Gach, M. M. Sidwell, J. E. Dykes, and J. R. Brubaker. 2019. "Am I Never Going to Be Free of All This Crap? Upsetting Encounters with Algorithmically Curated Content about Ex-Partners." *Proceedings of the ACM on Human-Computer Interaction* 3 (CSCW): 1. https://doi.org/10.1145/3359172.

Price, G. 2011. "Stress Resilience and the Power of Positive Acceptance." *Executive Support Magazine*, April 2011. https://executivesupport magazine.com/stress-resilience-the-power-of-positive-acceptance/.

Potegal, Michael, and Raymond W. Novaco. "A Brief History of Anger." International Handbook of Anger, 2009, 9–24. doi:10.1007/978-0-387-89676-2_2.

Pozzulo, J., Bunnell, C., Forth, A. (2022). Forensic Psychology, 6th edition. Toronto: Pearson Canada.

Rice, J. 2011. "Indian Residential School Truth and Reconciliation Commission of Canada." *Cultural Survival* 35:1. http://www.cultural survival .org/publications/cultural-survival-quarterly/Indian-residential-school -truth-and-reconciliation.

Robbins, A. 1997. *Personal Power*. San Diego: Anthony Robbins International.

Rodenhizer, K. A. E., and K. M. Edwards. 2017. "The Impacts of Sexual Media Exposure on Adolescent and Emerging Adults' Dating and Sexual Violence Attitudes and Behaviors: A Critical Review of the Literature." *Journal of Trauma Violence Abuse* 20 (4): 439–452. https://doi .org/10.1177/1524838017717745.

SAGE Publications. "Seeing and Experiencing Violence Makes Aggression 'Normal' for Children." *ScienceDaily*. Accessed April 23, 2023. www .sciencedaily.com/releases/2011/03/110329095742.htm.

Scott, H. D., and J. J. McWhirter. 2003. "Anger and Aggression Management in Young Adolescents: An Experimental Validation of the SCARE Program." *Education and Treatment of Children* 26 (3): 273. https://www.researchgate.net/publication/284428987_Anger_and

_aggression_management_in_young_adolescents_An_experimental
_validation_of_the_SCARE_program.

Seigel, D. J., and T. P. Bryson. 2011. *The Whole Brain Child: 12 Revolutionary Strategies to Nurture Your Child's Developing Mind.* New York: Bantam.

Smith, R. A. 2022. "Quiet Quitters Make Up Half the U.S. Workforce, Gallup Says." *Wall Street Journal.* https://www.wsj.com/articles/quiet -quitters-make-up-half-the-u-s-workforce-gallup-says-11662517806.

Stockly, L. 2020. *Mindful Monsters Therapeutic Workbook.* Bumble Press.

Swami, V., S. Hochstöger, E. Kargl, and S. Stieger. 2022. "Hangry in the Field: An Experience Sampling Study on the Impact of Hunger on Anger, Irritability, and Affect." *PLoS ONE* 17 (7): e0269629. https:// doi.org/10.1371/journal.pone.0269629.

Szklarski, C. 2022. "Toddlers Don't Need Firm Screen Time Limits, New Canadian Guidance Says." Global News Canada. https://globalnews .ca/news/9302391/screen-time-limit-guidance-kids-canada/.

Taylor, S. E., L. C. Klein, B. P. Lewis, T. L. Gruenewald, R. A. Gurung, and J. A. Updegraff. 2000. "Biobehavioral Responses to Stress in Females: Tend-and-Befriend, Not Fight-or-Flight." *Psychological Review* 107 (3): 411–429. https://doi.org/10.1037/0033-295x.107.3.411.

Thomas, S. P. 1989. "Gender Differences in Anger Expression: Health Implications." *Research in Nursing and Health* 12 (6): 389–398. https://doi .org/10.1002/nur.4770120609.

Thompson-Cannino, J., R. Cotton, and E. Torneo. 2009. *Picking Cotton: Our Memoir of Injustice and Redemption.* New York: St. Martin's.

Tibbits, D., G. Ellis, C. Piramelli, F. Luskin, and R. Lukman, R. 2006. "Hypertension Reduction through Forgiveness Training." *Journal of Pastoral Care and Counseling* 60 (1–2): 27–34.

Trofimova, I., and J. Christiansen. 2016. "Coupling of Temperament with Mental Illness in Four Age Groups." *Psychological Reports* 118 (2): 387–412.

University of Colorado at Boulder. 2020. "How Social Media Makes Break-ups That Much Worse: New Study Shows It's Hard to Get Distance in the Digital Age." *ScienceDaily*, February 14, 2020. www.sciencedaily .com/releases/2020/02/200214094404.htm.

WebMD. "Health Benefits of Essential Oils." https://www.webmd.com /diet/health-benefits-essential-oils.

Wood, S., E. Wood, D. Boyd, E. Wood, and S. Desmarais. 2014. *The World of Psychology, 7th Canadian Edition.* Toronto: Pearson Education Canada.

Williams, R. 2017. "Anger as a Basic Emotion and Its Role in Personality Building and Pathological Growth: The Neuroscientific, Developmental and Clinical Perspectives." *Frontiers in Psychology* 8 (1950): 1–9.